T0203561

Enterprise Interoperability

Enterprise Interoperability

IWEI 2011 Proceedings

Edited by
Martin Zelm
Marten van Sinderen
Guy Doumeingts
Pontus Johnson

First published 2011 in Great Britain and the United States by ISTE Ltd and John Wiley & Sons, Inc.

ISTE Ltd
27-37 St George's Road
London SW19 4EU
UK

John Wiley & Sons, Inc.
111 River Street
Hoboken, NJ 07030
USA

www.iste.co.uk

www.wiley.com

© ISTE Ltd 2011

Library of Congress Cataloging-in-Publication Data

IFIP International Working Conference on Enterprise Interoperability (3rd : 2011 : Stockholm, Sweden)
  Enterprise interoperability : IWEI 2011 proceedings / edited by Martin Zelm ... [et al.].
    p. cm.
  Papers of the IFIP International Working Conference on Enterprise Interoperability held March 22-24 at the Royal Institute of Technology in Stockholm, Sweden.
  Includes bibliographical references.
  ISBN 978-1-84821-317-3
  1. Management information systems--Congresses. 2. Information resources management--Congresses.
  3. Internetworking (Telecommunication)--Congresses. 4. Communication in organizations--Congresses.
  I. Zelm, Martin. II. International Federation for Information Processing. III. Title.
  T58.6.I1227 2011
  658.4'038011--dc23

                                                                                        2011021749

British Library Cataloguing-in-Publication Data
A CIP record for this book is available from the British Library
ISBN 978-1-84821-317-3

Printed and bound in Great Britain by CPI Antony Rowe, Chippenham and Eastbourne.

MIX
Paper from
responsible sources
FSC
www.fsc.org
FSC® C013604

Table of Contents

Foreword

The IFIP International Working Conference on Enterprise Interoperability (IWEI 2011) was held on March 22-24 at the Royal Institute of Technology in Stockholm, Sweden. A two-day working conference, the event attracted 50 participants from almost 20 countries.

Co-located with the conference were four workshops complementing the program of the working conference. The papers and discussions of the workshops are documented in these proceedings.

This working conference aimed at identifying and discussing challenges and solutions with respect to Enterprise Interoperability, both at the business and technical level, with a special focus on the use and realization of the Future Internet vision. The conference promotes the development of a scientific foundation for specifying, analyzing and validating interoperability solutions; an architectural framework for addressing interoperability challenges from different viewpoints and at different levels of abstraction; a maturity model to evaluate and rank interoperability solutions with respect to distinguished quality criteria; and a working set of practical solutions and tools that can be applied to interoperability problems to date.

The single-track IWEI conference program featured 15 full and 5 short papers on topics such as model transformation, enterprise architecture, ontologies, modeling languages, business processes, requirements, service monitoring, and trust models, all in the context of enterprise interoperability. All conference papers are published in the Springer Lecture Notes in Business Information Processing. Additionally, selected papers will be invited to a special issue in the academic journal Computers in Industry, published by Elsevier.

The IWEI began as a workshop in Munich in 2008 with a modest 13 participants, then was organized in Valencia (2009), where the number of participants increased to 30. As mentioned, the Stockholm event attracted 50 participants, thus maintaining a sizeable growth rate.

Pontus Johnson

April 2011

Preface

This book contains the short papers of the Third International IFIP Working Conference on Enterprise Interoperability, IWEI 2011, held March 22-23, 2011, in Stockholm, Sweden, and the papers of the co-located IWEI Workshops, held on March 21, 2011. IWEI 2011 was the third in a series of international events on enterprise interoperability. Previous events took place in Munich, Germany (2008) and Valencia, Spain (2009). The IWEI series of events aim at identifying and discussing challenges and solutions with respect to enterprise interoperability, with the purpose of achieving flexible cross-organizational collaboration through integrated support at business and technical levels.

The IWEI Working Conference highlighted developments in the following areas: scientific foundations for specifying, analyzing and validating interoperability solutions; architectural frameworks for addressing interoperability challenges from different viewpoints and at different levels of abstraction; maturity models to evaluate and rank interoperability solutions with respect to distinguished quality criteria; and working sets of practical solutions and tools that can be applied to interoperability problems to date. Furthermore, a special theme was chosen for IWEI 2011, which crosscuts the aforementioned areas, namely: "Interoperability and Future Internet for Next-Generation Enterprises". This means that special attention was given to the interoperability needs of Next-Generation Enterprises and how these needs are shaped and supported by the emerging Future Internet.

The IWEI Workshops complemented the topics of the IWEI Working Conference and explored new issues and solutions in enterprise interoperability. This was done in four separate workshops: (1) Enterprise 2.0 – Using Internet 2.0 Technologies in Enterprise Management; (2) Semantic Interoperability in the Scope of Future Energy Smart Grids; (3) Advanced Results in MDI/SOA Innovation; and (4) Standards Ensuring Enterprise Interoperability and Collaboration – State of the Art and Perspectives. More than the Working Conference, the Workshops offered opportunities to discuss issues raised during the paper presentations and to brainstorm about possible solution directions.

The first workshop explored the results, experiences, required action and potential value of the Enterprise 2.0 with industry practitioners and members of the academic community. Enterprise 2.0 is the use of emergent social internet focused software platforms within companies, or between companies and their partners or customers.

The second workshop elaborated emerging topics of enterprise architecture and semantic interoperability in the scope of the future Energy Smart Grids. In particular, it considered the Enterprise Architecture of Utilities focusing on Smart Grids and the semantic integration of Smart Grids layers, data models and transport technologies.

The third workshop presented the latest results in the domain of Model-Driven Interoperability (MDI) and Service Oriented Architecture (SOA) concerning research projects and the transfer towards industry. Topics of Interoperability Services, Reference Ontologies and Business-IT alignment were addressed. The workshop. is a follow-up of the I-ESA 2010 workshop in Coventry, UK.

The fourth workshop focused on awareness of interoperability standards enabling real life collaboration of enterprises. Furthermore, the workshop identified new approaches of the evolution of standards for services in the Future Internet perspective as well as implementation of standards in SME networks.

IWEI 2011 was organized by the IFIP Working Group 5.8 on Enterprise Interoperability in cooperation with INTEROP-VLab. The objective of IFIP WG5.8 is to advance and disseminate research and development results in the area of enterprise interoperability. The IWEI series of events provide an excellent platform to discuss the ideas that have emerged from IFIP WG5.8 meetings, or, reversely, to transfer issues that were raised at the conference to the IFIP community for further contemplation and investigation.

We would like to take this opportunity to express our gratitude to all those who contributed to IWEI 2011. We thank the workshop organizers for creating a stimulating environment for discussions; we thank the authors for presenting their papers and enabling a valuable information exchange; and we thank the attendants for their interest in this event. We are indebted to IFIP TC5 and WG5.8 for recognizing the importance of enterprise interoperability as a research area with high economic impact. Finally, we are grateful to KTH, the Royal Institute of Technology, for hosting IWEI 2011.

Martin Zelm

Marten van Sinderen

Guy Doumeingts

Pontus Johnson

April 2011

Organization

IWEI 2011 was organized by IFIP Working Group 5.8 on Enterprise Interoperability, in cooperation with INTEROP VLab.

Executive committee

General Chair:	Pontus Johnson	KTH, Sweden
Program Chair:	Marten van Sinderen	University of Twente, Netherlands
Workshop Chair	Martin Zelm	INTEROP-VLab, Germany
IFIP Liaison:	Guy Doumeingts	INTEROP-VLab/ Univ. Bordeaux 1, France
Local organization:	Joakim Lliesköld	KTH, Sweden

Workshop organizers

Enterprise 2.0 – Using Internet 2.0 Technologies in Enterprise Management
Ricardo Chalmeta — University of Jaume 1, Spain
Veronica Pazos — ESTIA II, Spain

Semantic Interoperability in the Scope of Future Energy Smart Grids
Mathias Uslar — OFFIS, Germany
Ulrike Steffens — OFFIS, Germany
Matthias Postina — OFFIS, Germany
Sebastian Rohjans — OFFIS, Germany

Advanced Results in MDI/SOA Innovation
Guy Doumeingts — INTEROP-VLab, University of Bordeaux 1
Jean-Pierre Bourey — Ecole Centrale Lille (F)
Stephan Kassel — University of Applied Sciences, Zwickau, Germany
Pontus Johnson — KTH, Sweden

Standards Ensuring Enterprise Interoperability and Collaboration – State of the Art and Perspectives
Piero De Sabbata — ENEA, Italy
Martin Zelm — INTEROP-VLab, Germany

International Program Committee

Stephan Aier	University of St. Gallen, Switzerland
Khalid Benali	LORIA – Nancy University, France
Peter Bernus	Griffith University, Australia
Jean-Pierre Bourey	Ecole Centrale Lille, France
Ricardo Chalmeta	University of Jaume I, Spain
David Chen	University of Bordeaux 1, France
Antonio DeNicola	LEKS-IASI-CNR, Italy
Guy Doumeingts	INTEROP-VLab/University of Bordeaux 1
Yves Ducq	University of Bordeaux 1, France
Ip-Shing Fan	Cranfield University, UK
Ricardo Goncalves	New Univ. of Lisbon, UNINOVA, Portugal
Claudia Guglielmina	TXT e-solutions, Italy
Sergio Gusmeroli	TXT e-solutions, Italy
Axel Hahn	University of Oldenburg, Germany
Jenny Harding	Loughborough University, UK
Roland Jochem	University of Kassel, Germany
Paul Johannesson	KTH, Sweden
Pontus Johnson	KTH, Sweden
Leonid Kalinichenko	Russian Academy of Sciences, Russian Federation
Bernhard Katzy	University of Munich, Germany
Kurt Kosanke	CIMOSA Association, Germany
Stephan Kassel	University of Applied Sciences, Zwickau, Germany
Lea Kutvonen	University of Helsinki, Finland
Jean-Pierre Lorre	PEtALS Link, France
Michiko Matsuda	Kanagawa Institute of Technology, Japan
Kai Mertins	Fraunhofer IPK, Germany
Jörg Müller	Technische Universität Clausthal, Germany
Philipp Offermann	Deutsche Telecom T-Labs, Germany
Andreas Opdahl	University of Bergen, Norway
Angel Ortiz	Polytechnic University of Valencia, Spain
Hervé Panetto	UHP Nancy I, France
Hervé Pingaud	École des Mines d'Albi-Carmaux, France
Raul Poler	Polytechnic University of Valencia, Spain
Raquel Sanchis	Polytechnic University of Valencia, Spain
Ulrike Steffens	OFFIS, Germany
Mathias Uslar	OFFIS, Germany
Piero de Sabbata	ENEA, Italy
Raymond Slot	Hogeschool Utrecht, Netherlands
Bruno Vallespir	University of Bordeaux 1, France
Alain Wegmann	EPFL, Switzerland
Xiaofei Xu	Harbin Institute of Technology, China
Martin Zelm	CIMOSA, Germany

Additional reviewers

Camlon Asuncion
Alexis Aubry
Luiz Olavo Bonino da Silva Santos
Markus Buschle
Moustafa Chenine
Michele Dassisti
Luís Ferreira Pires
Christian Fischer
Ulrik Franke
Bettina Gleichauf
Sven Glinizki
Hannes Holm
Frank Jaekel

Thomas Knothe
Holger Kohl
Mario Lezoche
Pia Närman
Matthias Postina
Waldo Rocha Flores
Brahmananda Sapkota
Teodor Sommestad
Vikram Sorathia
Sergey Stupnikov
Johan Ullberg
Sven Wusher
Esma Yahia

Sponsoring organizations

IFIP TC5 WG5.8
INTEROP-VLab
KTH, Royal Institute of Technology
CTIT, Centre for Telematics and Information Technology

Part 1
Workshop Proceedings

Workshop W1

Enterprise 2.0, Using Internet 2.0 Technologies in Enterprise Management

WORKSHOP W1 – REPORT

Ricardo Chalmeta, Verónica Pazos
University of Jaume, Spain

The workshop was held as the kick-off meeting for the new thematic group of the InterOP-Vlab Task Group, *TG12: Interoperability in Enterprise 2.0.* The meeting was structured in three parts, as described below.

Participants: Veronica Pazos, Guy Doumeingts, Sergio Gusmeroli, David Chen, Pontus Johnson, Stuart Short, Yves Ducq, Tomasz Debicki, Asuncio, Miguel Beca,

1) Introduction

Verónica Pazos (University of Jaume) provided an overview of previous work on the topic.

2) Discussion to identify issues, requirements and conclusions

The **concept** of Enterprise 2.0 must be defined. This means to identify the changes needed to make an enterprise become an Enterprise 2.0. The change must be defined at a strategic, tactical and operational level. Further, it is necessary to identify the benefits that an Enterprise may have when becoming an Enterprise 2.0.

Methodologies, methods and techniques: it is necessary to develop guidelines and maturity models of social networking in the enterprise. Namely, to define goals at all levels of the enterprise using a top-down approach complemented with a bottom-up one. 2.0 technologies seem to be oriented to operational information and hence it may be necessary to define methods to extract automatically strategic information from operational level. In addition, it is necessary to develop ROI methods to prove benefits and show enterprises quantifiable benefits of the Enterprise 2.0 approach. Finally, the structure, architecture, processes and specific rules of Enterprise 2.0 must be developed.

Regarding **corporate culture,** it is necessary to change enterprise mentality in a way that all the users of 2.0 technologies trust each other and develop privacy policies that facilitate the access to information.

3) Proposed actions for TG12

The following actions were agreed upon:

- White paper from Wolfgang Prinz (Fraunhofer FIT): Doc-ID: Web2.0 Whitepaper.

- Establish a common baseline on Enterprise 2.0, comprising Version: V2.0 Author(s): Wolfgang Prinz, Steffen Budweg, delivered in the frame of the COIN project Date: 31.07.2010.

- Write a white paper on Grai Model (David Chen and Yves Ducq), will be produced for the end of 2011. Referencing McAfee, A.: The Dawn of Emergent Collaboration.

- FInES position paper (2011 – 2009): published on the site of the European Commission.

- ENTERPRISE 2.0 DEFINITION

  o   Analyze various definitions

  o   Propose TG12 definition

- ORGANIZATION CHALLENGES FOR ENTERPRISE 2.0

  o   Define what type of organizations (segmentation, legal aspects, human resources, etc.)

  o   Description of the various types of Enterprise 2.0

  o   Comparison between the Enterprise 2.0 and the previous concepts of Enterprise.

- NEW TECHNOLOGY AND ENTERPRISE 2.0

  o   What is the influence of the technologies in Enterprise 2.0? Future Internet, social network, service web, SaaS, mashups. Disruption or evolution?

  o   What are the needs of Enterprise 2.0?

  o   Tangible and intangible benefits analysis

References

WhitePaper on Web 2.0 & Enterprise cooperation services based on Web 2.0 principles, Wolfgang Prinz, Steffen Budweg, 2010. Available on: http://www.coin-ip.eu/coin-community/community-documents/documents-available-from-the-community

McAfee, A. "Enterprise 2.0: The Dawn of Emergent Collaboration", MIT Sloan Management Review, vol.47, 2006, no 3, p 20-28

Future Internet Enterprise Systems (FInES) Roadmap, June 2010, available on http://cordis.europa.eu/fp7/ict/enet/documents/fines-researchroadmap-final-report.pdf

Workshop W2

Semantic Interoperability in the Scope of Future Energy Smart Grids

Interoperability between Temporal Domains in Real-time Control of Active Distribution Networks

Lars Nordström – Rune Gustavsson

KTH – Royal Institute of Technology
Stockholm, SWEDEN
larsn@ics.kth.se

ABSTRACT. *This paper describes ongoing work focused on the interoperability between systems for distributed control of power systems using industry standard automation and protection devices. The background to the work is the assumption that the interface to the power system will be a fail-safe layer of automation and protection functions optimized for safe operation of the power system in order to minimize the risk of injury to people and equipment. Above this layer, however, reside information system layers with the task of optimizing different aspects of the power system. This paper presents a layered model of the problem domain that illustrates and discusses the interfaces between the layers from an interoperability standpoint.*

KEYWORDS: Smart grids, interoperability, temporal, control, protection.

1. Active distribution networks

Active distribution networks are electric power distribution networks that have developed from a state of uni-directional power flow from generation to load point into a state where there are electric generation facilities distributed in the distribution system and where the loads are to some degree controllable. This transformation implies not only a technological development, but also the emergence of new actors in the value chain implying new interaction patterns between end-users, producers and service providers.

It is obvious that in such active distribution networks, there arise a number of situations that require collective problem solving. The prime example of such situations is of course balancing between supply and demand, which will have an impact on the electric characteristics of the network such as frequency and voltage. At the same time, demand and supply is affected by the price of the commodity, in this case electric energy. For such multi-dimensional problems with several stakeholders involved, multi-agent systems have been brought forward as an appropriate paradigm for developing the necessary control systems.

1.1. *Organizational actors in active distribution systems*

The exact types of actors and their responsibilities in an active distribution network cannot be uniformly defined. However, for the purpose of this presentation, some key actors based on the deregulated power industry that is becoming the norm in Europe have been identified.

Distribution Network Operator (DNO) is a company that operates the distribution grid in a specific geographic region. The DNO does not generate electricity and does not sell electricity to end-users. The operation of the distribution grid constitutes a natural monopoly since customers cannot switch to another electricity grid; therefore the DNO operates under the auspices of a governmental regulator.

System Operator (SO): the system operator is an organisation responsible for frequency control in a power system. The system operator does not operate any generation facilities, but instead fulfils its role through procuring auxiliary services from actors on the markets. In the perspective of this presentation it is not relevant whether the System Operator also owns and/or operates a power transmission grid.

The generating company (GenCo) owns and operates production facilities connected to the power system either at transmission or distribution level. From the perspective of a DNO, GenCos can be divided into two groups. The first is the

GenCos that operate production facilities connected to the specific DNOs grid, and the second group is GenCos that do not. We refer to the former group as Distributed Generating Companies (DisGenCo)

Consumer: a consumer is an entity that is connected to a specific DNO's grid, and that uses electricity for some purpose. The consumer purchases electricity from Energy Service Providers.

Energy Service Provider (ESP): an energy service provider is a company that provides some type of service to consumers. The most basic type of ESP is the retailer that resells electricity produced by GenCos to consumers.

1.2. Problem domain and interfaces

The overall control problem in an active distribution system can be separate into subdomains based on the temporal characteristics of different aspects of the problem.

Layer 1: protection of the distribution grid, its goal is safe operation of the power system to avoid damage to equipment or people. Timing requirements at this level are very strict and faults need to be cleared within the 50-100 millisecond range. Responsible for fulfillment is the DNO sometimes in cooperation with DisGenCos.

Layer 2: optimization of the distribution grid to current production and consumption patterns. This includes optimizing setting of parameters in Layer 1 based on operational situation. The time requirements are less strict than in Layer 1 being in the range of seconds to minutes. Responsible for operations at this layer are DNO and DisGenCos. In some markets there may be ESPs providing grid optimization services.

Layer 3: optimization of the power system from a business perspective to ensure that resources are used efficiently. The timing requirements on this layer are dependent on the market rules in the power system, which may vary from 15 minutes up to the order of hours or days. Actors at this layer are GenCos of both types, consumers, ESPs and the system operator.

To facilitate interaction between actors in the same active distribution network, the interfaces between the actors on all layers need to be well defined and restricted to allow only the type of interaction that is defined by external requirements such as market rules and safety requirements.

Figure 1 illustrates the three temporal layers and the two intermediate interfaces that are used to involve functions and exchange information between the layers.

Additionally, the actors presented are included at the layer in which they are potentially engaged.

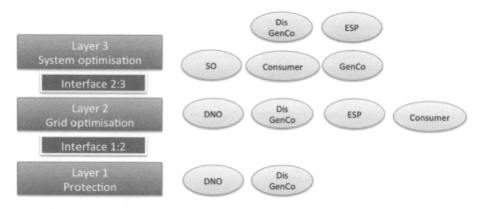

Figure 1. *A layered model of active distribution network control with a simplistic model of actors included*

2. Temporal domain interoperability

Based on the simple model presented in the previous section, use cases for interaction between the organizational actors across the layers can be outlined.

2.1. *Intra-layer – intra-organization*

Interaction and information exchange within a single organizational entity among systems supporting a business process within the same temporal domain. An illustrative example for this type of interaction, in this case on the protection layer, is differential protection that utilizes measurements from two distant IED (intelligent electronic devices) at separate substations, to perform its protection function. Data is then exchanged in accordance with for instance the IEC 60834 or 61850-90-1 protocols. This type of use case is relatively straightforward since the organization is in control of all end-points in the communication as well as the communication channels. Interoperability is achieved whatever protocol is used as long as the organization is consistent in implementation at all participating nodes.

2.2. *Intra-layer – inter-organization*

Data exchange within the same temporal layer but across organizational boundaries. This is normally not done at the protection layer, since such cross boundary interaction poses an additional risk to successful communication, and such risks are normally not acceptable at the protection layer. One example of information exchange at this level is exchange of network models between neighboring DNOs that can be used to create larger network models for Optimal Power Flow calculations. Another example is exchange of data from DisGenCos to the DNO whose network they operate within. The data that can be exchanged in those circumstances are for instance production forecasts for the coming 24 hours.

2.3. Inter-layer – intra-organization

Interaction between systems within single organizational entity among systems supporting a business process on one temporal layer, that requires interaction with systems residing on another temporal layer. An illustrative example is Automated Event Analysis that uses data from IEDs (residing on the protection layer) to support business processes, e.g. post-fault analysis within systems at the optimization layer.

2.4. Inter-layer – inter-organization

Finally, inter-layer inter-organization communication involves communication of data from one temporal layer at one organization to another organization's systems at another temporal layer. One example of a use case is grid optimization and updating of protection configuration. In this particular use case the DNO receives information from Layer 3 (the power market) that a DisGenCo within its grid will be delivering large amounts of active power at a point in the grid. From a grid optimization perspective (Layer 2) the DNO determines that the power flow on one line will be reversed. This results in a requirement to update the settings in the protective relays on the line, to be invoked via interface 1:2.

The use-cases serve to illustrate the interoperability challenges that appear when management of active distribution networks are studied. These challenges are of both an inter-organizational nature as well as an inter-temporal nature. This implies that the Quality of Service requirements for the information exchange are not one-dimensional, but instead shaped by the requirements from several organizations as well as temporal domains.

3. Interoperability aspects

To further understand the concept of interoperability, whether it is intra- or inter-layer or organization, we must distinguish between two kinds of interoperability; functional interoperability and non-functional interoperability. Functional interoperability involves the traditional interoperability of the application or business logic. Functional interoperability requires some kind of agreement on the interface: an API or contract. Non-functional interoperability involves interoperability cross-behavioral issues such as delay and security.

Implementation of systems taking into account functional and non-functional requirements as well as issues of flexibility and maintainability take into account models and methods of Service-Oriented System engineering. Applications are then not designed and implemented as stand-alone stovepipe systems, but as configurations of services. The transition from closely coupled systems to loosely coupled systems puts issues of coordination and communication in focus.

We also need to use middleware for implementation of Service-Oriented Systems. Middleware is a layer of software and services above the operating system but below the application program providing a common programming abstraction and system model across a distributed system. Middleware exists in part to help manage the complexity and heterogeneity inherent in distribute systems. Network researchers have of course developed layers of network protocols, where each layer builds on the one below and offers higher level of abstractions or service. Similarly, middleware researchers have developed multiple layers of middleware that build on the layer below it. Note that middleware typically overlays and enhances OSI layers above the transport (level 4) layer. The alternative to handle these layers in middleware is to hand code these layers in the application program. However, this is very time consuming and error prone; the best practices are very hard to recreate.

The following figures articulate some of the issues supporting cross-cutting security and privacy, as well as QoS aspects in the GWAC framework of network and syntactic categories. Interoperability is driven by the need of businesses (or business automation components) to share information between others. Business processes enable the necessary information exchange. At the organizational layers, interoperability requires agreement on the business process interaction that is expected to take place across an interface. Such an agreement would describe the service requests and responses that need to support a larger process picture that is shared by the collaborating parties. These processes must also be consistent with the tactical aspects of running the interacting businesses, the strategic aspects shared by the parties of the exchange, and the political environment embodied in economic and regulatory policy that governs such business.

Figure 2 depicts these categories of interoperability. The framework pertains to an electricity plus information (E+I) infrastructure. At the organizational layers, the pragmatic drivers revolve around the management of electricity. At the technical layers, the communications networking and syntax issues are information technology oriented. In the middle, we transform information technology into knowledge that supports the organization aspects of the electricity related business.

Within each horizontal category the information exchange can be implemented using the same technologies. However, information exchange across categories typically requires other technologies and/or transformation of data between data models. Particular challenges arise when we have a vertical shift in the E+I column. This reflects a transformation of the semantics of information between Energy Systems and Information Systems.

Figure 2. *GWAC Interoperability Framework Categories*

Cross-cutting issues are areas that need to be addressed and agreed upon to achieve interoperation. They are usually relevant to more than one interoperability category of the framework. Figure 3 from GWAC proposes to organize interoperability issues into a series of topics. These topics are introduced in this formative stage of developing the framework with the realization that each topic needs to be articulated in future developments and captured in detailed technical papers. These topics would then help organize specific work items for soliciting proposals to resolve issues where their impact to interoperability can be prioritized and where establishing agreement on specific directions for resolution can advance the cause.

Figure 3 depicts the cross-cutting issues spanning all categories. Deciding precisely which interoperability categories are relevant to each cross-cutting issue requires more review. Though a matrix of issues for each interoperability category would arguably be desirable, further clarification and analysis of the issues will be necessary. The GWAC interoperability model suggests that any implementation supporting interoperability must also support the following principles:

Principle I09: An interoperability framework must be practical and achievable:

- meets performance requirements;

- is reliable;

- is scalable;

- has sufficient breadth to meet the range of business needs.

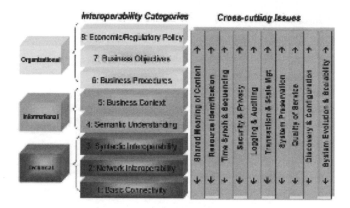

Figure 3. *GWAC Interoperability Context – Setting Framework Diagram*

Principle I10: An interoperability strategy must accommodate the coexistence of and evolvement through several generations of IT standards and technologies that will reside at any point in time on the grid.

In support of Principle I09, which essentially states that any solutions need to be effective from a variety of operational perspectives, it is essential that syntactic interoperability be incorporated across the board to its individual elements. We believe that having a comprehensive middleware architectural framework to deliver these services is the most effective way to ensure this in a comprehensive way, instead of a large collection of individual but narrow approaches, mechanisms, and evaluations. In order to support interoperability across organizations and in support of the "future proofing" articulated in Principle I10, it is essential that APIs for Quality of Service (including security) should be expressed at a middleware layer, which maps down onto the lower level mechanisms for providing a given property, in order to extend life cycle management across the evolution of these mechanisms. In order to support multiple non-functional/QoS properties (delay, rate, confidentiality, criticality/availability, and so on), it is essential that APIs be expressed in middleware so that they can be integrated and co-managed.

Resource allocation is an important part of resource management and is essential for providing non-functional properties. A given lower-level mechanism enables one or more non-functional properties that may be optimized (or, at minimum, appropriate) for some operating conditions and inappropriate or even considered "not working" under other conditions. At runtime, a given mechanism may utilize different levels of underlying resources (CPU, bandwidth, memory/storage). Different mechanisms providing the same property can provide different levels of non-functional service for given operating conditions; they also typically offer different trade-offs between the level of non-functional properties provided and resources consumed.

Examples of typical ways that non-functional properties can be supported include the following:

- Latency mechanisms: a chain of network level "reservations" for performance (see below for a more detailed view).

- Confidentiality mechanisms: encryption

- Integrity mechanisms: higher-level algorithms built on top of encryption (e.g. digital signatures).

- Availability mechanisms: replication (spatial, temporal, value) and end-to-end latency mechanisms per above.

Best practices dictate that the abstraction level for non-functional properties offered to the programmer be established as high as possible, rather than encouraging developers to bind directly into lower level mechanisms, for a number of reasons:

1. It is less error prone. Very few application programmers are expert in low level, non-functional property mechanisms.

2. Different lower-level mechanisms are available in different configurations in different deployments. The APIs of the lower-level mechanisms will change over time and perhaps with situation.

3. New lower-level mechanisms providing the same property or properties will become available over the lifetime of an application (which often can span many decades). Such new mechanisms will often be better than existing ones in one or more ways, including offering a higher level of non-functional property or being useable across a wider range of operating conditions

A stovepipe system is a legacy system that is an assemblage of inter-related elements that are so tightly bound together that the individual elements cannot be differentiated, upgraded or refactored. The stovepipe system must be maintained until it can be entirely replaced by a new system. From this, we propose the following new definition: QoS Stovepipe System (QSS): a system of systems whose subsystems are locked into low level mechanisms for QoS and security such that:

a)   it cannot be replaced in many reasonable configurations, or

b)   some programs cannot be combined because they use different lower level QoS mechanisms for the same property (e.g. latency) that cannot be directly composed, or

c)   it cannot be upgraded to "ride the technology" curve as better low level QoS and security mechanisms become available.

It is essential that any Smart Grid avoid enabling or perhaps even allowing QSS. This can be achieved using a proper set of middleware components.

4. Summary

We have presented a model of the control problem of active distribution networks that includes a temporal separation of the problem and small set of actors. With help of this model, use cases that involve interaction across the actors and temporal domains of the control problem can be identified. These use cases can then be analyzed with regards to their requirements in the framework of the Gridwise interoperability framework which adds the aspects of functional as well as non-functional interoperability to the temporal domains identified in the preceding discussion on active distribution networks.

5. References

Bakken D.E , Schantz, RE and Tucker, RD "Smart Grid Communications: QoS Stovepipes or QoS Interoperability?", *Proceedings of Grid-Interop 2009*, pp. 17–19.

GridWise® Interoperability Context- Setting Framework Prepared by The GridWise Architecture Council March 2008, Available at www.gridwiseac.org

Hussain S, Gustavsson R. Nordström, L. "Engineering of Trustworthy Smart Grids Implementing Service Level Agreements", submittted to *ISAP 2011*, Intelligent Systems Application to Power Systems.

Kezunovic,   M., Popovic,T. "Substation Data Integration for Automated Data Analysis Systems", in *Proceedings of IEEE Power & Energy Society General Meeting 2007*.

NIST Framework and Roadmap for Smart Grid Interoperability Standards, Release 1.0 NIST Special Publication 1108, Office of the National Coordinator for Smart Grid Interoperability.

Solving the Mismatches between the Electric System Ontologies

R. Santodomingo – J.A. Rodríguez-Mondéjar – M.A. Sanz-Bobi

Comillas Pontifical University. ICAI School of Engineering. Institute for Research in Technology (IIT)
26, Santa Cruz de Marcenado
28015 Madrid
Spain

rafael.santodomingo@iit.upcomillas.es
mondejar@dea.icai.upcomillas.es
miguel.angel@iit.upcomillas.es

ABSTRACT: *The heterogeneity between CIM and IEC 61850 ontologies is an important barrier for the semantic integration in the electric system domain. This paper proposes a new classification for the mismatches existing between such ontologies. This classification is based on the reasons that explain the existence of the mismatches rather than on their location in the ontologies. Moreover, solutions for all the types of mismatches identified are proposed. The interaction between these solutions will make it possible to solve all the heterogeneities without losing information and without modifying the original standards.*

KEYWORDS: *CIM, IEC 61850, Mismatches, Ontologies, Semantic Integration*

1. Introduction

The CIM (IEC 61968/61970) and the IEC 61850 are the two main standards that aim to achieve the semantic integration in the electric system domain. On the one hand, the CIM is focused on the remote energy management systems and, on the other hand, the IEC 61850 is focused on the local automation systems of the electric facilities.

An optimal management of the electric networks requires the interaction between remote energy management systems and local automation systems (EPRI, 2006). For that reason, the harmonization between CIM and IEC 61850 standards is a key issue for the development of future energy smart grids (NIST, 2010).

The problem is that such standards were developed by different working groups in the International Electrotechnical Comission Technical Committee 57 (IEC TC 57). This caused the information models defined by the standards to be heterogeneous, which means that there are incompatibilities or mismatches between them (Preiss *et al.*, 2006) (EPRI, 2006).

The alignment of heterogeneous ontologies is a major challenge for the Semantic Web development and also for the semantic integration in fields like Medicine and Biology. That is why the state of the art includes many works (Euzenat *et al.*, 2007), tools (Sirin *et al.*, 2007) and languages (Horrocks *et al.*, 2004) which are intended to detect, classify and solve the mismatches that appear due to the heterogeneities between the ontologies.

The work presented in this paper takes advantage of the solutions proposed in those fields (mainly in the Semantic Web) and adapts them in order to achieve the semantic integration in the electric system domain by harmonizing the CIM and the IEC 61850 as automatically as possible and without modifying the original standards (Saxton *et al.*, 2003). The paper includes: a) a new classification for the mismatches between the standards, b) the proposed solutions to solve each type of mismatch, c) a description of the interaction between the proposed solutions in order to solve all the heterogeneities, and d) the conclusions reached.

2. New classification for the mismatches between CIM and IEC 61850

In (Preiss *et al.*, 2006) the ABB group led by T. Kostic made an exhaustive analysis of the incompatibilities between the standards. This analysis was based on an envisioned unified model, recently proposed by the EPRI in (EPRI, 2010), which would modify the original CIM and IEC 61850 information models in order to solve their heterogeneities. That is why the classification of the mismatches proposed in

(Preiss *et al.*, 2006) focuses on where the incompatibilities occur in the original models, in order to detect the changes that had to be made on such models to design the unified one. Thus, (Preiss *et al.*, 2006) distinguishes three types of incompatibilities. Firstly, the *type (or class) level incompatibilities* that occur at the class level in the models. An example of this type of incompatibility is the one that stands for the fact that in CIM there is a class to represent the bus bar sections (*cim:BusbarSection*), whereas in IEC 61850 there is not. Secondly, the *relationship level incompatibilities* that occur at the relationship level. An example of a relationship level incompatibility is the one that exists because in CIM the class *cim:ConductingEquipment* is directly associated with the class *cim:Substation*, whereas in IEC 61850, the *scl:tCondutingEquipment* instances must be contained in a *scl:tBay* inside the substation. Finally, the *attribute level incompatibilities* occur at attribute level. An example of an attribute level incompatibility is explained in the following. The attribute *RSYN.DifHz* may not be included in an IEC 61850 device because it is optional in this standard. However, the equivalent CIM attribute, i.e. *cim:SynchrocheckRelay.maxFreqDiff*, could be mandatory in a CIM application.

The classification for the mismatches between CIM and IEC 61850 proposed in our work tries to find the solutions to those mismatches without modifying the original standards. In that way, this new classification is closer to those given in ontology mismatching works like (Euzenat, 2001), (Benerecetti *et al.*, 2001), and (Euzenat *et al.*, 2007) and is more focused on the reasons that explain the existence of the heterogeneities (Smart *et al.*, 2008) rather than on its localization in the models.

2.1. *Granularity mismatches*

Granularity mismatches occur when two ontologies describe the same region of a domain from the same perspective but at different levels of detail (Euzenat *et al.*, 2007). The *TapChanger* mismatch is an example of this type of mismatches between CIM and IEC 61850. In CIM there are three different classes for representing tap changers: *cim:TapChanger*, *cim:PhaseTapChanger* and *cim:RatioTapChanger*, whereas in IEC 61850 there is only one, the *scl:tTapChanger*. Thus, in CIM the tap changers are represented in a higher level of detail than in IEC 61850 and, for that reason, in a translation from the second standard to the first one a decision has to be made in order to translate an *scl:tTapChanger* as one of the three CIM classes that can represent different types of that element.

2.2. *Perspective mismatches*

Perspective mismatches occur when two ontologies describe the same region of a domain, at the same level of detail, but from a different perspective (Euzenat *et al.*,

2007). This type of mismatch appears between CIM and IEC 61850 when electric lines are represented. Thus, the CIM distinguishes two types of lines depending on the type of current, *cim:ACLineSegment* and *cim:DCLineSegment*, whereas the IEC 61850 differentiates two types of lines depending on its isolation, *LIN* (without isolation) and *GIL* (with gas isolation). In this type of mismatches there will be conflict situations during the translation in both directions.

2.3. *Coverage mismatches*

Coverage mismatches occur when two ontologies describe different, possibly overlapping, regions of a domain at the same level of detail and from a unique perspective (Euzenat *et al.*, 2007). This type of mismatches in our case refers to the information that is included in one of the standards, but not in the other one. An example of this type of mismatch is the *BusbarSection* mismatch explained above. Due to this type of mismatch there are going to be losses of information during the translation from one standard to the other.

2.4. *Flexibility mismatches*

Finally, flexibility mismatches occur when the ontologies are developed from standards that contain optional attributes and relationships. The conflict situations in this type of mismatch appear when an optional attribute or relationship is not included in the instance file of the source ontology and this attribute or relationship is required in the target ontology. These are the cases of the *RSYN.DifHz* and the *scl:tBay* mismatches explained above as the examples of *attribute level* and *relationship level* incompatibilities, respectively.

3. Proposed solutions to the mismatches

Once the mismatches between the CIM and the IEC 61850 standards are classified and the reasons that explain their existence are identified, the following section proposes solutions for each type of mismatch.

3.1. *Specific domain knowledge*

The only way to solve the conflict situations that appear due to the *granularity* and *perspective mismatches* is to employ specific domain knowledge in order to take the suitable decisions during the translation from one standard to the other (Figure 1). In some cases this specific knowledge can be found in the standards. This is the case of the *Disconnector* mismatch, which is a granularity mismatch that appears because in CIM there are three classes that represent different types of disconnectors: *cim:Disconnector*, *cim:LoadBreakSwitch* and *cim:GroundDisconnector*, whereas in IEC 61850 these elements can only be represented with the *scl:tConductingEquipment* class when its attribute *scl:type* takes the *DIS* value. In this mismatch, the information about the type of disconnector that it is represented in the IEC 61850 configuration file (SCL file) can be obtained directly from this file if the *scl:tConductingEquipment* instance which is representing a disconnector is associated with a *XSWI* logical node. In that case, the type of disconnector can be obtained from the *swTyp* attribute of the *XSWI* logical node. However, such association between the *scl:tConductingEquipment* and the *XSWI* logical node with the *swTyp* attribute is not always included in the SCL file. Moreover, the majority of the granularity and perspective mismatches cannot be solved employing only information contained in the standards. For that reason, additional domain knowledge is required.

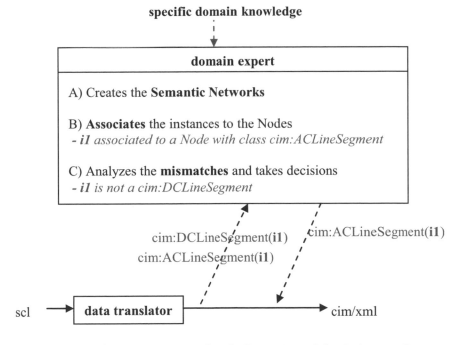

Figure 1. *The Domain Expert solves the Lines mismatch for the instance i1*

This section briefly describes the tool, called *Domain Expert*, and the methodology that makes it possible to automatically use additional knowledge about the electric system facilities in order to solve the granularity and perspective mismatches. The *Domain Expert* creates its knowledge base from two OWL[1] files containing information about how a specific type of facility (radial MV/LV substation, breaker and a half substation, electrified railway system DC substation, etc.) and its automation system should be represented in each standard. The knowledge base consists of two semantic networks (one for each standard) in which each node represents a type of element that have to appear, or at least, can appear in the output of the translation. Thus, when the data translator, for example, *ESODAT* (Santodomingo *et al.*, 2010), translates an instance file from one standard to the other, the *Domain Expert* analyzes the output of the translation and associates the instances of the file with their closer nodes in the corresponding semantic network. Such associations are based on the information about: a) the class to which the instances belong in the output of the translation, and b) the relationships and attributes that have the instances in the output of the translation. From these associations the *Domain Expert* is able to solve the conflict situations that appear in the granularity and perspective mismatches. For example, if in the SCL input file there is an instance representing a line, in the output of the translation that instance will belong to two different classes, *cim:ACLineSegment* and *cim:DCLineSegment*. The *Domain Expert*, depending on the class of the semantic network node associated with the instance, will decide to which of the two CIM classes the instance belongs.

3.2. *Buffer*

In the case that, once the instance file is translated from one standard to the other it is necessary to translate it back to the original standard, which is a common case in the interaction between CIM and IEC 61850 (EPRI, 2006), the lost information during the translation due to the *coverage mismatches* has to be retrieved.

The solution to this problem is based on a buffer which is able to detect the lost information by comparing the instances and values in the input and the output files of the translation. This lost information is loaded in an RDF/XML[2] file. During the translation to the opposite direction the buffer fulfils the output file of the translation with the information loaded in the RDF/XML file. In this process the buffer takes into account the possibility that an instance appearing in the RDF/XML file could have been removed in the target configuration tool. In this case the buffer will not add the information of the removed instance. For example, if the RDF/XML file contains a statement with the information about the *cim:Switch.normalOpen* attribute of a breaker and that breaker is removed in the SCL configuration tool, when the SCL file is translated back to the CIM the buffer will not add this statement.

---

1 Web Ontology Language: http://www.w3.org/TR/owl-guide.
2 RDF/XML syntax: http://www.w3.org/TR/REC-rdf-syntax.

In order to retrieve the lost information following the methodology explained above, the buffer has to previously retrieve the lost instance identifiers. The problem is that in CIM the instances are identified with the rdf:ID identifiers, whereas in SCL the instances are identified by the attributes defined in the SCL Schema. In that way, in the translation from CIM to IEC 61850 the rdf:ID identifiers are lost. When the files are translated back from IEC 61850 to CIM, in order to retrieve the lost information during the first translation, it is necessary to associate the instances included in the buffer with the instances described in the input SCL file. Such association is very complex if the instances employ different identifiers in the buffer and in the SCL file. In order to solve this problem, during the CIM to IEC 61850 translation, the data translator automatically generates in the output SCL file *scl:tPrivate* sections associated with each instance. These *scl:tPrivate* sections include the rdf:ID identifier of the corresponding instance and, following the IEC 61850 standard, will not be modified or removed in a SCL configuration tool. Thus, the process for recovering the rdf:ID identifiers could be easily done by the data translator at the beginning of the IEC 61850 to CIM translation.

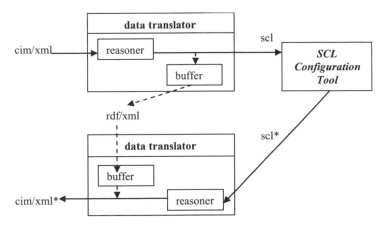

Figure 2. *The buffer included in the data translator solves the coverage mismatches by saving the untranslated parts*

3.3. Coordinated profiles

Flexibility mismatches appear due to the existence of optional attributes and relationships in the ontologies obtained from the standards. Such attributes and relationships are defined as optional in order to give the standards the flexibility required to be applied in different types of electric facilities. Thus, the solution to this type of mismatch will be given by the creation of coordinated profiles that select the optional attributes and relationships that have to appear in the instance files of each standard to guarantee the interoperability for a specific type of facility. In that way, the cases in which a profile does not include optional attributes or relationships included in the other profile have to be avoided.

Currently, the profile elaboration is not automated at all and has to be carried out by specialists on the standards. In order to improve this process, a tool, called *Profiler*, which processes the ontologies and alignments in order to guide the user in the coordinated profile elaboration, is being developed using Semantic Web resources. In the future, this tool will be able to generate the OWL files that are employed by the *Domain Expert* to solve the granularity and perspective mismatches following the methodology explained above, i.e. the profiles give the *Domain Expert* the specific domain knowledge required to solve the conflict situations. Such files are also employed by the data translator (*ESODAT*) to validate the instance files against the profiles.

4. Interaction between the solutions

This section shows how the different proposed solutions will interact in order to achieve the harmonization between the CIM and the IEC 61850 standards.

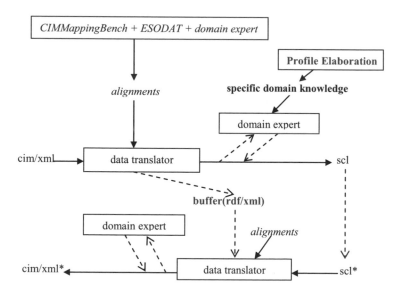

Figure 3. *Interaction between the solutions to achieve the harmonization*

The first step for the harmonization is to obtain the semantic correspondences (alignments) between the standards. In the state of the art there are may ontology matching contributions that aim to automatically find the alignments between ontologies, such as: (Euzenat *et al.*, 2007), the SEALS Project[3] and the Ontology Matching Organization[4]. In the particular case of the electric system domain, the OFFIS Institute of Oldenburg developed a methodology to align the ontologies created from the standards defined by the IEC TC57. This methodology, called COLIN (Uslar *et al.*, 2008), includes a tool (the *CIMMappingBench*) which semi-automatically obtains the alignments between the ontologies employing lexical-based, dictionary-based and string-based methods. Currently an interaction between the *CIMMappingBench*, *ESODAT* and the *Domain Expert* has been defined and will be implemented as part of a collaborative work between OFFIS and IIT. This interaction will improve the process of obtaining the alignments between the CIM and IEC 61850 ontologies and will consist of an iterative process in which the *Domain Expert* will check the validity of the translation obtained in *ESODAT* with the alignments found for a specific iteration. If the *Domain Expert* finds some mistakes in the output of the translation it will propose new alignments so that in the next iteration *ESODAT* obtains better results.

Once the alignments are obtained, they will be processed by the data translator (*ESODAT*) in order to translate instance files from one standard to the other. *ESODAT* contains a buffer that solves the coverage mismatches. Moreover this data translator is able to check if the instance files follow the definitions included in the coordinated profiles that solve the flexibility mismatches. During the translation the *Domain Expert*, which creates its knowledge base from specific knowledge defined in the coordinated profiles, analyzes the output of *ESODAT* and solves the granularity and perspective mismatches.

5. Conclusion

To achieve harmonization between CIM and IEC 61850 standards it is necessary to solve the mismatches that appear due to its heterogeneity. Previous works (Preiss *et al.*, 2006) classify the mismatches attending to their localization in the ontologies: *class level, relationship level* and *attribute level* incompatibilities. Such classification seeks to detect the modifications that have to be made in the original standards in order to create a unified model (EPRI, 2010) for both standards without mismatches between them.

The work presented here gives a different approach that is closer to the ontology matching contributions mainly developed for the Semantic Web and proposes a new classification for the mismatches based on the reasons that explain their existence. Moreover, this work proposes solutions for all the types of mismatches that were

---

3 SEALS Project: http://www.seals-project.eu.
4 Ontology Matching Organization: http://www.ontologymatching.org.

identified and describes how these solutions should interact in order to harmonize the CIM and IEC 61850 standards.

6. References

Benerecetti, M., Bouquet, P. & Ghidini, C., "On the Dimensions of Context Dependence: Partiality, Approximation, and Perspective". In *Proc. 3rd International and Interdisciplinary Conference on Modeling and Using Context (CONTEXT)*, volume 2216 of Lecture notes in computer science, pages 59-72, Dundee (UK), 2001.

EPRI, Harmonization of IEC 61970, 61968, and 61850 Models. Palo Alto, CA: 2006.

EPRI, Harmonizing the International Electrotechnical Comission Common Information Model (CIM) and 61850 Standards via a Unified Model: key to achieve Smart Grid Interoperability Objectives. Palo Alto, CA: 2010.

Euzenat, J. & Shvaiko, P., *Ontology Matching*, Springer-Verlag. 2007.

Euzenat, J., "Towards a Principled Approach to Semantic Interoperability", *Workshop on Ontologies and Information Sharing, IJCAI'01*, pages 19-25, Seattle (WA US), 2001.

Horrocks, I., Patel-Schneider, P.F., Boley, H., Tabet, S., Grosof, B. & Dean, M., *SWRL: A Semantic Web Rule Language Combining OWL and RuleML*, World Wide Web Consortium; National Research Council of Canada, Network Inference, and Stanford University, 2004.

NIST, Framework and Roadmap for Smart Grid Interoperability Standards, Release 1.0, January, 2010.

Preiss, O. & Kostic, T., "Unified Information Models in Support of Location Transparency for Future Utility Applications", *39th Hawaii International Conference on System Sciences (HICSS)*, Kauai, Hawaii, USA, 4-7 January 2006

Santodomingo, R., Rodríguez-Mondéjar, J.A. & Sanz-Bobi, M.A., "Ontology Matching Approach to the Harmonization of CIM and IEC 61850 Standards", *First IEEE International Conference on Smart Grid Communications (SmartGridComm)*, 2010.

Saxton T. & Schimmel G., IEC 61970 and IEC 61850 harmonization issues. IEC TC57 Draft Technical Report, 2003.

Sirin, E., Parsia, B., Grau, B.C., Kalyanpur, A. & Katz, Y. "Pellet: A practical OWL-DL reasoner", *Journal of Web Semantics*, vol. 5, no. 2, pp. 51-53, 2007.

Smart, P.R. & Engelbrecht, P.C., "An Analysis of the Origin of Ontology Mismatches on the Semantic Web", *Proceedings of the 16th International Conference on Knowledge Engineering: Practice and Patterns*. Springer-Verlag, Berlin, pp. 120., 2008.

Uslar, M., Rohjans, S., Schulte, S. & Steinmetz, R., "Building the Semantic Utility with Standards and Semantic Web Services", *Lecture Notes in Computer Science - On the Move to Meaningful Internet Systems: OTM Workshops*, eds. A. Hofmann, B. Apfel, U. Barth, *et al.*, Springer-Verlag, Computer Science Editorial, 2008.

Dynamic Virtual Enterprises – The Challenges of the Utility Industry for Enterprise Architecture Management

Sabine Buckl[1] – Rolf Marliani[2] – Florian Matthes[1] – Christian M. Schweda[1]

[1]*Chair for Software Engineering for Business Information Systems*
Technische Universität München, 85748 Garching
Germany
{sabine.buckl,matthes,christian.m.schweda}@mytum.de

[2]*E.ON IT GmbH, Humboldtstr. 33, Hanover*
Germany
Rolf.marliani@eon.com

ABSTRACT: *Driven by the rapidly changing markets conditions, organizations from the utility and energy industry sector have to cope with increasing demand for change. This demand for change not only arises from external forces as legal regulations and emerging innovations but also originates from strategic objectives within the company. Thereto, organizations from the industry sector strive for a flexible enterprise architecture (EA) that provides a holistic overview on the overall make-up of the organization and fosters adaptation to changing situations.*

In this paper, we present characteristics of the energy industry sector and the resulting challenges with respect to enterprise transformation, discuss how prevalent approaches could contribute to a solution, and propose future research areas and topics.

KEYWORDS: *Dynamic virtual enterprises, enterprise architecture management, utility industry, smart networks*

1. Motivation

Today's organizations in general and those from the energy and utility sector in particular are confronted with rapidly changing market situations and conditions resulting in an increasing demand for change. A holistic overview on the overall make-up of the organization, its constituents and interdependencies is typically regarded as a prerequisite to cope with this demand for change. The strategic management of the enterprise architecture (EA) is a commonly accepted instrument to support the transformation of the organization (see Aier and Gleichauf, 2010 or Doucet *et al.*, 2009). The EA according to the International Organization of Standardization (2007) is the fundamental conception of the organization in its environment, embodied in its elements, their relationships to each other and to its environment, and the principles guiding its design and evolution.

The following excerpt from the strategy description of E.ON emphasizes the challenges organizations in the energy and utility sector are confronted with:

> *In today's world of global competition, rapid business change, legal regulation impacts and narrowing margins, E.ON is under increasing pressure to simultaneously grow revenue and market share while reducing costs, simplifying infrastructure and speeding up processes.*

The driving forces for adaptation of organizations thereby do not only originate externally as changing legal regulations or technology innovations but also arises within the organization. Typical internal demands for adaptation are increasing responsiveness via reduced project duration (van Raadt and van Vliet, 2008), risk management (Ross *et al.*, 2006), enhanced standardization (Bird, 1998), or mergers and acquisitions (Buckl *et al.*, 2009). This demanding environment requires a new quality of partnership between distinct parts of the organization to which we refer in this paper as dynamic virtual enterprises. A dynamic virtual enterprise emphasizes the situation in which an organization has to cope with challenges of dynamically re-organizing its overall make-up with respect to legally independent parts.

The idea of a dynamic virtual enterprise can be exemplified along the typical value chain from the utility and energy industry sector as illustrated in Figure 1. Instead of optimizing the overall value chain due to a change demand, the transformation focuses on a dedicated part of the value chain. This results in different virtual enterprises as different parts of the value chain within one organization can even be managed with different business models. Thereto, the utility and energy industry sector can be described by the following set of characteristics:

- legal regulations demand a flexible adaptation of the structure of the overall organization or parts thereof resulting in different business models used in distinct units;

- information needs to be managed throughout the lifecycle and classified with respect to confidential information and information that needs to be shared among distinct units of the virtual enterprise;

- a need for secure information exchange to fulfil audit and compliance regulations;

- information about already existing ICT infrastructures and related business processes need to be available; as well as

- a clear understanding of the organizational interconnections and dependencies.

Figure 1. *Typical value chain from the energy industry sector*

In this paper, we sketch how a strategic management of the EA can support an organization in (re-)building dynamic virtual enterprises. We reflect prevalent approaches to EA management against the above discussed characteristics of the utility and energy sector and discuss the provided support in section 2. Based on the findings, we delineate future areas of research in the area of EA management accounting for the characteristics of the utility and energy industry in section 3.

2. Contributing work

Smart networks are (virtual) organizational structures of high flexibility. This means that for all three levels of collaboration, namely organizational, knowledge, and ICT (Filos, 2006), new partners can easily be integrated or dismissed. Lau *et al.* (2009) analyze how EA management can be applied to manage smart networks, more precisely to establish such networks. Critical to the EA-based approach to smart network establishment is the distinction between three categories of knowledge that is exchanged between the different participating organizations (see Rehm, 2007):

- *public knowledge* which is available to everyone;

- *community knowledge* available to the participants of the smart network; and

- *internal knowledge* which is kept privately by the owning organization.

Once an organizational network is set up, i.e. the collaborating organizations have decided to jointly pursue a business opportunity; the knowledge network has to be established. For this particular network, the different participating organizations decide which internal knowledge is promoted to community knowledge. Such knowledge can be strategic and tactical planning knowledge, as well as operational knowledge. In a final step, the knowledge exchange is supported by an appropriate ICT network. For the development of such a network, the EA management patterns of Lau *et al.* (2009) provide a valuable basis. They outline a method to decide whether decentralized and non-automated or ICT-supported communication means should be employed. The method is further supported by an EA modeling language spanning both knowledge and ICT level of the smart network.

The often cited analogy of EA management with city planning or urban development (see Pulkkinen, 2006) can further contribute to solving the challenges of the utility and energy sector discussed in section 1. Thereby, an organization is logically divided into:

- a *managed core*, i.e. the city center for which detailed rules regarding the construction of new and reshaping of existing buildings exist; and

- an *unmanaged periphery*, i.e. suburb where fewer rules exist and buildings can be (re-)constructed with more liberties.

The challenge in the context of EA management nevertheless is the establishment and adaptation of dynamic integration points between these independent areas within an organization, i.e. the dynamic virtual enterprises. Thereby, it must be ensured that a) reliable interfaces between the different areas exists, which remain stable during the future evolution; b) the "right" information is exchanged between these areas to ensure that the dynamic virtual enterprises can effectively collaborate with each other; c) the integration points must be completely deconstructable to allow dynamic allocation and reorganization of new virtual enterprises; and a d) capability-oriented dynamic EA management federation which provides a stable structure along with the long term evolution and vision of the organization can be organized.

3. Future research topics

In recent years, many of today's utility companies have re-structured themselves in respect to their organization. On the one hand, mergers and acquisitions have consolidated the market and have made the remaining companies more competitive. New regulations have forced on the other hand the companies to "unbundle" their different business roles, i.e. to separate the energy provider from the energy distributor. Mergers and acquisitions have led to heterogeneous enterprise architectures, in which similar business capabilities are implemented by different business applications. Vertical consolidation projects leverage potential synergies from homogenization. The organizational unbundling contrariwise demands the companies to rethink and re-structure integrated business applications that support business capabilities owned by different business roles. Horizontal modularization projects seek to establish a clear separation of the business support pertaining to different business roles of the company. Future research in this respect has to answer the following research question:

How can EA management support vertical consolidation and horizontal modularization of the business support?

The new regulations in respect to the separation of business roles have opened the utility sector for new competitors. Energy resellers, for example, that do not operate power plants or distribution facilities can supply electric power to households and businesses, offering additional services as "smart metering". Such services have implications to both the enterprise architecture of the reseller, but also of the distributor. While the former company requires additional facilities, as the smart meters, to offer such services, latter company has to support the routing of corresponding end-user specific information. This raises twofold implications. On the one hand, the distributor and the reseller have to negotiate and establish a linkage between their enterprise architectures. The reseller on the other hand has to ensure privacy of the obtained information, while it is routed through the distributor infrastructure. We expect the market of energy resellers to be volatile, such that both of the above implications demand a dynamic federation of enterprise architectures between changing distributors and resellers, while preserving privacy of end-user information as well as of business-critical information about the single architectures. EA research can in this area target the following research question:

What management methods and models are necessary to support dynamic federation of EAs, while keeping sensitive or business-critical EA and operation information private?

4. References

Aier, S., Gleichauf, B., "Application of enterprise models for engineering enterprise transformation", *Enterprise Modelling and Information System Architectures* 5, 2010, p. 56-72.

Bird, G.B., "The business benefit of standards", *StandardView* 6, 1998, p. 76-80.

Buckl, S., Ernst, A.M., Kopper, H., Marliani, R., Matthes, F., Petschownik, P., Schweda, C.M., "EAM pattern for consolidations after mergers", *SE 2009 – Workshopband*, Kaiserslautern, Germany, 2009, p. 67-78.

Doucet, G., Gotze, J., Saha, P., Bernard, S.A., "Introduction to coherency management: The transformation of enterprise architecture", Doucet, G., Gotze, J., Saha, P., Bernard, S. (eds.) *Coherency Management – Architecting the Enterprise for Alignment, Agility, and Assurance*. AuthorHouse, Bloomington, USA, 2009.

Filos, E., *Smart Organizations in the Digital Age. Integration of ICT in Smart Organizations*, 2009, p. 1-39.

International Organization for Standardization: ISO/IEC 42010:2007 Systems and software engineering { Recommended practice for architectural description of software-intensive systems, 2007

Lau, A., Fischer, T., Buckl, S., Ernst, A.M., Matthes, F., Schweda, C.M., "EA management patterns for smart networks", *SE 2009 – Workshopband*, 2009, p. 79-90.

Pulkkinen, M., "Systemic management of architectural decisions in enterprise architecture planning. four dimensions and three abstraction levels", *39th Hawaii International Conference on System Sciences (HICSS 2006)*. vol. 8, 2006, p. 179c.

van Raadt, B.d., van Vliet, H., "Designing the enterprise architecture function", Becker, S., Reussner, R., (eds.) *4th International Conference on the Quality of Software Architectures (QoSA2008)*. Lecture Notes in Computer Science, vol. 5281, Springer, Karlsruhe, Germany, 2008, p. 103-118.

Rehm, S.V., *Architektur vernetzter Wertschöpfungsgemeinschaften der Textilwirtschaft. (Architecture of Networked Value Added Communities of Textile Industries)*. Dissertation, Universität Stuttgart, 2007, http://elib.uni-stuttgart.de/opus/volltexte/2007/3197.

Ross, J.W., Weill, P., Robertson, D.C., *Enterprise Architecture as Strategy*. Harvard Business School Press, Boston, MA, USA, 2006.

Coping with Smart Grid

Standardization and Enterprise Architecture at your Service

Matthias Postina — Mathias Uslar — Sebastian Rohjans — Ulrike Steffens

OFFIS
Institute for Information Technology
Escherweg 2
D-26121 Oldenburg Germany

firstname.lastname@offis.de

ABSTRACT. *This paper shows how beneficial a close collaboration between Standardization and Enterprise Architecture can be in terms of the future Smart Grid IT architecture. We motivate the current trends in ICT for Smart Grids and bring in existing EA approaches and architectures from other domains. Starting with the IEC 62357 Seamless Integration Architecture, we identify five key issues to cope with Smart Grid challenges.*

KEYWORDS: *Smart Grid, Standardization, Enterprise Architecture, IEC 62357*

1. Introduction

The future Smart Grid is one of the biggest infrastructure changes being discussed today. While certain companies think of it as an even bigger market for hardware and equipment in terms of Information and Communication Technology (ICT) use than the Internet, the reality is much more pragmatic. Within standardization organizations, different roadmaps have evolved focusing both technical and organizational dimensions. In Europe, the European Committee for Standardization (CEN), the European Committee for Electrotechnical Standardization (CENELEC) and the European Telecommunications Standards Institute (ETSI) have been given a Smart Grid mandate and will provide recommendations for technical standards for Smart Grids. While the European initiative is slightly lagging behind other international work [ROH 10b] like the US National Institute of Standards and Technology (NIST), national initiatives like the German E-Energy/Smart Grid roadmap [DKE 10], the Chinese Strong and Smart Grid Roadmap [SGC 10], or recommendations of the International Electrotechnical Commission (IEC) [SMB 10], now major recommendations are to be expected.

One of the key recommendations of each individual aforementioned roadmap is the IEC TC 57 Seamless Integration Architecture (SIA). It is a Service Oriented Architecture (SOA)-based viewpoint and layered architecture taking into account all the relevant vertical and horizontal functions and layers of an electric utility. The current version with European focus is depicted in Figure 1. Other relevant standards include security being imposed by IEC 62351, field communication using IEC 60870, substation automation and Distributed Energy Resources (DER) control using IEC 61850, and Energy Management Systems (EMS) using IEC 61970/61968. In order to provide a proper seamless integration for the Smart Grid, all layers have to be interoperable, imposing changes to the Enterprise Architecture (EA) in the classic electric utility.

Coping with Smart Grid architectural visions like IEC TC 57 will be an inter-organizational effort. The NIST Smart Grid roadmap [NIS 10] identifies various stakeholders and, due to governmental regulations like for example legal unbundling in the German market, single utilities will not cover the entire Smart Grid supply chain (any more). Besides well-established standards for the architecture of the automation layer, more holistic architectural considerations need to be taken into account including business and process layers to foster intra- and inter-enterprise communication [POS 10a]. Moreover, Smart Grid architecture management has also to adhere to rules and regulations such as legal issues and social integration since the Smart Grid will become an ultra large-scale sociotechnical system.

EA and standardization will be of value for both architectural challenges of future Smart Grids, inter-enterprise collaboration and intra-enterprise architecture changes. The situation is comparable to sectors like the telecommunications industry in the 1990s or more recently the financial industry, even though the Smart Grid seems to become much more complex in scale. Architectural standardization, especially

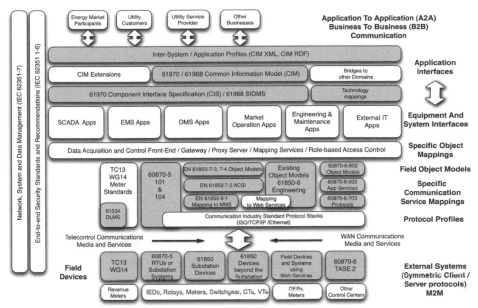

Overview on IEC/TR 62357 Seamless Integration Architecture - CENELEC adopted Standards in light gray

Figure 1. *IEC TR 62357 Seamless Integration Reference Architecture*

for SOA-like architectures took and still takes place at the TeleManagement Forum[1] (Frameworx – eTOM, SID, TAM) or the Banking Industry Architecture Network[2] (BIAN). We consider these industry solutions as an inspiring starting point for coping with similar challenges that utilities are facing in Smart Grid. An integrated conceptual framework for a canonical data model, standard payloads and interfaces, transport layers and well defined processes – this is where IEC can benefit a lot from existing approaches.

2. As-is status of utilities

2.1. *Standardization*

Within the electric utility, different standards have already been deployed at IT, Supervisory Control and Data Acquisition (SCADA), field device and home-area-network level. As Figure 1 shows, different standards have to be seen in context with this topic. Different Smart Grid standardization studies and roadmaps exist all around the world [ROH 10b, USL 10]. Because most of them rely on standards and technologies from international standardization bodies like International Telecommunication Union (ITU), International Organization for

---

1. http://www.tmforum.org
2. http://www.bian.org

Standardization (ISO) or IEC, a consensus on the most important standards for the future electric and ICT side of the Smart Grid could be reached. [ROH 10b, USL 10] provide an overview of the most important national, international and Standards Developing Organization (SDO)-based roadmaps worldwide. Consensus has been reached on some very basic levels. Most of the standards are from the IEC TC 57 group with some further standards from IEC TC 13 on metering (like DLMS/COSEM[3]). For security, the IEC 62351 family has been ruled out to be setting the most important security issues in terms of communication for the Technical Report (TR) 62357 family standards. At IT level, the Common Information Model (CIM) (IEC 61968/61970) has been identified to be the most suitable domain ontology and EMS-API interface for SCADA, Distribution Management System (DMS) and EMS applications. At field automation level, the IEC 61850 provides data communications and object models for substation and DER. With the upcoming integration of automation, IT and substation Intelligent Electronic Devices (IEDs), the new OPC Unified Architecture (UA) IEC 62541 gains more and more attention as service-oriented architectures within the distributed IT in the Smart Grid get more and more important.

Utilities nowadays are both open to accept and implement those standards but also regulators and legislators (e.g. Federal Energy Regulatory Commission (FERC) and North American Electric Reliability Corporation (NERC) in the US or the European Commission with the EU mandates M/441 on smart metering, M/468 on electric vehicles an M/490 on Smart Grids) try to enforce technical infrastructure and solutions in order to provide a proper and resilient infrastructure for the end-customer.

2.2. *Architectural situation*

System landscapes in electric utilities used to be rather monolithic and mostly dominated by one single vendor providing the whole infrastructure. As the Smart Grid introduces new systems, applications and markets, new players come into the market. The overall amount of system interfaces and data being exchanged increases and the shift from datapoint-oriented SCADA-focused communication changes to more bus-oriented structures. This leads to a shift in the overall data being exchanged now with the IT department where the data gathered is processed. Services emerge and must be orchestrated and aligned to business processes. The IEC TC 57 SIA is meant to be implemented using the SOA-paradigm, but little work has been done so far regarding the applicability in the electric utility domain in general. This contribution wants to come up with issues to be addressed and propose solutions.

2.3. *Smart Grid readiness*

It is not easy to measure how well a utility and its infrastructure performs in terms of Smart Grid maturity. The Software Engineering Institute at the Carnegie

---

3. http://www.dlms.com/index2.php

Mellon University has, alongside IBM, created a so-called Smart Grid Maturity Model (SGMM) which addresses 8 different dimensions: Grid Operations, Value Chain Integration, Work and Asset Management, Customer Management and Experience, Organization, Technology, Societal and Environmental and finally Strategy, Management and Regulatory. Those eight domains have been assigned to roughly 175 indicators which are assessed to distinguish between five levels. Those levels are exploring and initiating, functional investing, integrating cross-functional, optimizing enterprise-wide and innovating – next wave of improvements [TOG 10]. With some adaptation, this model can be used at European utilities, too. When looking at the different dimensions, the technical aspect left alone cannot solve the Smart Grid problems. As EA also takes into account Organization and Value Chain Integration, the aspect of IT can be better aligned to the technology dimension using this paradigm to assess the Smart Grid readiness at IT-level in the utility. The next section is going to provide more insight to the overall topic of Enterprise Architecture and how it should be seen in context with Smart Grids.

3. Enterprise Architecture

Enterprise Architecture has a long tradition reaching back into the late 80th of the last century where pioneers in the field of EA like Zachman [ZAC 87] were introducing first frameworks for information systems architecture. Today EA is well known among enterprise architects in large companies and tools are supporting them in their daily work of enterprise evolution management. In practice, such information integration often corresponds to the usage of a centralized architecture repository providing data to architecture management software which provides support for description [IEE 00] and analysis (for example graphical analysis like in [WIT 07]) of complex enterprise environments.

However, architecture is changing over time and architecture management has to follow. Especially with the advent of SOA complexity has grown compared to classical application-silo architectures [ERL 06]. Following the SOA paradigm, services seem to become the central building blocks of entire enterprise architectures with multiple stakeholders involved. This trend changes the characteristics of enterprise architectures, since the subject matter is shifting from applications towards services and leads to a number of new challenges like:

– Applications were considered as black-boxes with hidden internal functionality offering a limited number of interfaces to the environment. Internal integration was generally assured by data integration on a common database. In SOA-like environments also former internal functionality is made available externally for multiple purposes. This leads to a new level of granularity, the need for a formalization of interface descriptions and explicit data transfer between services. Also formally hidden aspects like security, transaction and error handling and assured Service Level Agreements (SLAs) need to be externalized.

– Applications were usually reflecting organizational structures. A billing application was managed and used by the billing department for instance. This led to a "natural" alignment of systems and responsibility. In SOA environments, services can be used in various contexts to assemble temporary composites. Responsibilities need to be modeled explicitly in such environments.

– The possibility to exchange services easily fosters the development and usage of alternative services. Functional and non-functional requirements need to be clearly stated by all involved stakeholders in order to find an appropriate match.

– Applications were also logical entities with "natural" borderlines for architectural rules and standards. Protocols, data models, technology specification as well as version and release control were bound to an application or at least modules of an application. Service management needs to support these issues for much more and smaller entities.

EA as a discipline has just begun to reflect the SOA paradigm in EA frameworks (for example in [USD 09]), architecture description languages [TOG 09a] or as part of industry consortia activities like Frameworx, which was formally known as New Generation Operations Systems and Software (NGOSS) for the telecommunication industry or BIAN for banks.

Smart Grid goes beyond the scope of single enterprises and the IT dimension of Smart Grid forms an ultra-large-scale system (ULS system) as described in [NOR 06] affording even more challenges like:

– **Design and evolution:** Designing ULS systems requires much more coordination of design capabilities and reaches beyond traditional enterprise boundaries. The entire utility industry and further stakeholders are affected by Smart Grid as a complex design space. Thus, traditional blueprint design approaches will fail, since the "nature" of such a system is not about initial design but evolution management of "decentralized design activities spread across the economy" [NOR 06].

– **Orchestration and control:** Orchestration is defined by [NOR 06] as "the set of activities needed to make the elements of a ULS work in reasonable harmony" as part of "an emergent whole". Since for Smart Grid single organizations will not be able to control the emergent whole other forms of control mechanisms have to be established on different levels. Standardization, general policies and commonly agreed regulations will become more important and will also affect the internal structures of organizations.

– **Monitoring and Assessment:** Measuring the "health" of the entire Smart Grid requires different monitoring and assessment capabilities than necessary to observe smaller systems. Indicators have to be found to "reflect the conditions not only of the technological but also human, organizational, economic and business elements of the system" [NOR 06].

However, EA has been dealing with complex systems ever since and provides adequate methods and techniques for large scale architecture management. Moreover, first experience for EA management of large SOA environments has been integrated in the form of best-practices into EA frameworks and industry solutions. In combination with standardization efforts EA can contribute significantly to cope with Smart Grid.

4. Key issues for applying standards and EA methods in the Smart Grid sector

We have identified the following issues and key aspects on where EA and standardization efforts can provide significant benefits for architecture development in the electric Smart Grid:

– **Well-defined business processes:** Whereas typical Smart Grid scenarios lack the urgent need of well-documented business processes, the Smart Grid has a strong need for documenting use cases. Because business models are new and infrastructure and processes must be developed, there is a high acceptance for spending money on documenting use cases and mapping them to services. Especially for inter-enterprise collaboration, standardized business processes providing well known interfaces to all participants are important. Regarding the business layer as part of the overall context is an aspect where EA techniques serve well and for example Phase B of the The Open Group Architecture Framework (TOGAF) [TOG 09b] Architecture Development Method (ADM), which is dedicated to Business Architecture, is a good starting point.

– **A canonical data model with common semantics:** The IEC 61970 Common Information Model provides all the needed objects for EMS data exchange and interfaces within the semantic utility. For a SOA in the Smart Grid, this is a huge leap forward – services should rely on common sense data objects as part of a well understood data architecture for seamless automated processing. Organizing the data architecture in complex systems is a typical challenge EA is dealing with – for example being part of the TOGAF Information Systems Architecture.

– **Well-defined function and building blocks:** Standards like the IEC 61968 Interface Reference Model provide both standardized semantics and payloads with defined interfaces. This supports stripping down systems to functions to services which can then be recombined, but also provide an opportunity for vendors to provide specialized applications which are interoperable with standard interfaces. Vendors like IBM, SAP and Oracle are prepared to put their utility strategy in this direction getting into the markets of classic automation vendors. Understanding building blocks as essential elements of the entire application landscape and especially make or buy considerations for these building blocks are everyday business for enterprise architects. An approach where IEC 61968 was used to identify architectural building blocks is presented in [POS 09].

– **Standardized Technology Spaces:** Upcoming trends like OPC Unified Architecture with technology mappings for both IT and automation domain will have a huge impact on transforming utilities IT landscapes, making previous separated systems merge and business processes have a larger vertical impact [ROH 10a]. First approaches like [KÖN 10] already show the applicability of the EA language ArchiMate [TOG 09a] to describe parts of the standardized automation layer (IEC 61850).

– **Creating reference frameworks and models:** Just as the telecommunication industry has benefited from reference models, the standards provide a head-start to do this kind of work for creating an EA strategy in the Smart Grid sector. Different viewpoints for Smart Grid applications have to be defined, covering processes, data models, functional aspects, and technical infrastructure. A first classification approach aiming in this direction is outlined in [GON 10]. Moreover, Smart Grid viewpoints have to be broken down into fine grained viewpoints. Especially for SOA viewpoints, EA can provide guidance on how to develop such viewpoints (for example in [POS 10b]).

5. Future work and conclusion

Within this paper, we provided an overview on the most important Smart Grid reference architecture, the IEC Seamless Integration Architecture. Our research aims at providing a meaningful architecture for the upper IT part of SIA. With the focus on horizontal and vertical integration, it is fully suitable for most electric utilities around the world providing different architecture styles which could be implemented. To reach a proper implementation of this architecture, we propose the use of known and established EA practices. We suggest multi-perspective service management (MPSM) for both the automation layer using the OPC-UA and the process layer. Therefore, we outlined five key aspects on where EA could provide input to the most recognized IEC standards and architectures and where a useful joint can be anticipated. Within our research agenda, we address each of those five key factors to resolve the layer integration and architecture instantiation problem for the Smart Grid.

6. Bibliography

[DKE 10] DKE, *The German Standardization Roadmap E-Energy/Smart Grid*, VDE, 2010.

[ERL 06] ERL T., *Service-Oriented Architecture: Concepts, Technology, and Design*, Prentice-Hall, Upper Saddle River, NJ, 2006.

[GON 10] GONZÁLEZ   J.   M.,   APPELRATH   H.-J.,   ""Energie-RMK"   Ein Referenzmodellkatalog für die Energiewirtschaft", *GI-Modellierung 2010*, 2010, p. 319–334.

[IEE 00] IEEE Std 1471-2000, IEEE - 1471 Recommended Practice for Architectural Description of Software-Intensive Systems, 2000.

[KÖN 10] KÖNIG J., ZHU K., NORDSTRÖM L., EKSTEDT M., LAGERSTRÖM R., "Mapping the substation configuration language of IEC 61850 to ArchiMate", *Enterprise Distributed Object Computing Conference Workshops, 2010 14th IEEE International*, October 2010, p. 60–69.

[NIS 10] NIST, NIST Framework and Roadmap for Smart Grid Interoperability Standards, Release 1.0, Technical report, 2010, National Institute for Standards and Technology.

[NOR 06] NORTHROP L., FEILER P., GABRIEL R. P., GOODENOUGH J., LINGER R., KAZMAN R., SCHMIDT D., SULLIVAN K., WALLNAU K., Ultra-Large-Scale systems-the software challenge of the future, Technical report, 2006.

[POS 09] POSTINA M., GONZALEZ J., SECHYN I., "On the architecture development of utility enterprises with special respect to the gap analysis of application landscapes", STEFFENS U., STREEKMANN N., ADDICKS J., POSTINA M., Eds., *MDD, SOA and IT-Management (MSI 2009) Workshop*, Berlin, 2009, Gito Verlag, p. 17–33.

[POS 10a] POSTINA M., ROHJANS S., STEFFENS U., MATHIAS U., "Views on service oriented architectures in the context of smart grids", *First IEEE International Conference on Smart Grid Communications*, Gaithersburg, 2010, IEEE, p. 25–30.

[POS 10b] POSTINA M., TREFKE J., STEFFENS U., "An EA-approach to develop SOA viewpoints", *Enterprise Distributed Object Computing Conference (EDOC), 2010 14th IEEE International*, October 2010, p. 37–46.

[ROH 10a] ROHJANS S., USLAR M., APPELRATH H.-J., "OPC UA and CIM: Semantics for the smart grid", *Transmission and Distribution Conference and Exposition, 2010 IEEE PES*, 2010, p. 1–8.

[ROH 10b] ROHJANS S., USLAR M., BLEIKER R., GONZÁLEZ J., SPECHT M., SUDING T., WEIDELT T., "Survey of smart grid standardization studies and recommendations", *First IEEE International Conference on Smart Grid Communications*, 2010.

[SGC 10] State Grid China, SGCC Framework and Roadmap for Strong & Smart Grid Standards, 2010.

[SMB 10] SMB Smart Grid Strategic Group (SG3), IEC Smart Grid Standardization Roadmap, 2010.

[TOG 09a] The Open Group, Archimate 1.0 Specification - Technical Standard, 2009.

[TOG 09b] The Open Group, TOGAF Version 9, 2009.

[TOG 10] The SGMM TEAM, Smart Grid Maturity Model - Model Definition - A framework for smart grid transformation, 2010.

[USD 09] United States Department of Defense, The DoDAF Architecture Framework Version 2.0, 2009.

[USL 10] USLAR M., ROHJANS S., BLEIKER R., GONZÁLEZ J. M., SUDING T., SPECHT M., WEIDELT T., "Survey of smart grid standardization studies and recommendations - Part 2", *IEEE Innovative Smart Grid Technologies Europe*, 2010.

[WIT 07] WITTENBURG A., Softwarekartographie: Modelle und Methoden zur systematischen Visualisierung von Anwendungslandschaften, PhD thesis, TU München, Faculty of Informatics, 2007.

[ZAC 87] ZACHMAN J. A., "A framework for information systems architecture", *IBM Systems Journal*, vol. 26, no. 3, 1987, p. 291–296.

A Standards-Based Security Approach with Interoperable Interfaces for the Smart Grid

P. Beenken – C. Pries – S. Abels – M. Uslar

OFFIS – Institute for Information Systems
Escherweg 2
26121 Oldenburg
Germany

Petra.beenken@offis.de
Christine.Pries@offis.de
Uslar@offis.de

Ascora – Consulting Development Research
Langeooger Strasse 2
27755 Delmenhorst
Germany

abels@ascora.de

ABSTRACT: *Within this contribution, we outline the need for an end-to-end vertical solution for Smart Grid security. With the upcoming new devices and interfaces, both interoperability and security issues arise. The data needed and gathered from the field devices and metering devices (e.g. smart meters) impose new problems in terms of general data security and privacy. Within this paper we summarize existing standards related to security aspects and challenges for Smart Grid. Afterwards, we introduce the so-called Enertrust framework which copes with the data security problem and shows possible solutions and restrictions for the new ICT infrastructure. We also describe the usage of additive homomorphic encryption within the Smart Metering domain and we describe potential benefits that arise from its usage.*

KEYWORDS: *IEC 62351, Security Ontologies, Security Measures, Integration*

1. Introduction

With the upcoming envisioned Smart Grid, the transition of the existing transmission and distribution grid to a more resilient, self-monitoring, and self-optimizing grid with better overall efficiency is intended. Within this future Smart Grid, the usage of ICT alongside the classic filed automation and electric generation and distribution technology becomes more and more prominent. One main aspect of the future Smart Grid will be the meaningful introduction of ICT sensors, communications and metering equipment to know more information about the load flows, the exact state of the grid at any level and the control or distributed and dispersed generation or storage.

Within this environment, the need for performing interoperable systems that may seamlessly communicate within the Smart Grid, is crucial. One possibility to cope with those challenges is using a standardized architecture like the IEC TC 57 Seamless Integration Architecture SIA [NIS10a]. But standardizing syntax and semantics interfaces is only aspect, also communication and control is of highest interest. The grid has to be considered a critical infrastructure; therefore, it has to be protected. With new interfaces introduced, and new data being generated and exchanged, security problems may arise [URS08]. Typical solutions today focus on the security at transport or communication level. Data protection and security aspects at the storage and database label are not in the current focus of interest. For the new optimization processes, data is used in a different context. Within some EU member states, such as Germany, laws enforce the informational unbundling, making data protection in Smart Grids even more important. Distributed actors and systems have to act with different views and roles for accessing and viewing the data, data leakages preventions become more and more important. Also, the trend is to go from monolithic security by obscurity solutions to more interconnected, standard-hardware (COTS), IP-based networks and data exchange. Therefore, there will be a shift of the protection goals. Integrity and confidentiality have always been of the highest importance for IT infrastructures, whereas confidentiality and availability of data have always been of the highest importance in the utility sector.

Within this contribution, we focus on the protection goal of confidentiality and the commercially sensitive data like customer data, load profiles, market data, metering data and general personal data according to the German law "BDSG".

The rest of this contribution is organized as follows. Section 1 provided a short introduction to the Smart Grid and the upcoming ICT interfaces challenge with the protection goal of data confidentiality. Section 2 provides an overview on existing security standards and measures in the context of the IEC TC 57 SIA and outlines current challenges. In section 3, the concept of ontology-based information security management systems (ISMS) is introduced, providing an overview on our ontology and concepts developed. A feasible technological concept for smart metering security based on this approach is presented in section 4. Section 5 concludes the paper, outlining the concept of privacy by design and using reasoning on our ontology-based ISMS for finding out more about the current security status of data and system landscape.

2. Existing security standards and challenges for the Smart Grid

There are established as well as drafted security standards for diverse target groups and different domains. All these security standards have the goal to harmonize and simplify the procedures of IT security as well as to increase the common security level. In this section security standards, which can be applied in the energy and the Smart Grid domain, will be described shortly and additionally categorized into the eight different domains of the value chain for the energy sector: generation, trading, retail, transmission, storage, distribution, metering and application (see Table 1).

Security standard	generation	trading	retail	transmission	storage	distribution	metering	application
IEC 62351	■	■	■	■	■	■	■	■
ISA99/IEC 62443	■	■	■	■	■	■	■	■
IEEE 1686	■			■	■	■	■	
NERC-CIP 002-009	■	■	■	■	■	■	■	■
BDEW Whitepaper	■	■		■	■	■	■	■
ISO/IEC 27000	■	■	■	■	■	■	■	■
VDI/VDE 2182	■	■	■	■	■	■	■	■
AMI-SEC							■	

Table 1. *Security standards and their scope in the Smart Grid*

IEC 62351: IEC 62351 has the title "Data and Communications Security" and is included in the aforementioned SIA as a cross-section for data and communication security. This standard is divided into nine parts. The first part provides a general introduction and the second part includes some definitions used in the standard. The following parts three to six provide security enhancements for profiles including TCP/IP, profiles including MMS, IEC 60870-5 and derivatives and IEC 61850 profiles. The seventh and eighth part of the standard deals with domain specific data models for network management and role-based access control. This eighth part is actually in a draft version and shall be published in 2012. A ninth part is planned and will contain key-management issues for this domain.

ISA99 / IEC 62443: The standardization activities for the standards ISA 99 and IEC 62443 were combined because there is a high correlation. The standard deals with IT security for industrial automation and control systems. It specifies a process model for IT security in this domain. This standard is divided in different parts. Not all parts are published yet.[1] The first three parts are summarized as "Common" and contain an introduction, a glossary and a part about security metrics. The next three parts are entitled "Security program" and describe how to establish, how to operate and how to do the patch management for the security program. The next four parts specify the "Technical – System" with security technologies, security assurance levels, different security requirements and product development requirements. The last four parts named "Technical – Component" describe technical requirements for embedded devices, host devices, network devices and applications, data and functions.

IEEE 1686: The standard IEEE 1686 with the title "IEEE Standard for Substation Intelligent Electronic Devices (IEDs) – Cyber Security Capabilities" describes the fundamental security requirements for devices in substations. These requirements can also be used in other scopes in the electric domain. The main goal is to support the secure exchange of information for all devices, for example in the updating- or configuration-process. For this, the following measures are specified: electronic access control, audit trail, supervisory monitoring and control, configuration software and port access.

NERC-CIP: The NERC-CIP 002 to 009 standards arise from the "Critical Infrastructure Protection-Program" of the North American Electric Reliability Corporation (NERC) and present some mandatory guidelines for the utilities. This standard provides a framework for the utilities to identify and protect assets.

BDEW Whitepaper: The BDEW-Whitepaper was published in 2008 in German and English and has the title "Requirements for Secure Control and Telecommunication Systems". The Whitepaper describes some requirements for this domain, for example requirements for the base system or the networks/communication. There are no concrete implementation recommendations but there are some references to the ISO/IEC 27002, where this can be found. It is planned to publish this whitepaper as a domain specific version in the ISO/IEC 27002.

---

1 See http://isa99.isa.org/ISA99%20Wiki/Work%20Products.aspx.

ISO/IEC 27000: The ISO/IEC 27000 is international series of standard for common information security issues.[2] This series contains of some standards, for example the ISO/IEC 27001 which is the standard for information security management systems. Another example is the before mentioned ISO/IEC 27002 which contains codes of practice for information security.

VDI/VDE 2182: The VDI/VDE 2182 is a standard of two German organizations and is published since 2007. It contains guidelines for information security in the industrial automation. To reach an adequate security level they developed and provided in the standard a common process model. Additionally there are some examples of use, for example for programmable logic controller (PLC).

AMI System Security Requirements: The "AMI-SEC" document, published in 2008, contains more than 500 different requirements separated in different categories, for example integrity or availability. These requirements support the power industry to secure the Advanced Metering Infrastructure.

In addition to these described standards and recommendations there are some more security standards, which can be applied in the energy domain. In Table 1 the most relevant security standards for the Smart Grid domain are listed. In the list above, we mention security standards that enhance protocols of the energy domain, and we also mention some standards for security management. There are many aspects one has to consider when building overall security for a Smart Grid. The complexity of involved IT systems, actors and exchanged data is growing, and therefore, one main challenge for Smart Grid security is the maintenance of this complexity from a security perspective. In the next section we present an ontology-based approach to face the complexity challenge. Another facet of the security consideration in the Smart Grid is privacy, especially for smart metering. Section 4 will outline a security concept which mentions privacy by design for smart meter.

3. Ontology-based information security management for the Smart Grid

Information security is not a state but a process. Therefore, information security management defines rules and methods for an enterprise in order to control and continuously maintain information security. Most information security management systems hold different documents, so the company's information objects are not integrated in one data source and reviewed in an overall knowledge base. This makes it very difficult to get a quick overview of the enterprises' information security. It gets even more complex when different and concurring requirements exist, e.g. in the Smart Grid domain. The energy domain has a bunch of unique requirements. For example, a high availability of IT systems and information are

---

2 See http://www.27000.org.

crucial in the energy domain and may sometimes even lead to real-time requirements. As such it may happen that security conditions are in conflict with domain specific requirements. For example, the installation of a virus scanner as a security enhancement can have negative impacts to the requirements of high availability or to their response time [GrK06]. Especially, a Smart Grid needs an adequate overall security concept because it is a critical infrastructure with direct control of industry facilities.

The *Enertrust* ontology integrates Smart Grid-specific requirements and security needs into an enterprises semantic information network as follows. There are different requirements for information objects in the Smart Grid domain. Some non-functional requirements that can be named are originating from laws, standards or domain-specific requirements like high availability [NIS10b]. For example, in Germany – like in most other European countries – commercially sensitive data like "customer load" has a security requirement defined within the law. This law usually enforces companies to treat commercially sensitive data as confidential. As such, confidentiality can be named a "security goal" for this type of data. The appropriate realization of security mechanisms in a specific context for a corresponding security goal is important for a cost-benefit-optimization. Whether or not the confidentiality of an object is threatened – and therefore an implementation of a security mechanism is necessary – depends on the context or system in which the specific object appears. Therefore, subjects, contexts, processes or concurring requirements of a specific object are essential information in order to define security requirements.

Within the described approach of this paper, we are proposing an ontology for defining this essential information and for modeling connections. Machine-readable standards and security policies are used to introduce a holistic ontology-based security management concept for the energy domain [BAE10]. Existing knowledge bases such as data models from CIM and security policies are transformed into ontologies and used within the holistic concept. An overall ontology integrates different existing ontologies and standards and connects them with each other. Consequently, a re-use of existing knowledge and existing ontologies is fostered within our proposed approach. Ontology alignment can be used for integrating security requirements in the semantic net of enterprise information objects [Euz01]. There are many security ontologies to describe concepts like threats, countermeasures, etc. in the literature. [BLV08] gives an overview of different security ontologies. In addition to integrated security ontologies, the overall ontology contains energy-specific possibilities to adequately represent functional and non-functional requirements as well as security concepts coming from the energy sector.

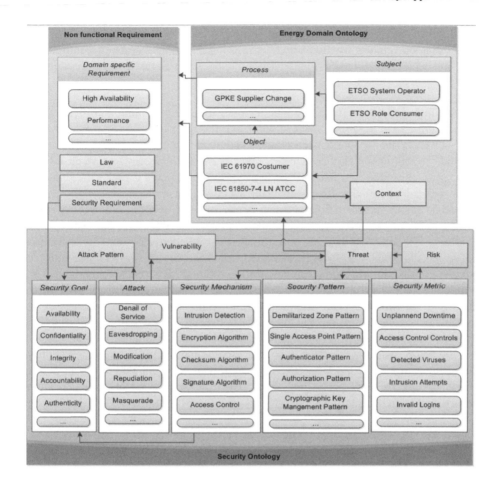

Figure 1. *Main concepts of the Enertrust ontology*

As such, the resulting ontology consists of three different parts shown in Figure 1: domain-specific data models (in the upper right box), non-functional requirements (in the upper left box) and security concepts (in the lower box). In order to keep the figure readable, Figure 1 only shows a few main concepts of the overall ontology and has just a few hints of connections. A central point is the concept *object*. This is a (meta)model for (information) objects within the energy domain. Security requirements or domain specific requirements are defined for each instance of object or object group/type.

There are some sub-concepts of *object* like IEC 61970 Customer data models as an example in the box. Ontologies are extensible, so that new metrics or mechanisms can be integrated (Open World Assumption). The overall ontology provides important information which can allow users to gain additional information by allowing search and reasoning facilities and by making knowledge accessible and interpretable by IT systems.

Figure 2 shows how the ontology concludes through reasoning facilities whether an enterprise's information object is security relevant or not. Within the figure, one can see concepts in rounded rectangles and instances in rectangles. The dotted rounded rectangle shows the concept *security relevant object*, which is an inferred concept. A reasoner can deduct the security relevant objects through the following rules. Domain-specific requirements bring sanctions for an enterprise, especially for a specific object category. Such a sanction can lead to a security requirement which corresponds to a security goal. For example, if the reasoner knows that commercially sensitive data has to be treated confidentially because of restrictions defined within the ontology and originated from the law, the reasoner can draw the conclusion that object A, which is of the commercially sensitive type, has the protection goal "confidentiality". Moreover it can reason that object A should be protected via an encryption algorithm as a security mechanism because of the security goal *confidentiality*. Figure 3 depicts that the presence of a protection goal for an object might be inferred. An object has the protection goals that are relevant for its object category through non-functional requirements. One can see these connections in a curve over the different concepts on the right side in Figure 3. If an object has one or more protection goals, then it belongs to the class or concept of security-relevant objects.

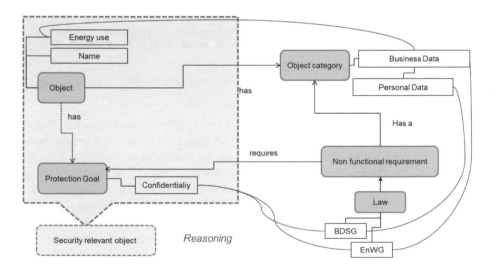

Figure 2. *Security relevance*

The necessity to realize a security mechanism is not automatically given through the property of security relevance. The need for protection is also a concept of our ontology. An object has a need for protection when it is security relevant, so it has a protection goal, and when furthermore for this protection goal known threats are given, which are used by a weakness that appears in a system context where the object is stored or transferred. In the Smart Grid domain, a protection need might be given for smart meter data stored in a MS SQL Server database, which has known weaknesses. In the next section, we present a security concept, which protects such smart meter data by a specific encryption.

4. Technology concept for smart metering privacy

Within the domain of cryptology, the so called fully homomorphic encryption is a research field which has only been mathematically proven in 2009 by Craig Gentry [Gen09]. This relatively new encryption concept is based upon specific algebraic structures that allow operations on encrypted data. The practical relevance of this methodology has so far mainly been seen within the domain of digital voting and eParticipation. However, it also provides interesting benefits for the energy domain when handling data. Especially within the area of transferring information from smart meters, the additive homomorphic and asymmetric encryption of Paillier [Pai99] is quite promising. Metering operators may manage encrypted data for their customers and may aggregate information without needing the key to decrypt information and without ever being able to decrypt and see the information hidden in the encrypted datasets.

The following figure shows a potential usage of the additive homomorphic encryption within the smart metering domain. The image shows three different actors: energy customer, metering operator and energy provider. The arrows displayed in the figure show the data flow of measured information of a smart meter between the actors.

Energy consumer 1 of the figure owns the public key of energy provider 1. The corresponding private key is only known by energy provider 1. Energy consumers may now use the public key to encrypt the data of their energy meter with the public key of energy provider 1. This process is basically a typical asymmetric encryption. What is new in the Pallier approach is the possibility the billing provider has at this scenario. Thanks to the approach, the metering operator may pre-process the information of the energy consumer without needing the corresponding key and without needing to work with decrypted information. The metering operator is able to manage the energy information of many energy consumers without needing to have the possibility to actually "understand" (decrypt) the data.

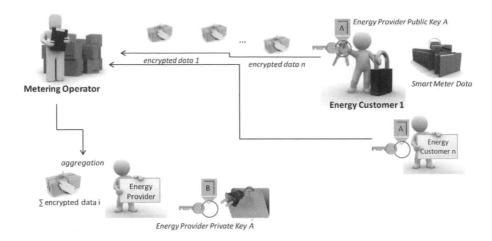

Figure 3. *Usage of additive homomorphic encryption for smart metering*

The additive homomorphic encryption allows aggregation on encrypted data. This aspect has a significant importance from a data privacy law perspective as it allows a data storage and processing (i.e. the provision of data related services) on the one hand without the need to decrypt private information from customers. Only the energy provider will be able to decrypt the data and to view the original information.

5. Conclusion

Firstly, the Enertrust ontology enables information security management for the energy domain. Therefore, ontologies are used for integrating existing knowledge from the energy and the security domain. To manage the huge size of highly connected concepts, semantic query languages can help in order to get a quick overview of the requirements, security mechanisms, etc. In addition, reasoning and rules can be used to conclude new knowledge like the need for implementing a certain security mechanism.

Secondly, the approach of using an additive homomorphic encryption allows a new approach for energy providers, consumers and service providers to work together and to exchange information by allowing better privacy protection. We strongly believe that privacy should be a key element within the smart metering domain and that the above aspects contribute to this goal.

6. References

[BAE10] Beenken, P.; Appelrath, H.-J.; Eckert, C.: "Datenschutz und Datensicherheit in intelligenten Energienetzen", in: P. Schartner, E. Weippl (eds) *D•A•CH Security 2010*, Vienna, Austria, 2010

[BLV08] Blanco, C.; Lasheras, J.; Valencia-Garcia, R.; Fernández-Medina, E.; Toval, A.; Piattini, M.: "A Systematic Review a Comparison of Security Ontologies", in: *Proceedings of the Third International Conference on Availability, Reliability and Security*, IEEE, 2008

[Euz01] Euzenat, J.: "Towards a Principled Approach to Semantic Interoperability", *Workshop on Ontologies and Information Sharing, IJCAI'01*, Seattle (WA US), 2001

[Gen09] Gentry, C.; A Fully Homomorphic Encryption Scheme, PhD Thesis, Stanford University, Sept. 2009

[GrK06] Gresser, C.; Kubik, S.: "IT-Sicherheit für Leittechnik", in: *Die Zeitschrift für Informationssicherheit*, Heft 1/2006, SecuMedia Verlag, 2006

[NIS10a] NIST, Framework and Roadmap for Smart Grid Interoperability Standards, Release 1.0, January, 2010

[NIS10b] NIST Smart Grid Cyber Security Strategy and Requirements, Draft NISTIR 7628, Feb 2010

[Pai99] Paillier, P.; "Public-Key Cryptosystems Based on Composite Degree Residuosity Classes", *EUROCRYPT'99*, Prague, Czech Republic, 1999

[URS08] Uslar, M.; Rohjans, S.; Schulte, S.; Steinmetz, R.: "Building the Semantic Utility with Standards and Semantic Web Services", in: *Lecture Notes in Computer Science – On the Move to Meaningful Internet Systems, OTM Workshop*, eds. A. Hofmann, B. Apfel, U. Barth, *et al.* (eds), Springer-Verlag, Computer Science Editorial, 2008

Workshop W3

Advanced Results in
MDI/SOA Innovation

Reference Ontologies for Manufacturing-based Ecosystems

R. Young[*] – N. Chungoora[*] – Z. Usman[*] – N. Anjum[*],
G. Gunendran[*] – C. Palmer[*] – J. Harding[*] – K. Case[*] –
A.-F. Cutting-Decelle[**]

[*] *Loughborough University-Wolfson School of Mechanical & Manufacturing Engineering, Loughborough, Leicestershire, UK*

[**] *CODATA France, 5, rue A. Vacquerie, F-75016 Paris, France and Univ-Lille Nord de France, F-59000 Lille, France, LM2O, Ecole Centrale de Lille, Cité Scientifique -- BP 48 -- 59651 Villeneuve d'Ascq*

Email contact: r.i.young@lboro.ac.uk

ABSTRACT: *There is a clear need for improved semantic communication to support information sharing across engineering groups and their systems in the manufacturing industry. This work presents the progress towards the development of a reference ontology for a manufacturing ecosystem, focusing particularly on the design and manufacture of aerospace parts, explained in the context of Model-Driven Architectures. A concept is presented which illustrates how knowledge, captured from a manufacturing engineer's perspective, can be shared back into the product design process through the use of reference ontologies and appropriate mapping mechanisms. An experimental test case is used to illustrate the success of the approach*

KEYWORDS: *knowledge sharing, manufacturing, ontologies, mappings.*

1. Introduction

This paper provides a contribution to understanding how to improve information and knowledge sharing within manufacturing businesses and especially in relation to interoperability amongst the many software systems that support key activities within a manufacturing organization. The understanding presented in this paper comes as a result of the Interoperable Manufacturing Knowledge Systems (IMKS) research project (Young *et al.*, 2010).

The traditional approach to systems integration through the use of a neutral or common data model is still typically seen as the most effective current commercial basis for information sharing in systems. This is restrictive to manufacturing businesses due to the complexity of the information requirements, combined with the difficulties of understanding the semantic relationships between multi-domain concepts (Young *et al.*, 2007).

Manufacturing is a complex ecosystem, with many interacting systems, operating over a wide range of time cycles and with a wide variety of lifecycles for products, processes and systems. We argue in this paper that the provision of a reference ontology, based on heavyweight ontological concepts, provides an effective basis for concept specialization across a range of manufacturing systems. We show such concepts can be defined, constrained and used in an experimental program targeted at sharing a manufacturing perspective of knowledge with that required by product designers. These arguments build on the ideas of foundation ontologies (Oberle *et al.*, 2007, Borgo & Leitão, 2007), but with a specific ecosystem focus.

The methodology employed has been to determine through industrial investigation the key concepts that need to be specified to meet the needs of specific industrial scenarios and then to design and implement an experimental environment to test the resulting ideas. The experimental environment is based on the use of the IODE ontology development environment and XKS knowledge base from Highfleet Inc, based on Common Logic, along with Siemens' PLM software as a source and repository for relevant product and manufacturing facility information.

2. A manufacturing ecosystem in the context of MDA

While an ecosystem is normally considered to be a biological community of interacting organisms and their physical environment (Oxford English dictionary) we consider a manufacturing ecosystem to be a manufacturing community of interacting people, processes, products and systems along with their physical environment. There is a huge variety of activities which process information and knowledge in different ways and at vastly different timescales. There are also multiple lifecycles not just for products but also for processes and systems. All of these must interact effectively and changes in any one can have substantial consequences for the overall manufacturing ecosystem. An illustration of the sorts of levels of process, timescales and software systems involved in a simple manufacturing ecosystem is provided in Figure 1.

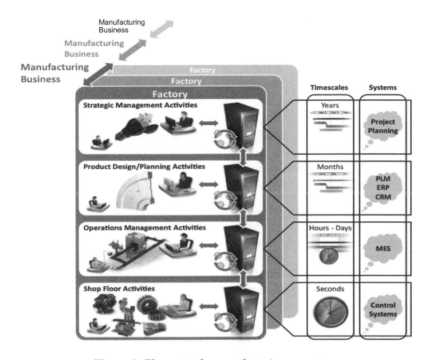

Figure 1. *Elements of a manufacturing ecosystem*

Model-Driven Architectures (MDA) is an approach to IT system specification that separates the specification of system functionalities from the implementation specification for a specific technology platform (Almeida *et al.*, 2005). The MDA approach should enable the same model functionality to be achieved on multiple platforms through mappings to specific platforms. The architecture defines a hierarchy of models from three different points of view: the Computation Independent Model (CIM), the Platform Independent Model (PIM), and the Platform Specific Model (PSM). The computational independent viewpoint focuses on the environment and the requirements of the system. The platform independent viewpoint focuses on the operation of a system while hiding the details necessary to a particular platform. A platform independent view shows the part of the complete specification that does not change from one platform to another. The platform specific viewpoint combines the platform independent viewpoint with an additional focus on the detail of the use of a specific platform by a system. For MDA to be effective, model transformations are needed which define the process by which a model is converted into another model of the same system.

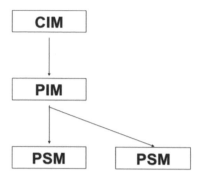

Figure 2. *Multi-system development*

The traditional approach to multi-system integration is to identify a common PIM for two or more PSM as illustrated in Figure 2. We argue that multiple Platform Independent Models are needed in complex manufacturing ecosystems. However, a level of common semantic understanding is still necessary across these multiple PIMs if any form of information sharing is to be possible. This leads to the need for a heavyweight ontology to underlie these models in order to provide a formal set of concepts which can be utilized across the full range of models needed in a manufacturing ecosystem. In addition, when concepts are specialized to suit specific domain requirements, e.g. product design or manufacturing planning, there is a need to evaluate the differences in concept specializations across domains in order to verify the extent to which knowledge across these domain concepts is sharable. This basic idea is illustrated in the context of MDA in Figure 3.

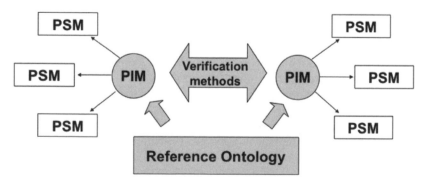

Figure 3. *Sharing across multiple platform models*

3. The development of a manufacturing reference ontology

The process for the development of a manufacturing reference ontology has been to work firstly with our industrial collaborators to understand the concepts of interest to their design and manufacturing engineers. Also to exploit the understanding already available from previous research and especially the understanding that is available from existing international standards and in particular ISO 10303, 13584, 15531, 18629, 13399 and 19439.

3.1. *A lightweight view of necessary key concepts and relationships*

From the understanding gained from this research we have developed and progressively refined a lightweight high level view of the ontology represented in UML as illustrated in Figure 4. This figure not only captures key concepts for manufacturing facilities, products, part families, features and manufacturing methods but also starts to develop the critical relationships that exist between each of these concepts.

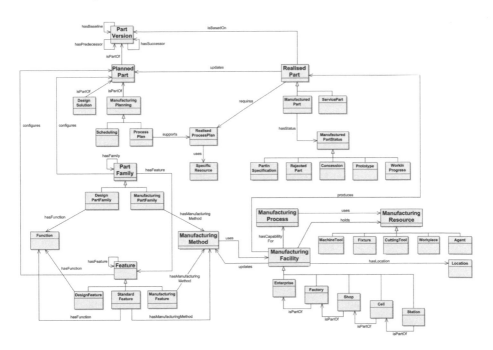

Figure 4. *A high level view of a manufacturing reference ontology*

From this model the subsequent heavyweight reference ontology has been developed using Highfleet's IODE ontology development environment. This offers the general ability to constrain the meaning of each concept through the use of appropriate axioms. Two particular aspects of constraint are particularly worthy of consideration in the development of our reference ontology: these being "Concept Specialization" and "Second Order Relations". Concept specialization is discussed in detail in the following section. The importance of second order relations is described briefly in the next section.

A second-order relation is a relation that connects two properties or a property and an instance. Properties here are equivalent to classes in standard ontological terminology. This capability allows us to model relations typical of a meta-class -> class -> instance relationship which arise on numerous occasions in manufacturing concepts. For example, during process planning it is common to need to instantiate a type of cutting tool or a type of machine where that type of tool or machine will later be further instantiated to identify a specific cutting tool or machine. Similarly, the manufacturing method concept illustrated in Figure 4 has multiple instantiations at the class level dependent on whether the manufacturing method is associated with a feature, a part family or a process plan. These relations have been modeled in IODE but are not represented here.

3.2. Concept specialization

A further issue in developing a reference ontology for manufacturing is to determine the breadth of applicability of concepts and then to provide appropriate constraints on their use. To illustrate the use of concept specialization here we use the concept of "feature" and its domains of applicability. This is a concept which has been explored for over 30 years as an important factor in linking computer aided design and manufacture. However, it often leads to confusion due to the many interpretations of its meaning. An illustration of a range of features and levels of specialization is provided in Figure 5. This highlights that at a very general level a feature is any "distinctive or noticeable quality of a thing" (Oxford English Dictionary). This can be specialized through form into product features and then into either design or production features.

This range of variation in the feature concept can be represented in the Knowledge Frame Language (KFL) that is the IODE implementation of Common Logic. Listed below can be seen first the representation for a feature where "Every feature has an Attribute of Interest". This is followed by a form feature where the attribute of interest is the form. The subsequent code then captures the difference between a design feature and a production feature such that a design feature must have a function while a production feature must have a manufacturing method.

(=> (Feature ?f)
    (exists(?AOI)
    (and (AttributeOfInterest   ?AOI)
   (hasAttributeOfInterest   ?f ?AOI))))
:IC hard "Every feature has an Attribute of Interest

 (=> (FormFeature ?ffeature)
    (exists (?form)
   (and (Form ?form)
   (FormFeature   ?ffeature)
   (hasAttributeOfInterest ?ffeature ?form))))
:IC hard "A Form exist as an Attribute of Interest for a FormFeature"

(=> (DesignFeature ?df)
    ((exists(?function)
   (and (Function ?function)
 (hasAttributeOfInterest ?df ?function)))))
:IC hard "A function exists for a DesignFeature"

(=> (ProductionFeature ?Turningf)
(exists (?mfgmethod)
(and (ManufacturingMethod ?manufacturingmethod)
   (hasAttributeOfInterest ?Turningf ?mfgmethod))))
:IC hard "ManufacturingMethod exists for every Productionfeature"

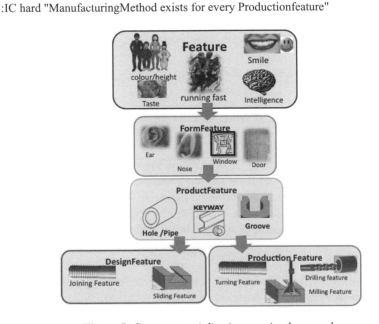

Figure 5. *Concept specialization – a simple example*

By using this heavyweight representation it is possible to constrain the meaning of each concept to avoid it's misuse or misunderstanding. This representation has been applied to examples of design and production features drawn from our industrial collaborators. Figure 6 illustrates an example of this showing how function is linked to a design feature and how a manufacturing method from the equivalent manufacturing feature leads to the relevant manufacturing knowledge that can then be fed back to the product designer. This example captures manufacturing knowledge that is a) necessary for the design process and b) not easily understood by the designers.

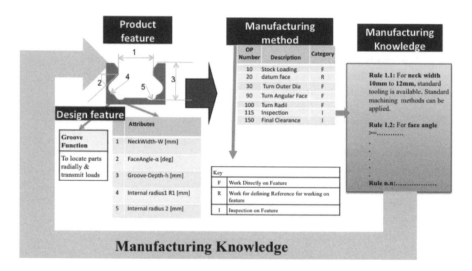

Figure 6. *An example design and production feature*

4. The experimental system: sharing manufacturing knowledge with product designers

An experimental manufacturing reference ontology has been constructed and is used to explore the provision of manufacturing knowledge into the product design process, based on the example illustrated in Figure 6. This is effectively a tightly constrained manufacturing ecosystem, but offers the opportunity to explore some of the fundamental issues concerning a reference ontology for manufacturing. An outline of the experimental system is illustrated in Figure 7.

The experimental reference ontology is the heavyweight implementation of the concepts shown in Figure 4, utilizing the concept specializations and second order relations also described in section 3. These have been captured in Highfleet's IODE ontology development environment. The geometry of the features and parts has been modeled in Siemens NX and the tooling and manufacturing methods are being implemented in the Siemens Teamcenter PLM system. This is interfaced into Highfleet's knowledge system (XKS) where facts about tooling constraints on manufacturing features have been implemented.

At this stage in the experimental development we are able to provide simple feedback of manufacturing knowledge to product designers, when they make changes to design feature parameters. We are currently extending the implementation so that more comprehensive sets of concepts and more complex knowledge relationships can be explored.

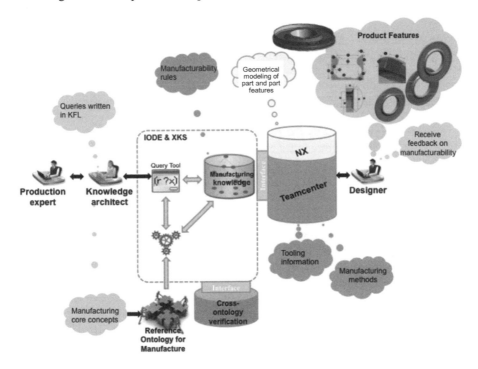

Figure 7. *The experimental system*

5. Discussion and conclusions

This paper has discussed the complexity of manufacturing ecosystems and the subsequent need for more effective methods to capture the underlying semantics of such systems through reference ontologies.

An initial lightweight view of such a reference ontology has been shown in a UML class diagram and the key methods by which this ontology has been developed to capture heavyweight constraints has been illustrated. An example, based on feature concepts, has been used to illustrate how design and manufacturing concepts can be used to drive the feedback of manufacturing knowledge into the product design process. The experimental system that we have developed has been described along with simple initial experiments.

The current phase of this work is to further develop the experimental system to be able to undertake more extensive experiments to demonstrate the extent to which the idea of the reference ontology, along with captured manufacturing knowledge can be exploited to support product design.

We are currently starting research into extensions of the reference ontologies to support other critical multi-perspective issues within manufacturing ecosystems.

6. Acknowledgements

This research is funded by the EPSRC through the Innovative Manufacturing and Construction Research Centre in Loughborough University (IMCRC project 253).

7. References

Almeida, J.P., Dijkman, R., Sinderen, M.V., Pires, L.S., (2005), "Platform-independent modelling in MDA: supporting abstract platforms," in: *Model Driven Architecture: European MDA Workshop, MDAFA*, June 10-11, 2004, Linkping, Sweden.

Borgo, S., Leitão, P., (2007), *Foundations for a Core Ontology of Manufacturing*, 1 Laboratory for Applied Ontology, ISTC-CNR, Trento, Italy, 2 Polytechnic Institute of Bragança, Bragança, Portugal. 1134, 5301-857

ISO 10303-1, (1994), Industrial Automation Systems and Integration – Product Data Representation and Exchange – Part 1: Overview and Fundamental Principles. Geneva, Switzerland: International Organization for Standardization (ISO).

ISO 13399, (2006), Cutting tool data representation and exchange. Geneva, Switzerland: International Organization for Standardization (ISO).

ISO 13584, (2001), Industrial automation systems and integration – Parts library. Geneva, Switzerland: International Organization for Standardization (ISO).

ISO 15531-1, (2004), Industrial automation systems and integration – Industrial manufacturing management data – Part 1: General overview. Geneva, Switzerland: International Organization for Standardization (ISO).

ISO 19439, (2006), Industrial automation systems – Framework for enterprise modeling. Geneva, Switzerland: International Organization for Standardization (ISO).

ISO 18629-1, (2004), Industrial Automation System and Integration — Process Specification Language: Part 1. Overview and Basic Principles. Geneva, Switzerland: International Organization for Standardization (ISO).

ISO/IEC-24707, (2007), International Standard, First edition 2007-10-01 Information technology — Common Logic (CL): a framework for a family of logic based languages. Geneva, Switzerland: International Organization for Standardization (ISO).

Oberle, D., *et al.* (2007), "DOLCE Ergo SUMO: On Foundational and Domain Models in the SmartWeb Integrated Ontology (SWIntO)", *Web Semantics: Science, Services and Agents on the World Wide Web*, 5.3: 156-74.

OMG. Object Management Group http://www.omg.org/mda.

Young, R.I.M, Gunendran, A.G, Cutting-Decelle, A.F, Gruninger, M, (2007), "Manufacturing knowledge sharing in PLM: a progression towards the use of heavy weight ontologies", *International Journal of Production Research*, Vol. 45, No. 7, 1 April, 1505–1519

Young, R., Chungoora, N., Usman, Z., Anjum, N., Gunendran, G., Palmer, C., Harding, J., Case, K., and Cutting-Decelle, A-F., (2010), "An exploration of foundation ontologies and verification methods for manufacturing knowledge sharing", *Interoperability for Enterprise Software and Applications*, H. Panetto and N. Boudjlida (eds), ISTE, London and John Wiley & Sons, New York, pp 83 – 92.

Interoperability for Product Design and Manufacturing Application in the Aeronautical Industry

Yves Ducq[1] – Nabila Zouggar[1] – Jean Christophe Deschamps[1] – Guy Doumeingts[1,2]

[1] *University of Bordeaux - IMS/LAPS*
351 cours de la libération
33405 Talence cedex

{*nabila.zouggar, yves.ducq, Jean-Christophe.Deschamps*}@ims-bordeaux.fr

[2] *INTEROP-VLab*
351 Cours de la Libération
33405 Talence cedex
guy.doumeingts@interop-vlab.eu

ABSTRACT. *The aeronautical industry is a fragile and highly competitive sector in which the relationships between the different partners are supported by numerous IT applications which must be interoperable in a flexible manner and at low cost. This is particularly true for the sub-contractors of rank 2 and following which are small enterprises (around 50 employees). This paper presents the ISTA3 methodology based on MDI and SOA principles using a progressive approach in order to define technical services based on business models at the highest level. After the presentation of SOA and MDI principles, the method is presented and illustrated by a case study of ISTA3 Project presenting the models used to characterize interoperability nodes. The last part of the paper presents the method to define indicators used to evaluate interoperability level.*

KEYWORDS: *Aeronautics sub-contractors; GRAI Methodology; Model-Driven Interoperability; interoperability performance measurement*

1. Introduction

The design and manufacturing of aircraft parts is a hard process that requires the association of several big, medium and small size companies working together, very often certified and organized in a complex supply chain. Design activities imply numerous exchanges of data between multi-disciplinary experts that complicate their execution and lead to many reworks due to technical data misunderstanding or inaccuracy.

This paper presents a methodology to characterize interoperability nodes between partners and to evaluate the interoperability level for each node. An interoperability node is an activity done by one partner and using inputs from another partner. This activity can be a process activity or a decision activity. In this case, this decision activity uses information or decision frame (objectives, action means, constraints) provided by another partner.

The proposed method, based on Model Driven Interoperability intends to characterize activities required for interoperability through process modeling and performance measurement of non-interoperability. This work is led in the frame of the ISTA3 project funded by the French Ministry of Industry.

In the first part of this paper, the industrial context and ISTA3 project will be slightly reminded. Part 2 presents the general method with the application to a specific case study derived from the project. Part 3 describes the performance evaluation principles applied to the case study, before concluding and discussing future research works.

2. Problem statement

The aeronautical industry operates on the logic of sharing objectives and risks. This logic brings up long-term relationships between industrial partners involved in a complex network called a supply chain.

In this sector, the structure of the supply chain is not vertical in the sense that principals would cover the complete and hierarchical organization of sub-contractors network. Relations between different actors in the network are relatively horizontal, where an enterprise can be simultaneously principals and sub-contractors of each other.

To strengthen the competitiveness of the enterprises network and their business performance, it is important to establish a better use of information technology and communication. Nevertheless, enterprises implied in collaborative works are faced with managing multiple types of information systems: those imposed by the client, its own internal system and those of its own sub-contractors. The multiplicity and heterogeneity of these information systems make collaboration difficult, mainly during exchange of documents. The objective of the ISTA3 project is then to propose organizational and technical solutions to facilitate and accelerate the collaboration through the aeronautic supply chain.

The ISTA3 (*Interopérabilité de 3ème génération pour les Sous-Traitants de l'Aéronautique* – Interoperability of 3rd generation ($I3^{rd}G$) for the Aeronautics Sub-contractors) project is funded by the French Ministry of Industry and supported by the "Pole de Compétitivité" Aerospace Valley located in both the Midi-Pyrénées (Toulouse) and Aquitaine (Bordeaux) regions. Considering that aeronautical supply chains are multi-stage networks (Figure 1), ISTA3 does not focus on the relationships between order makers (e.g. Airbus or Boeing) and rank 1 subcontractors (considering that the problem is different), but considers collaborative works involving sub-contractors of ranks 2 and 3. The industrial case presented in this paper is more particularly formed by one sub-contractor producing composite materials (called SC 2) and one of its sub-contractors in charge to manufacture molds (called SC 3).

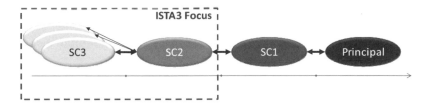

Figure 1. *ISTA3 industrial case*

Indeed, subcontractors of rank 1 of the aeronautic sector have often adopted information system used by the principals when sub-contractor of rank 2 and 3 can not invest in costly Information Systems. The collaboration between those sub-contractors then may have different levels of maturity [1]: communication (ability to exchange and share information), open (ability to share business services and functionalities with others), federated (ability to work with others by following collaborative processes in order to pursue a common objective, as well as objectives of the enterprise itself), and interoperable (ability to work with others without a special effort; the enterprises involved are seen as a seamless system). This federated level of maturity seems to be the most appropriate, because it requires fewer investments and enables long- as well as short-term relationships between partners [2]. However, sub-contractors working in a collaborative network rarely want to disclose their whole knowledge and internal business processes. Data exchange interfaces then require a public part that publishes information accessible to other partners and a secure domain which protects private information [3]. In fact, the expectations of subcontractor of rank 2 and 3 are:

- a collaboration with changing at the minimum their information systems;

- a dissemination to its partners limited to the public part of their information systems.

In this context, the ISTA3 project aims to meet these expectations by providing a platform allowing for information systems to interoperate by taking into account the "private/public" relationship. It leads to the development of a complete methodology and the associated IT applications for I3rdG.

I3rdG characterizes the third generation of interoperability (also called the federated approach) which uses ontology principles to adapt dynamically the exchange of information, and to bring more flexibility in the workflow linking industrial partners. This approach differs from the first and second generation of interoperability which respectively refers to the use of standard formats and meta-models to exchange information. The proposed approach is then based on MDI (Model Driven Interoperability), supported by Enterprise Modeling Techniques, and SOA (Services Oriented Architectures), combined with Ontology to develop ISUs (Interoperability Services Utilities: services solutions adaptable and reusable).

3. Proposed ISTA3 methodology to characterize interoperability nodes and evaluate interoperability level

3.1. *Why combine the MDI and SOA techniques?*

The ISTA3 methodology refers to various approaches presented in this part.

The first choice was done to use the MDI (Model-Driven Interoperability) approach. This choice was done in order to develop flexible interfaces between information systems of both parts and to facilitate the use of a common platform without leading to strong investments at the beginning of the collaboration. The main advantage of MDI is also to develop these flexible interfaces based on enterprise models, from the business level to the platform specific level. The enterprise levels will enable us to identify the interoperability nodes from the process and decision points of view. Based on these interoperability nodes, computerization will be proposed and will be done through SOA techniques. SOA techniques will define the technical services that will be supported and orchestrated by the service bus. The SOA techniques enable this flexibility with providing numerous services which are chosen based on the models derived from the MDI approach. This is the interest to that 3rd generation approach of interoperability to combine both techniques to have an automatic and then a flexible generation of services based on specific models of collaboration and to have a performance evaluation of interoperability in order to verify if the implemented services are appropriate in comparison with the expected running and the expected performance in the collaboration between partners.

3.2. *Overview of MDI*

So, first of all, ISTA3 methodology is based on MDI principles, developed within the INTEROP NoE network. As explain previously, this approach aims to define technical services based at the highest global level on business representation of the collaboration [5]. For this, 3 modeling levels are defined:

-   The CIM: model enable to collect needs and characteristics of the enterprise. This is the most global level of representation using enterprise modeling formalisms taking into account the system theory. The results of this level is to characterize interoperability nodes from a process and decision points of view, that will be used to define future services supporting specific collaboration.

-   The PIM: derived from business models defined in the CIM level, the PIM level will focus of generic services that will be included in the repository.

-   The PSM: represents several application models using the technology chosen.

A strong impact of MDI is the fact that it starts from the business modeling that allows us to understand the context of collaboration but also the needs and expectations of each partner in implementing new solutions. These needs, identified at the CIM level, are then transformed and then derived at the technical levels (PIM and PSM) using model transformation tools. This will ensure a continuum between a global vision of the collaboration and a very detailed vision of the technical services that must be developed and orchestrated to support this collaboration.

3.3. *Overview of SOA*

SOA is an architectural approach, guideline and pattern to realize a system through a set of provided and required services [6]. SOA is technology independent; it means that the choice of technologies and tools is secondary. Various technologies might be used to support SOA implementation [7]. According to a recent research [8], "to achieve its potential, an SOA needs to be business-relevant, thus driven by the business and implemented to support the business". Because most of SOA implementations were not done based on the global vision of the collaboration, the implemented and orchestrated services are often too narrow. This totally justifies the combination between SOA and MDI techniques, the second one bringing this business vision.

The choice of using SOA is that it contributes to the scalability, flexibility and durability of the information system which enables to reduce the difficulty to work, which is the aim of interoperability.

Also, SOA can facilitate the abstraction of information systems [3]. Indeed, services ignore the information system: partners communicate with services in terms of input and output, without knowing the specifics of the system with which they communicate. The company then connects to the collaborative network through the public part of its information system [1]. This answers to the second expectation of subcontractors, which is not disclosed its expertise and its business processes.

3.4. *ISTA3 structured approach*

As explain previously, most of the proposed methodologies to implement SOA approach start from the information level. In order to align information systems on business processes, we propose to start the methodology from the business level in order to understand and to analyze the companies from several points of view (physical and decision) and not only from IT one. The methodology starts from business level (CIM Models) to PIM and PSM level to produce the solutions using SOA techniques and ESB (Enterprise Service Bus) to orchestrate the services. The proposed methodology is composed of five phases (Figure 2):

- Phase 1: evaluate the potentiality of the collaborations between the sub-contractors. Before launching the collaboration, it is necessary to roughly evaluate the potentiality of each partner to work together. This is particularly important in the aeronautical industry driven by the strong quality level and standards which must be respected in order to answer calls coming from principals. In this phase, the method does no enter very deep in detail in the running of each system neither in the way the collaboration will be implemented and computerized. This is performed through a bearing questionnaire on the knowledge of partners concerning their past collaborations with other partners. This is a short phase (no more than one day) which allows us to quickly determine the potentiality of the sub-contractors to collaborate with others and then to minimize risks for the principals.

- Phase 2: determine the requirements according a CIM level modeling. This is the first level of modeling. This CIM level is decomposed in ISTA3 approach in two levels: TOP CIM and BOTTOM CIM that will be detailed later in the paper.

- Phase 3: produce solutions using SOA techniques and ESB to orchestrate the services according the PIM and PSM level modeling. This phase is using PSM models in order to derive the services that will be orchestrated. When the service already exists, it will be then only called. Otherwise, the service will be developed based on the PSM models.

- Phase 4: implement the solutions inside the sub-contractors. In this phase, the IT system of both partners will be modified in order to support the new interoperable services.

- Phase 5: measure the interoperability performance in order to check if the initial objectives are reached and to maintain a continuous check.

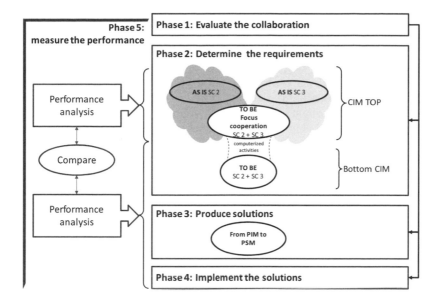

Figure 2. *ISTA 3 methodology*

In the following, the application of the methodology is presented based on the case study given by the project partners. The case study is composed of two sub-contractors working together in the design and industrialization of composite parts for the aeronautical industry.

This presentation starts from phase 2. Indeed, the results of the questionnaire assessing sub-contractor 2, has shown that it is in collaboration with four customers and four suppliers among is which the considered sub-contractor 3 with whom the interoperability will be analyzed. We can conclude after combining the responses of subcontractor 2 with interoperability indicators defined above that this subcontractor is consistent with the development on the 3rd generation interoperability. This evaluation will be extended to the other sub contractors.

Even if the first version of process models have been presented in [9], the second version is presented hereafter as well as the decision models elaborated in the mean time.

3.5. Results of CIM level modeling

The objective of the CIM level is to model business processes and the decision model of the collaboration between sub-contractors. The modeling approach is here decomposed into two phases: Top CIM and Bottom CIM. The advantage of this decomposition into two descriptive levels is first to acquire a global understanding of companies in analyzing their running, from several viewpoints (business process, decisions, IT). The second modeling level makes it possible to focus on the subset of processes and decisions that must be implemented and computerized to improve interoperability. Indeed, some activities and decisions are not supported by IT tools and should be standardized and computerized in order to improve the interoperability. This computerization which supports the future interoperability is then precisely located within the entire business processes, and implemented only when it is relevant. So, again, the interoperability is progressively implemented.

–   Top CIM modeling: the result of this phase is an AS IS model of each sub-contractor and a common TO BE model focusing on the collaborative activities and decisions which will be implemented between sub-contractors and which will require interoperability. For this task, GRAI modeling is used to build different models: physical, decisional, and information [10], [11], [12]. GRAI was chosen for several reasons: the skill of the partners in this method, the systemic approach provided by the methods which enable us to consider the systems from the global to the local points of views, and the stability of the GRAI Meta model, which enables us to have valid models during the whole project and the fact that GRAI models are easy to understand and enable to detect strong points and points to improve using specific rules.

–   Bottom CIM modeling: the result of this phase is a part of the previous TO BE model which focuses on the future collaborative activities and decisions which will be computerized. This part is selected based on return on investment, on technical possibilities…This Bottom CIM model uses the same formalisms to ensure the coherence between both levels of description. This phase is the first step for providing I3rdG models that will be transformed to code and program functions. Then, the bottom CIM models are transformed into BPMN in order to prepare the transformation at the PIM level. BPMN models enable us to go deeper into the modeling of business processes depicting the exchanges between partners in order to facilitate the identification of detailed interoperability nodes. So, by this way, we start from the global point of view using GRAI to the detailed point of view using BPMN. Of course, it would be possible to use only BPMN at the Top CIM level but it would not be possible to detect collaborative decisions and to relate the control and the controlled systems.

4. Application to the aeronautical industry

4.1. *Top CIM*

Data collection was done through various meetings with the synthesis group and interviews with various actors in charge of controlling processes which must interact with those of the partner.

For the purpose of the project, the modeling of SC 2 was completely done and not limited to the single design activities that involve cooperation with SC 3. The modeling result of SC 2 contains essentially:

- Business Process Modeling using GRAI extended actigrams. The Business Process concerns any activity that provides added-value to products. The BP models represented in our case study include the following activities: industrialization and manufacturing, customer relationships management, delivery and supply management.

- Decision Model, based on a GRAI Grid. It contributes to bring a global and structured representation of the main decisional functions of each company pointing on treatment and data that should be shared. Indeed, an efficient level of interoperability should be reached only if partners have common objectives and accept to share information on decision variables, constraints and criteria that define their own individual decision frameworks.

- Information system Model using UML.

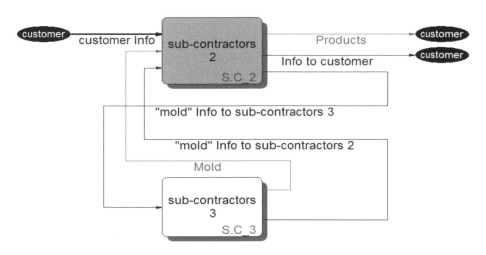

Figure 3. *TOP CIM model*

The AS IS process model of SC 3 concerns exclusively the collaborative activities with SC 2. It is then possible to verify the coherence of links between SC 2 and SC 3 presented in both SC2 and SC3 AS IS Models. All the activities of the process were decomposed for a better understanding of the link between both partners. However, these AS IS models are not presented hereafter in order to focus our presentation on the TO BE models (Top CIM and Bottom CIM). The AS IS models have demonstrated that even if the quality of final products are quite good, the number of iterations are important due to misunderstanding problems and problems to transform CAD files between different software versions of SC2 and SC3.

The cooperation model (TO BE TOP CIM) is done by analyzing SC2 and SC3 AS IS models and also with taking into account the strategy of collaboration of SC2 and SC3. It represents the target situation of collaboration between both partners. This global model presented in figure 3 represents the "macro links" (i.e. the main exchanges) between both partners. Of course, the links with other partners are not represented in this model in order to focus the representation to a specific collaboration.

This very global TOP CIM model shows that the main exchanges between SC2 and SC3 concerns the mold and information of these molds.

Then, a detailed description of this model, also named TOP CIM Level, enables to clearly identify the various points of interoperability between the partner activities.

4.2. Bottom CIM level: I3rdG model

The Business Process I3rdG model is extracted from the previous detailed TO BE TOP CIM model. It concerns the modeling of the "computerized activities" of the cooperation between the two sub-contractors (Figure 5). The TO BE TOP CIM also includes the decision model of the collaboration (Figure 6). In order to build this collaborative decision model, we decided to carry out the complete decision TO BE model of SC2 (Figure 4). This was necessary to understand clearly how the collaborative decisions are connected to periodic decisions internal to SC2.

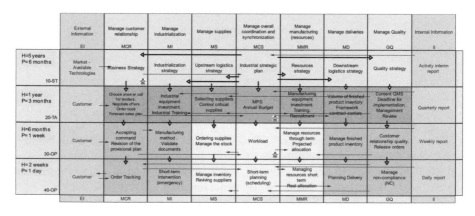

Figure 4. *I3rdG TO BE decision model of SC2*

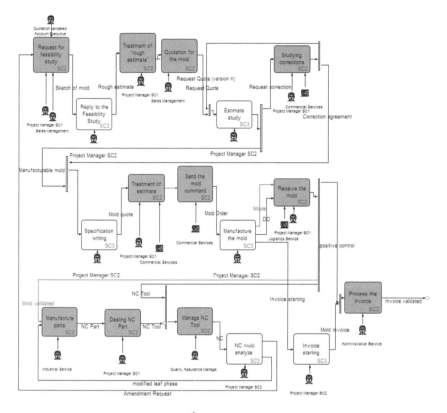

Figure 5. *I3rdG Business Process model*

	External Information	Manage Industrialization	Manage overall coordination and synchronization	Manage Quality	Manage Manufacturing	Manage deliveries	Manage Quality	Internal Information
	EI	SC2	SC2	SC2	SC3	SC3	SC3	II
H=5 years P=6 months	Market - Available Technologies	Industrialization strategy	Industrial strategic plan	Quality strategy	Manufacturing strategy	Delivery Strategy	Quality strategy	Activity interim report
10-ST								
H=1 year P=3 months	Customer	Industrial equipment investment. Industrial Training	MPS Annual Budget	Content QMS Deadline for implementation. Management Review	Manufacturing equipment investment. Training.	manage inventory and carriers	Management Review	Quarterly report
20-TA								
H=6 months P=1 week	Customer	Manufacturing method . Validate documents	Workload	Customer / SC relationship quality. Release orders	Manage resources: Projected allocation	Manage finished product inventory	Customer relationship quality	Weekly report
30-OP								
H=2 weeks P=1 day	Customer	Short-term intervention (emergency)	Short-term planning (scheduling)	Manage non-compliance (NC)	Managing resources: Real allocation	Planning Delivery	Manage non-compliance (NC)	Daily report
40-OP								
	EI	SC2	SC2	SC2	SC3	SC3	SC3	II

Figure 6. *I3rdG TO BE collaborative decision model between SC2 and SC3*

The I3rdG model is composed of:

- processes model of cooperation in which are indicated sub-contractor 1 (in grey), sub-contractor 2 (in white) and the exchanges of information;
- the associated Information System model with additional details (example of exchanged documents);
- the decision model of collaboration between SC2 and SC3.

The model of Figure 5 above highlights the various interoperability nodes that will exist in the future collaboration between partners. The model also shows the iterations of activities.

The decision model of Figure 6 shows the decisions of SC2 which are connected to decisions of SC3. For instance, at the strategic level, the decisions of SC2 concerning quality influence strongly the decisions of SC3 concerning the quality (decision frame between both decision centers). At level 30 (tactical level), the decisions on industrialization of SC2 strongly influence the decisions of SC3 concerning the manufacturing. Then, at the operational level, the decisions of synchronization of SC2 influence strongly the decisions of delivery of SC3.

But in order to define priorities in the actions to implement to improve interoperability, and in order to control the interoperability of activities in the exploitation of the system, it is necessary to develop and implement a relevant method to measure interoperability performance. Of course, the performance on interoperability is driven by the decisions. So, this is why the model of Figure 6 is useful for performance definition.

Because the project is not finished, the BPMN model is in the process of achievement.

5. Interoperability performance measurement

The domain of performance measurement has been investigated for more than 20 years leading to a lot of methods around the world, developed either by researchers or more pragmatically by practitioners, in order to define and implement indicators. All these methods have been developed independently based on system theory, production management theory or accounting methods, according to the background of developers. Among all these 30 methods, more or less used and well known, one can cite the famous ones or the most used or disseminated around the world as Balanced Score Card [13], the Performance Prism [14], ECOGRAI [15], QMPMS [16], or IDPMS [17].

The fact that interoperability can be improved means that metrics for measuring the degree of interoperability exist. Measuring interoperability allows a company knowing its strengths and weaknesses to interoperate and prioritize actions to improve their partnership ability. The proposed methodology proposes to decompose global business activities in two activities as shown in Figure 7: interoperation activity required to enable interoperability between two systems or two practices, and regular business activity. The performance of each of these activities will be measured with specific indicators: interoperation PIs for interoperation activities and physical (or business) PIs for the regular added value activities.

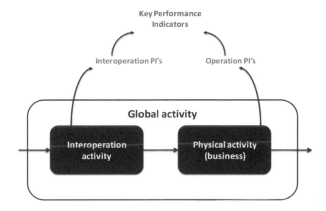

Figure 7. *The decomposition of global activities and measurement*

Based on this assertion, the framework of performance measurement of Figure 8 is proposed.

In this framework, it is proposed to measure several kinds of interoperability: intrinsic interoperability inside each enterprise and extrinsic interoperability in the collaboration of both enterprises.

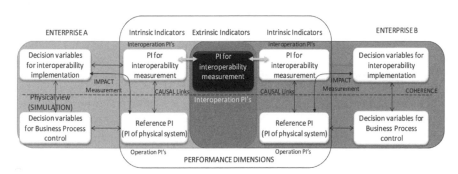

Figure 8. *The general framework for interoperability measurement*

For each enterprise, it is then possible to measure interoperability but also to implement reference PIs to measure physical (business) activity performances.

Then, some decision variables are used to control interoperability and other to control business processes. Of course, interoperability decision variables have an impact of the traditional business performance and there are also causal links between both kinds of PIs.

Finally, the Figure 9 below shows examples of each kind of PI.

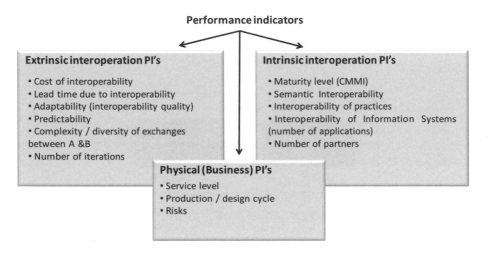

Figure 9. *Examples of PI's*

6. Conclusion

We present in this paper the methodology developed to solve interoperability problems. This method aims to characterize interoperability nodes and evaluate interoperability performance. This method is based on MDI and SOA techniques in order to define and orchestrate services based on high level business models with using continuum of models thanks to transformations from the TOP CIM level to the PSM Level. The first results of modeling of the two sub-contractors were shown and the work on interoperability performance measuring has been tackled.

The case study focuses on the cooperation of both partners, but in the future we provide to demonstrate that the addition of a new partner to the ISTA3 platform is possible and can be achieved at lower cost.

Modeling performed using GRAI methodology has shown the importance of business level. Indeed, this step provides a corporate image based on a graphical formalism that helps to understand and analyze the models.

Also, evaluation and measurement of interoperability performance is necessary.

The development of phase 3 will start soon; it aims to produce the I3rdG solutions, and it will be followed by phase 4 and phase 5 to implement the solution and the performance indicators in order to measure the interoperability performance.

7. Acknowledgments

The authors of this paper would like to thank the ISTA3 Project partners and the French Ministry of Industry for the financial support to this project.

8. References

[1] Touzi, J., Aide à la conception de Système d'Information Collaboratif support de l'interopérabilité des entreprises, PhD Thesis, INPT. (2007)

[2] Monateri, J.C., Sapina, M., "Dynamique des relations entre entreprises, stratégies manufacturières et arrangements contractuels durables", *3° Congrès international de génie industriel.* (1999)

[3] Vanderhaeghen, D., Werth, D., Kahl, T., Loos, P., "Service and process matching: An approach towards interoperability design and implementation of business networks", *Enterprise Interoperability: New Challenges and Approaches*, Springer, pp. 189-198. (2006)

[4] Chen, D., Doumeingts, G., "European initiatives to develop interoperability of enterprise applications–basic concepts, framework and roadmap", *Annual Reviews in Control*, 27, pp. 153-162. (2003)

[5] Bourey, J.P., Grangel, S.R., Doumeingts, G., Berre A., Report on Model Driven Interoperability. INTEROP NoE Deliverable DTG2.3. (2007)

[6] Raymond, G., SOA: architecture logique, principes, structures et bonnes pratiques, www.softeam.fr. (2007)

[7] Lemrabet, Y., Bigand, M., Clin, D., Benkeltoum, N., Bourey, J.P, "Model driven interoperability in practice: preliminary evidences and issues from an industrial project", in *Proceedings of the First International Workshop on Model-Driven Interoperability*, pp. 3-9. (2010)

[8] Amsden, J., Modeling with SoaML, the Service-Oriented Architecture Modeling. http://www.ibm.com/developerworks/rational/library/09/modelingwithsoaml-1/index.html. (2010)

[9] Zouggar, N., Romain, M., Doumeingts, G., Cazajous, S., Ducq, Y., Merlo, C., Grandin-Dubost, M., "ISTA3 Methodology application case", *I'ESA (The International Conference on Interoperability for Enterprise Software and Applications)*, Coventry. (2010)

[10] Doumeingts, G., Ducq, Y., Vallespir, B., Kleinhans, S., "Production Management and Enterprise Modelling", *Computer in Industry*, vol. 42, N° 2, pp. 245-263. (2001)

[11] Doumeingts, G., Chen, D., Vallespir, B., Fénié, P., Marcotte, F., "GIM (GRAI Integrated Methodology) and its Evolutions - A Methodology to Design and Specify Advanced Manufacturing Systems", *DIISM (Workshop on the Design of Information Infrastructure Systems for Manufacturing)*, pp. 101-120, Tokyo. (1993)

[12] Doumeingts, G., Vallespir, B., Chen, D., "GRAI Grid Decisional Modelling", in *Handbook on Architecture of Information System. International Handbook on Information Systems*, pp. 313-337, Springer Verlag. (1998)

[13] Kaplan, R.S., Norton, D.P., *The Balanced Scorecard*, Harvard Business School Press. (1996)

[14] Neely, A., Adams, C, Kennerley, M., *The Performance Prism – The Scorecard for Measuring and Managing Business Success*, Edition Prentice Hall. (2002)

[15] Ducq, Y., Vallespir, B., "Definition and aggregation of a Performance Measurement System in three Aeronautical workshops using the ECOGRAI Method", *International Journal of Production Planning and Control*, pp. 163-177. (2005)

[16] Bititci, U.S., Carrie, A.S., Mcdevitt, L., "Integrated Performance Measurement System: a development guide", *International Journal of Operations & Production Management*, n° 5-6, pp. 522-534. (1997)

[17] Ghalayini, A.M., Noble, J.S., Crowe, T.J., "An integrated dynamic performance measurement system for improving manufacturing competitiveness", *International Journal of Production Economics*, pp. 207-225. (1997)

Knowledge-based System for Semantics Adaptability of Enterprise Information Systems

Joao Sarraipa – Ricardo Jardim-Goncalves

Departamento de Engenharia Electrotécnica, Faculdade de Ciências e Tecnologia, FCT, Universidade Nova de Lisboa, 2829-516 Caparica, Portugal
Centre of Technology and Systems, CTS, UNINOVA, 2829-516 Caparica, Portugal

jfss@uninova.pt
rg@uninova.pt

ABSTRACT: *In the current global and competitive business context, it is essential that enterprises adapt their knowledge resources to seamlessly interact with others. However, one of the main problems found in the interoperability between enterprise systems and applications is related to semantics. Its integration, sharing and adaptability on the enterprise knowledge representation elements play an important role in the research challenges of the enterprise interoperability area. This paper proposes a knowledge-based system to endorse the semantics adaptability capability of enterprises information systems from a technical perspective.*

KEYWORDS: *Enterprise Interoperability; Information Systems; Knowledge; Semantics; Reference Ontology and Mapping mechanism*

1. Introduction

It is widely accepted that systems that possess knowledge and are capable of decision making and reasoning are regarded as "intelligent" (Meystel *et al.*, 2001) (Saridis *et al.*, 1988). There are recognized techniques, such as fuzzy logic, artificial neural networks, machine learning and evolutionary algorithms that contribute to increase a system's "machine intelligence quotient" (Zadeh, 1994). The rationale behind the intelligent label of those techniques is their ability to represent and deal with knowledge (Kasabov *et al.*, 2006). These branches form the triad of the so-called computational intelligence (Sarraipa *et al.*, 2010-A) (Panetto *et al.*, 2006).

Ontologies play an important role in intelligent systems. An ontology is an explicit specification of a conceptualization (Gruber, 1993) that refers to the shared understanding of some domain interest, which may be used as a unifying framework to facilitate knowledge sharing and interoperability between independently developed subsystems (Hayek, 1945). Thus, ontologies allow key concepts and terms relevant to a given domain to be identified and defined in a structure able to express the knowledge of an organization. Its recognized capacity to represent knowledge, to facilitate reasoning, use and exchange knowledge between systems contributes to increasing computational intelligence and consequently to its semantics adaptability.

Due to the relevance of the **knowledge** use and interpretation in semantics adaptability of information systems, a careful background observation on its nature is required. As with any substantive concept, it emerges that knowledge is a multi-faceted and interconnected entity (Brinklow, 2004). Thus, (Bellinger *et al.*, 2004) defined knowledge through its related concepts, establishing a hierarchy between them. This hierarchy is composed by Data, Information, Knowledge and Wisdom, with understanding achieving the transition through the categories. However, the authors, similarly to the (Ackoff, 1989) categorization of the human mind content, propose the use of the "understanding" as a new stage to the (Bellinger *et al.*, 2004) DIKW hierarchy. With this new stage ("Understanding"), is established the DIKUW hierarchy. The reason is related to the level to which the information systems are actually able to represent. Today they are able to represent some knowledge but they are far away from reaching wisdom. Consequently, the authors introduced the level understanding since it is a kind of middle stage between the knowledge and the wisdom level. These hierarchies study the knowledge concept, providing a foundation for exploring the dimensions of knowledge creation and representation.

2. DIKUW hierarchy

DIKUW hierarchy represents the knowledge creation chain from the simple data to wisdom. Each of the chain concepts is described through the conceptualization of the previous concept on the chain. They are:

Data. Data is raw. It simply exists, and has no significance beyond its existence, in and of itself. It can exist in any form, usable or not. It does not have meaning of itself (Bellinger *et al.*, 2004) (Keller *et al.*, 2005). *For instance, if we are not looking at any specific object, the affirmation, "That object is a regular chair", does not tell us anything.*

Information. On the other side, Information is data that has been given meaning, by the way of a relational connection. This "meaning" can be useful, but does not have to be. Information embodies the understanding of a relationship of some sort, possibly cause and effect (Bellinger *et al.*, 2004). *For instance, "If a person can sit on that object, then it is a chair", this affirmation gives us one idea. The next time we see a person sat, no matter where, we will predict that he, or she, is sat on a chair.*

Knowledge. Knowledge is the appropriate collection of information, such that its intent is to be useful (Bellinger *et al.*, 2004). *For instance, "If the object is not heavy; has legs; has a back rest; and a person could sit on it, making more or less 90 degrees between the legs and the body. That's a regular chair (Figure 1a)". This is a collection of information that almost certainly is useful.* There are two kinds of knowledge: (1) Explicit knowledge, is knowledge that has been, or can be, articulated, codified, and stored in certain media (Wikipedia, 2010); and (2) Tacit knowledge, is knowledge that people carry in their minds, which provides context for people, places, ideas, and experiences (United States Army, 2008).

Figure 1. *a) Regular Chair[1]; b) Strange Chair[2]; c) Planetary System?[3]*

---

1 Image retrieved from the web at August 2010:
http://brainaudit.com/blog/2008/08/understanding-patterns-how-your-brain-thinks.
2 Image retrieved from the web at August 2010: ttp://www.bentfabrication.com/suitcase.html.
3 Image retrieved from the web at August 2010: http://www.cribcandy.com/list=strange-chairs/175a5310d9ffe39c1b05ae14906517cc&pageoffset=0.

Understanding. Understanding is an interpolative and probabilistic process. It is cognitive and analytical. It is the process by which one can take knowledge, and synthesize new knowledge from the previously held knowledge. The difference between understanding and knowledge is the difference between "learning" and "memorizing" (Bellinger *et al.*, 2004) (Willcocks *et al.*, 2007). *From the previous example, we could say: "The object illustrated in Figure 1b seems to accommodate a person to sit on it, making more or less 90 degrees between the legs and the body. Then, it is a regular chair, even if we think it is a strange chair". This statement proves that we learned from the knowledge acquired earlier.*

Wisdom. Wisdom is an extrapolative and non-deterministic, non-probabilistic process. It beckons to give us understanding, about which there has previously been no understanding. It is the essence of philosophical probing. It asks questions to which there is no easily-achievable answer, and in some cases, to which there can be no humanly-known answer period (Bellinger *et al.*, 2004) (Willcocks *et al.*, 2007) (Ackoff, 1989). *For instance, if we look to the object illustrated in Figure 1c, at the first glance we do not know if it is a chair or a planetary system. However, since we have been talking about chairs, we can start thinking that perhaps, it could be a regular chair. Why not? Well, it is not a usual format, so it couldn't be a regular chair. We could state that we are concluding that "regular" is equivalent to "usual", thus a regular chair is something usual, where a person could sit, making more or less 90 degrees. All these thoughts indicate a presence of certain wisdom. Once again, is the picture presented in Figure 1c, a regular chair? What's the size of each of the balls? Could a person sit on the bottom ball? From these statements, we can conclude that we are in a presence of wisdom since we are making a kind of philosophical probe of the previous acquired knowledge. Thus, wisdom could change the way we understand something.*

2.1. *The "understanding" phase*

Today's research community is battling with the best way to collect data and information, in order to build knowledge bases with the focus in reaching the understandability. Understandability is the ability of the systems to understand what is happening around. Using the presented DIKUW hierarchy, it could be said that researchers are now focused on the Understanding phase. Understandability will allow a computer system to draw conclusions, from knowledge patterns represented in a machine-interpretable form.

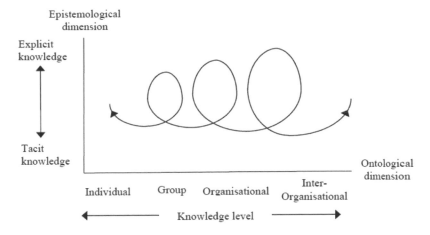

Figure 2. *Nonaka and Takeuchi's Spiral of Organizational Knowledge Creation (Nonaka et al., 1995) (Brinklow, 2004)*

(Diamantini, 2009) stated that the Science of Interoperability developed several theoretical models to formalize the concept of understanding. Most, if not all, of them rely on the notion of mapping. Mappings can link directly two units of information, or the mapping can be indirectly defined through a third element acting as a common reference model (like an ontology concept, a meta-model construct, or the element of a global schema) (Diamantini, 2009) (Halevy, 2003) (Lenzerini, 2002) (InteropWP8 Partners, 2004) (Missikoff *et al.*, 2006) (Jardim-Goncalves *et al.*, 2007). This affirmation emphasizes the need of mappings establishment between existent information units or in third elements defined with the purpose of being the common reference to the involved organizations. This explains the importance of the knowledge creation and especially its reuse by organizations/enterprises, through the use of appropriate mappings.

In the pursuit to organize the knowledge creation process, Nonaka and Takeuchi stated that knowledge is created in a cyclical trajectory simultaneously between ontological and epistemological planes, with spiral progression defining the conversion and mobilization of tacit knowledge (Figure 2) (Nonaka *et al.*, 1995) (Brinklow, 2004).

To reach understandability, systems have to have intelligence able to manage knowledge and consequently to learn from it. The path is to define a system able to create and re-use knowledge using mappings if needed, and following Nonaka and Takeuchi's Spiral of Organizational Knowledge Creation.

3. Semantics Interoperability Enhancer System

The purpose of the proposed Semantics Interoperability Enhancer System is to contribute to make other systems interoperable by defining how semantics adaptability could be accomplished. The knowledge creation dynamics compliant with the semantics adaptability objective can be represented as a system in the sense that encloses a set of interrelated components working together towards the interoperable system. Thus, it can be designed based on the Integration Definition for Function Modeling (IDEF0) standard structure. IDEF0 is a method intended to model the decisions, actions, and activities of an organization or system. This standard structure comprises a system based on inputs, outputs with feedback, controls and mechanisms of a determined function (NIST, 1993) (Figure 3). This system architecture is also based on the training development management system proposed by (Sarraipa *et al.*, 2010-B).

The Semantics Interoperability Enhancer System has as inputs, knowledge, tacit and explicit on a specific domain. It has mechanisms able to supply knowledge representation elements to be used; and an entry control composed by the Enterprise Interoperability (EI) directives, which will conduct the system to the defined focus. Finally, it has the output which through appropriate knowledge reasoning is able to execute decisions. Such output functionalities communicate back to provide essential feedback on performance and quality of reasoning, thus enabling semantics adaptation towards excellence. These system elements are described in the following sections.

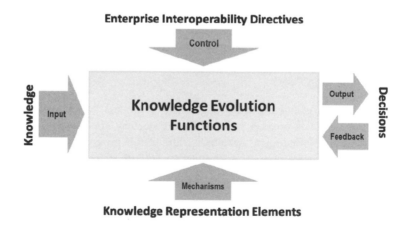

Figure 3. *Semantics Interoperability Enhancer System*

3.1. *EI directives (control)*

The control of the proposed system is ruled by a set of directives, which are defined from the grand challenges identified by the EI roadmap in (Charalabidis *et al.*, 2008). Such directives encourage the way to which the control of the system should be led. This is accomplished by bringing directions/ideas identified by the EI roadmap and impose them to be used by the functions of the system. As an example: directive 1 denotes that the overall system to provide enterprise interoperability should act as a utility-like capability. Thus, this leads to the implementation of interoperability functions (used by the proposed system) to be developed as a set of utility-like services. Therefore, the proposed system is synchronized with the overall EI research demands.

Directive 1 - Interoperability Service Utility (ISU). This directive denotes the overall system to provide enterprise interoperability as a utility-like capability. It pursues the creation of services to minimize the need and associated costs of enterprises, notably SMEs, to create information infrastructures that enable integration with different original equipment manufacturers in different sectors. It supports the use of basic information infrastructure that has information objects, ontologies, and metadata repositories as its core.

Directive 2 - Future Internet and Enterprise Systems. This directive is about researching new Web technologies for Enterprise Interoperability. It seeks to apply the concepts, technologies and solutions flowing from developments in Web technology to address the problems of EI. This will contribute to the advance of the implementation and uptake of Future Internet Services, establishing European-scale markets for smart infrastructure with integrated communications functionality (The European Future Internet Initiative, 2010).

Directive 3 - Knowledge-Oriented Collaboration and Semantic Interoperability. This directive supports the need for research in advanced technologies able to enable semantic interoperability and knowledge-based collaborations. They could be new methodologies, techniques and tools for the discovery, capture and re-use of knowledge collaborative capabilities and services (e.g. folksonomies); next generation knowledge management systems, which are able to provide advanced knowledge services (identification, collection, representation, processing and exploitation) in support of knowledge-based collaborations; and ontology development and management approaches able to furnish the semantics for the Semantic Web and to committed practice communities.

Directive 4 - A Science Base for Enterprise Interoperability. This directive is focused on provide a science base for engineering EI, to support solutions of higher quality, dependability, and reliability. For this it relies on making EI more demonstrably cost-effective for end users; laying a long-term foundation for coherent and visionary Enterprise Interoperability research with broad impact; enabling the establishment of a multi-disciplinary Enterprise Interoperability research community; and by providing an infrastructure to support the diffusion of ideas, education, research, and training.

3.2. Knowledge (input)

Traditionally, knowledge and information are fragmented among many different places in organizations. For instance, knowledge such as best practice accounts, lessons learned and experiences about particular processes or procedures resides with the professionals, managers and engineers, while, customer information, reports and procedures are often scattered across paper files and electronic databases. To leverage this scattered knowledge and increase organizational performance it is imperative to enable the flow of knowledge among and between individuals and groups within an organization (Rocket Project, 2002). Knowledge acts as the input to the proposed system independently of its format (explicit or not). Once inside such system knowledge has to be transferred or distributed among the organization members, thereby promoting learning and producing new knowledge or understanding to enable semantics interoperability of systems.

3.3. Decisions (output/feedback)

An enterprise knowledge-based system includes semantic features able to exchange decision-making information across its stakeholders. The knowledge from any domain can be modeled for decision-making and applicable to building specific decision support tools (Miah et al., 2007).

The output of the proposed system will be used to facilitate reasoning from the users. Such output is directly connected to the system's knowledge base that would be represented by ontologies. Thus it is able to support decisions or "answer" specific user's questions. It also acts as an interface to receive feedback from users. This feedback could be for instance obtained though the usage patterns of the ontology (Staab et al., 2001). The prototype system has to track the way users navigate for searching or reasoning the concepts and relations of the ontology. With an appropriate "ontology log analysis" it could be traced what areas of the ontology are often "used" and others which were not navigated.

3.4. *Knowledge representation elements (mechanisms)*

A knowledge representation element is an element that facilitates the formal representation of the knowledge in a specific domain. Dictionary, glossary, taxonomy, thesaurus, ontology, and data representation standards are some of its examples. They are introduced here as technological solutions (mechanisms) able to represent knowledge and to be used by the proposed system.

4. Knowledge evolution functions

The Semantics Interoperability Enhancer System is rooted by a function based on the knowledge lifecycle. A knowledge cycle is the process that knowledge passes through an organization as knowledge is identified, created, captured, shared, transferred, and utilized (Kirsch, 2008). The authors defined for such a system a four phase knowledge lifecycle composed of: acquisition; modeling; use; and maintenance (Figure 4). Although, the function of the Knowledge Interoperable System was correlated not only with the proposed four-phase knowledge life-cycle model but also with the Nonaka and Takeuchi's "Knowledge Spiral Conversion Model". In this way, the function performs an entire knowledge lifecycle, synchronized to the spiral conversion of knowledge cycle. The knowledge of the proposed Interoperable System is acquired, modeled, used and improved on its way from a smaller view (individual or group) to a wider view (inter-organizational) (Figure 5). Thus, for each flow from identification to capture, store, share and maintain, knowledge is converted from tacit to explicit and then to tacit again. To avoid having the use of Nonaka and Takeuchi's model reduced to the learning model; authors identified the use of training as a way to apply the knowledge evolution in the opposite direction. However, since this paper is mainly focused in the semantics adaptability from a technical view such part is not fully addressed.

4.1. *Knowledge acquisition*

Knowledge acquisition is the process of knowledge identification and its capture to an explicit format to enable further digital use. Automated tools to knowledge identification and capture have been developed by the research community. However, the more informally the knowledge is represented on its source, the more its results decrease on efficiency. Moreover, if the process is focused on semantics of data even lighter solutions are available due to the complexity of the process of acquiring embedded meaning of a simple business domain concept. In addition, this phase aggregates processes/methodologies able to acquire tacit knowledge to explicit through a human formalization process.

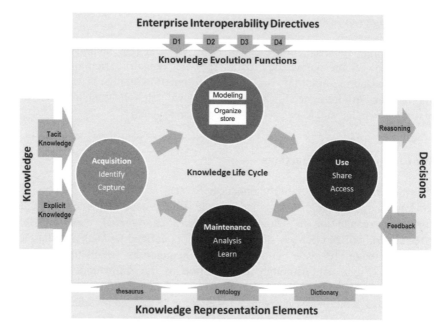

Figure 4. *Knowledge evolution functions of the Semantics Interoperability Enhancer System*

4.2. *Knowledge modeling*

The way the knowledge is stored and organized implies its further use. This stage receives the formal knowledge from the previous stage and organizes it in a knowledge base able to store and to enable further reasoning over the semantics of the concepts. The process, the knowledge base architecture, the tools, and the formal languages used to model the knowledge are the main point of the knowledge modeling stage. The use of appropriate technologies as glossaries, thesaurus and ontologies should be considered depending on the purpose to which such knowledge will be used for.

4.3. *Knowledge use*

This stage is centralized on the use of the stored knowledge to facilitate interoperability of the systems. Thus the way the knowledge could be shared and accessed by the various actors of a community is the main point of this stage. The formalism able to represent mappings between information models could facilitate the integration and use of various knowledge sources to the semantics adaptability of the information systems. This requires the ability of reasoning over the knowledge bases to be the support services of the knowledge sharing. In additional, this stage is also related to use of the knowledge by reasoning functions like, for instance, for specific products search.

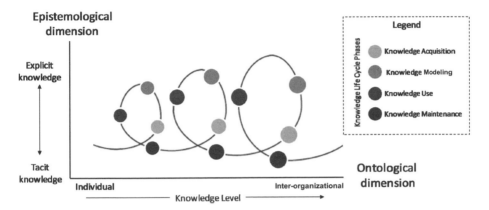

Figure 5. *Correlation between the knowledge lifecycle stages and Nonaka and Takeuchi's Knowledge Spiral Conversion Model*

4.4. *Knowledge maintenance*

The knowledge maintenance stage is focused on the improvement of the knowledge base in order to be alive and updated accordingly to the knowledge evolution to which the system could be related to. Knowledge maintenance is ruled by the analysis of the users' interactions patterns (feedback), which works as the main trigger to the learning process that such knowledge-based system could have.

5. A knowledge cycle example

A knowledge cycle of the proposed interoperable system can be exemplified by a set of enterprises from the mechanical domain that started to collaborate and consequently they have to harmonize and adapt their semantics in order to communicate (Jardim-Goncalves *et al.*, 2006a).

Through appropriate methodologies and tools, enterprises involved domain knowledge is acquired, stored and organized by establishing mappings between the various enterprises knowledge sources, to enable semantics interoperability. MENTOR is able to accomplish such a described action, since it is a methodology defined for enterprises reference ontology development, to help organizations to build and adapt a domain reference ontology (Sarraipa *et al.*, 2008) (Sarraipa *et al.*,

2010-A). Thus, MENTOR was used to build the reference ontology from the two enterprises (A and B) ontologies, whose are represented respectively on the left and right part of Figure 6. MENTOR uses a Mediator Knowledge Base (MKB) for supporting the mapping establishment, since it is able to represent such mappings through a tuple approach. The mapping tuple is defined accordingly to (Agostinho *et al.*, 2011); consequently, its expression is of the form: *<ID, MElems, KMType, MatchClass, Exp>*, where *ID* is an identifier; *MElems* is the pair *(a,b)* that indicates the mapped elements; *KMType* represents the Knowledge Mapping Type (e.g. *Conceptual*; *Semantics*; and *Instantiable Data*); *MatchClass* stands for Match/Mismatch Classification depending on the *KMType*, where some of its possible values are *"Equal"*, *"MoreGeneral"*, *"Disjoint"* etc.; finally *Exp* represents the formal expression that relates the mapping elements.

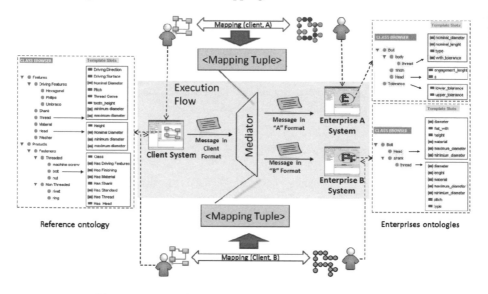

Figure 6. *Knowledge organization and use in a collaborative data exchange execution flow (Agostinho et al., 2011)*

MKB fills up a mapping tuple per each map identified on the semantic harmonization process conducted. Taking an example in the mechanical domain specifically related to the *tolerance* characteristic of a *bolt*, it is stated that in the client system (reference ontology) such a *tolerance* characteristic is defined by two properties, *maximum diameter* and *minimum diameter*. These are equally used by Enterprise B. However, Enterprise A uses the concepts *upper tolerance* and *lower tolerance*, which represents the same expected result but using different data values. *Nominal diameter* and *diameter* concepts have the same value and semantics in all the ontologies (Agostinho *et al.*, 2011). Thus, the transformation equations related to the *tolerance* properties from Client to Enterprise A, are the following:

maximum diameter = nominal diameter + upper tolerance

minimum diameter = nominal diameter - lower tolerance

Consequently the mapping tuple related to the *maximum diameter* concept (first of the above expressions) is composed by the values represented in Figure 7. Note that the elements presented in *MElems* and *Exp* fields are presented with their respective path in the ontologies to which they belong.

ID		*Client*2.1.1.2.7.8_2
MElems	*a*	$((Thread)Products.Fasteners.Threaded.bolt.HasThread).maximum\ diameter$
= (a, b)	*b*	$Bolt.body.thread.nominal\_diameter$
KMType		*InstantiableData*
MatchClass		*Granularity*
Exp		$"a = b + ((Tolerance)Bolt.body.thread.with\_tolerance).upper\_tolerance"$

Figure 7. *Mapping tuple values example (Agostinho et al., 2011)*

This approach to represent the mappings establishment between the ontologies enables a subsequent "mapping records" querying and reasoning. One of its applications is for the querying of a correspondence to a reference term in one specific enterprise ontology. As a result MKB is able to work as a "mediator" acting as a semantic translator of messages for the communications between the client system (left part of Figure 6) to one of the enterprises systems (right part of Figure 6).

In addition, in order for the system to contribute to the knowledge maintenance of the organization, it uses a product search functionality able to identify users' interactions patterns. As an example, if all customers start to adopt using a new term "*screw*" to an existent product "*bolt*", the system will be able to determine the adoption of the "*screw*" term in the communications and the replacement of such term on the reference ontology to the term "*bolt*".

The previous statements describe an entire knowledge cycle example of the proposed system. However, in order to have the knowledge cycle completely aligned to Nonaka and Takeuchi's model, it is needed to enforce the knowledge transfer in the opposite direction to what is presented in Figure 5; this means, from an inter-organizational to individual view. Such an action can be accomplished, by training execution. Since the proposed system is dedicated to computational information systems, the inter-organization to individual knowledge transfer is less in demand. But skills related to knowing how to contribute to such system knowledge management always need to be addressed among individuals that have to interact with it. Another need is related to knowing the "new" common view, which the reference concepts were defined. Thus, training is also a topic to be addressed in the deployment of systems as the proposed one in enterprises, to warrant also the semantics interoperability between human actors. This is aligned with the mentioned fourth EI directive.

6. Conclusions and future work

Authors have been developing methodologies and prototyping tools to manage each of the knowledge lifecycle four-phases of which the proposed system is composed. They defined and prototyped MENTOR to the knowledge acquisition and modeling phases. Concerning knowledge use, authors defined a tuple able to represent semantics and structural mappings between information models accomplished by traceability features to facilitate the knowledge re-use and share (Agostinho *et al.*, 2011) (Jardim-Goncalves *et al.*, 2006b). In addition, they have developed a knowledge maintenance application, which uses machine learning techniques in the support to ontologies learning. This is accomplished through attribution of weights to each ontology element in a similar way to the learning mechanisms, through which the human brain processes information. Thus, when there is any change in the information systems, detected from users' interaction patterns (feedback), ontologies will learn from it adapting its elements' weights as the human brain modifies the synaptic connection strengths (or weights) between the neurons that process information (Rolls, 2000).

With a full implementation of the proposed system authors envisage to contribute to the advance of the interoperability solution, in accordance with the European EI research roadmap affirmation: "Enterprises of the future will be nodes in innovation ecosystems, thereby requiring 'interoperability to become 'interoperable', to allow the creation of large-scale ecosystems and to avoid forming islands of ontologies in different business domains and application scenarios".

7. Acknowledgments

The authors would like to thank all involved in the CoSpaces - IST-5-034245 and CRESCENDO - 234344 projects that in some how could have contributed to this work. The research leading to these results has received funding from the European Community's Seventh Framework Programme (FP7/2007-2013) under grant agreement n°234344 (www.crescendo-fp7.eu<http://www.crescendo-fp7.eu/>).

8. References

Ackoff, R. L. (1989). "From Data to Wisdom", *Journal of Applies Systems Analysis*, Volume 16, 1989 p 3-9.

Agostinho, C.; Sarraipa, J.; Goncalves, D.; and Jardim-Goncalves, R. (2011). "Tuple-based semantic and structural mapping for a sustainable interoperability", in *Proceedings of: DOCEIS'11 2nd Doctoral Conference on Computing, Electrical and Industrial Systems* – Costa de Caparica, Lisbon, February 2011.

Bellinger, G.; Castro, D.; Mills, A. (2004). Data, Information, Knowledge and Wisdom, Retrieved from the web http://www.systems-thinking.org/dikw/dikw.htm at August 2010.

Brinklow, T. (2004). Domains, Ontologies, Models and the Knowledge Creation Cycle, published at Brighton Business School - Occasional / Working paper series - BBSW04-3; 2004.

Charalabidis, Y; Gionis, G; Hermann, K; Martinez, K. (2008) Enterprise Interoperability: Research Roadmap. Update Version 5.0. March 5th, 2008.

Diamantini, C. (2009). "Is "Understanding" a Misunderstanding?", in *Proceedings of the 15th International Conference on Concurrent Enterprising*, Leiden – The Netherlands, 22-24 June 2009.

Gruber, T.R., 1993. "A translation approach to portable ontology specifications", *Journal of Knowledge Acquisition*, 5 (2), 199–220.

Halevy, A. Y. (2003). "Data Integration: A Status Report", in *Datenbanksysteme für Business, Technologie und Web*, Leipzig Germany, February 2003.

Hayek, F., (1945). "The use of knowledge in society", *The American Economic Review*, 35 (4), 519–530. IEEE Computer Society, New York –USA, 1995. IEEE Guide for Software Quality Assurance Planning. Std. 730.1-1995.

InteropWP8 Partners (2004). State of the Art and State of the Practice Including Initial Possible Research Orientations. INTEROP project, FP6-IST-2002-508011, Deliverable D8.1, 2004.WWW page http://interopvlab.eu/ei_public_deliverables/interop-noe-deliverables/do-ontology-for-interoperability.

Jardim-Goncalves, R.; Agostinho, C.; Malo, P.; and Steiger-Garcao, A. (2007). "Harmonizing Technologies in Conceptual Models Representation", in *International Journal on Product Lifecycle Management, IJPLM*, 2007.

Jardim-Goncalves, R.; Figay, N.; and Steiger-Garcao, A. (2006b). "Enabling interoperability of STEP Application Protocols at meta-data and knowledge level", in *International Journal of Technology Management (IJTM)*, 2006.

Jardim-Goncalves, R.; Grilo, A.; and Steiger-Garcao, A. (2006a). "Challenging the Interoperability in the Construction Industry with MDA and SoA", in *Computers in Industry*, Vol. 57, Issues 8-9, 2006.

Kasabov, N.; and Filev, D., 2006. "Evolving intelligent systems: methods, learning, & applications", *Proc. Int. Symposium on Evolving Fuzzy Systems*, pp. 8–18.

Keller, T.; and Tergan, S.O. (2005). "Visualizing Knowledge and Information: An Introduction", in *Knowledge and Information Visualization: Searching for Synergies*. Springer 2005: p. 1-23.

Kirsch, D. (2008). Knowledge Cycle. Retrieved from the web at August 2010: http://it.toolbox.com/wiki/index.php/Knowledge_Cycle.

Kolski C., *Interfaces homme machine*, Paris, Editions Hermès, 1997.

Lenzerini, M. (2002). "Data Integration: a Theoretical Perspective", in *ACM Symposium on Principles of Database Systems*, 2002, p. 233-246.

May, P., Ehrlich, H.C., Steinke, T.: "ZIB Structure Prediction Pipeline: Composing a Complex Biological Workflow through Web Services", in Nagel, W.E., Walter, W.V., Lehner, W. (eds.) *Euro-Par 2006*. LNCS, vol. 4128, pp. 1148-1158. Springer, Heidelberg (2006).

Meystel, A.M. and Albus, J.S., (2001). *Intelligent Systems: Architecture, Design, and Control*. New York: John Wiley and Sons.

Miah, S. J.; Gammack, J.; Kerr, D. (2007). "Ontology development for context-sensitive decision support", in *Proceedings: Third International Conference on Semantics, Knowledge and Grid* – SKG2007 Xi'an, China, 29-31 October 2007 - Publisher IEEE.

Missikoff, M., D'Antonio, F., Lenzerini, M., Jeusfeld, M., Johannesson, P. (2006) Enterprise Modelling and Ontologies for Interoperability. INTEROP project, FP6-IST-2002-508011, Deliverable   D8.2,   2006.   WWW   page   http://interop-vlab.eu/ei_public_deliverables/interop-noe-deliverables/do-ontology-for-interoperability.

NIST, Integration Definition for Function Modeling (IDEF0): Draft Federal Information Processing Standards Publication 183, 1993 December 21. In: Federal Information Processing Standards Publications No 183. Gaithersburg, Md, USA: National Institute for Standards and Technology.

Nonaka, I.; Takeuchi, H. (1995). *The Knowledge-Creating Company*. Oxford University Press.

Panetto, H.; Jardim-Goncalves, R.; and Pereira, C. E. (2006). "E-Manufacturing and Web-Based Technology for Intelligent Manufacturing and Networked Enterprise Interoperability", in *Journal of Intelligent Manufacturing*, vol. 17, p. 639-640, 2006.

Rocket Project WP2 Partners (2002). Deliverable D 2.1 State-of-the-Art of Knowledge Management, from project ROCKET - Roadmap to Communicating Knowledge Essential for the Industrial environment - IST-2001-38245.

Rolls ET. (2000). "Memory systems in the brain", in *Annu Rev Psychol*. 2000; 51:599-630

Saridis, G.N.; and Valavanis, K.P., (1988). "Analytical design of intelligent machines", *Automatica*, 24 (2), 123–133.

Sarraipa, J.; Silva, J.; Jardim-Goncalves, R.; and Monteiro, A. (2008). "MENTOR – A Methodology for Enterprise Reference Ontology Development", in *2008 4th International IEEE Conference on Intelligent Systems*.

Sarraipa, J.; Figueiredo, D.; Maló, P. and Jardim-Goncalves, R. (2010-B). "An Inter-Organisational approach to Industrial e-Training", in *Collaborative Knowledge Management - CKM 2010: Inter-Organizational Collaboration, Collaborative Software Development, and Knowledge Management (I) - Invited Session (0000014) (KGCM) of the 3rd International Multi-Conference on Engineering and Technological Innovation: IMETI 2010*.

Sarraipa, J.; Jardim-Goncalves, R.; and Steiger-Garcao, A. (2010-A). "MENTOR: an enabler for interoperable intelligent systems", *International Journal of General Systems*, 39: 5, 557-573, http://dx.doi.org/10.1080/03081079.2010.484278.

Staab, S.; Schnurr, H.-P.; Studer, R.; and Sure, Y.; (2001). "Knowledge processes and ontologies", *IEEE Intelligent Systems, Special Issue on Knowledge Management*, 16(1), January/Febrary 2001.

The European Future Internet Initiative (2010). The European Future Internet Initiative (EFII). In: White paper on the Future Internet PPP Definition, January 2010.

United States Army (2008). In annex A: Glossary of Terms of the "Army Knowledge Management Principles" publication. Retrieved from the web at August 2010: http://www.army.mil/ciog6/docs/AKMPrinciples.pdf

Wikipedia   (2010).   Retrieved   from   the   web   at   August   2010: http://en.wikipedia.org/wiki/Explicit_knowledge.

Willcocks, Leslie P. and Finnegan, David (2007) *Implementing CRM - From Technology To Knowledge*. John Wiley series in information systems, Chichester, UK.

Zadeh, L.A., 1994. "Fuzzy logic, neural networks, and soft computing", *Communications to the ACM*, 37 (3), 77–84. ISSN:0001-0782.

A Model-Driven Approach to Interoperability in B2B Data Exchange

Dumitru Roman – Brice Morin – Sixuan Wang – Arne J. Berre

SINTEF, Norway

Forskningsveien 1, Oslo, Norway
{firstname.lastname}@sintef.no

ABSTRACT: *With the B2B data exchange becoming ubiquitous nowadays, automating as much as possible the exchange of data between collaborative enterprise systems is a key requirement for ensuring agile interoperability and scalability in B2B collaborations. Semantic differences and inconsistencies between conceptual models of the exchanged B2B data hinder agility, and ultimately the interoperability in B2B collaborations. In this paper we introduce a model-driven technique and prototype that support humans in reconciling the differences between the data models of the parties involved in a data exchange, and enable a high degree of automation in the end-to-end data exchange process. Our approach is based on the use of OMG Model-Driven Architecture (MDA) for abstracting platform-specific schemas and instances to platform-independent metamodels and models, specification of transformations at the platform-independent level, and generation of executable mappings for run-time data exchange. This paper presents the MDA-based data exchange framework we have developed, and focuses on the mapping metamodel and the generation of executable mappings from platform-independent transformations. Benefits of the proposed framework include the possibility of the mappings creator to focus on the semantic, object-oriented model behind the different platform-specific schemas and specify the mappings at a more abstract, semantic level, with both specification and execution of data mappings (i.e. design- and run-time mapping) provided in a single, unifying framework.*

KEYWORDS: *MDI, MDA, data exchange, mapping, transformation*

1. Introduction

Improving the level of automation of data exchange between B2B systems is widely regarded as a key enabler for agile interoperability and scalability in B2B collaborations (Bussler, 2003). Techniques and tools have been proposed to improve automation in data exchange in particular for concrete representation formats such as XML, however, generic approaches that can easily handle different data formats are currently missing, hindering the agility and scalability of B2B data exchange, and in general the interoperability of B2B systems and applications.

Rather than focusing on a specific data representation format, we introduce a generic technique and tool for design- and run-time support of B2B data exchange, based on the OMG Model-Driven Architecture[1] approach. The use of model-driven approaches for data mapping/exchange has not been yet widely investigated in the community. With this paper we aim at providing a solution to the end-to-end data exchange problem based on the use of OMG MDA framework which we use for high-level, abstract specification of schemas and mappings between them, as well as for run-time execution of mappings.

Figure 1 provides an overview of the elements involved in a typical B2B data exchange between two companies X and Y. Company X, the initiator of the exchange, wants to send the Source Instance (e.g. an invoice document) to Company Y. The Source Instance document is compliant with a schema, Source Schema (e.g. an invoice schema), made available by Company X such that the receiver of its instance document, Company Y, can understand the structure and meaning of such a document. nhema, then company X is faced with the problem of having to process the Source Instance document which it does not understand.

The core challenge in such a scenario is to generate the Target Instance document from the Source Instance document, given the Source Schema and the Target Schema. A Transformation Layer is usually designed to address this challenge by providing means to map the Source Schema to the Target Schema at design time, and by providing an engine that implements the schema mappings at run time when the Target Instance needs to be generated from Source Instance. Since the transformation cannot be fully automated, the core question is how to design the transformation layer in such a way that the human intervention in the specification and execution of mappings is kept at a minimum.

The OMG Model-Driven Architecture (MDA) approach appears attractive for addressing the problem of data exchange, in particular for its support in modeling schemas and transformations at a technology-independent level and its capabilities

---

1 http://www.omg.org/mda.

for automatic generation of executable run-time transformations. The OMG MDA approach, in essence, facilitates the mappings creator to focus on the semantic, object-oriented model behind the different schemas and specify the mappings at a more abstract, semantic level, and potentially enables both specification and execution of data mappings (i.e. design- and run-time mapping) in a single, unifying framework. Rather than having to deal with technicalities of specific data formats and their transformations at lower levels, this paper uses the MDA approach to provide a generic a solution to the end-to-end data exchange problem.

The remaining of this paper is organized as follows. Section 2 gives an overview of our proposed generic MDA data exchange framework. Section 3 describes the transformation metamodel – a core element of our framework – and its use in the specification of transformations. Section 4 focuses on the run-time aspects of the data exchange framework, and provides details on the generation of executable mapping rules. Section 5 concludes this paper, together with some relevant related work and potential extensions.

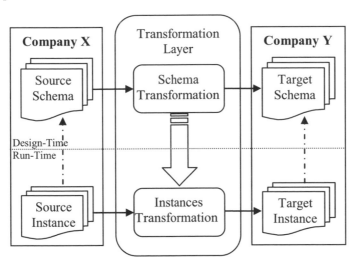

Figure 1. *Generic design-time and run-time data transformation*
(adapted from Liao et al., 2010)

2. Generic MDA Data Exchange Framework

Figure 2 below gives an overview of our proposed data exchange framework. The shadowed box in the center of the figure (which we refer to as *MDI Transform Engine*) is the core part of the framework, where all the specifications and transformations take place at the platform-independent level. The elements outside the shadowed box (source and target schemas, their transformation, the source instance, and the generated target instance) represent platform-specific models and transformations.

In our approach, source and target schemas (e.g. XSDs, database schemas, etc.) are abstracted as platform- and technology-independent models. In our framework (and current implementation), they are abstracted as ECore[2] metamodels (depicted as Source MM and Target MM in the figure), which are very closed to UML class diagrams. Both ECore and UML provide advanced object-oriented mechanisms to data modeling (inheritance, references, compositions, etc.). In a similar way, the source instances are abstracted to platform-independent models (depicted by Source M in the figure), which are processed by our run-time executable transformations to generate platform-independent target models (depicted by Target M in the figure), which are then serialized in platform-specific Target Instances.

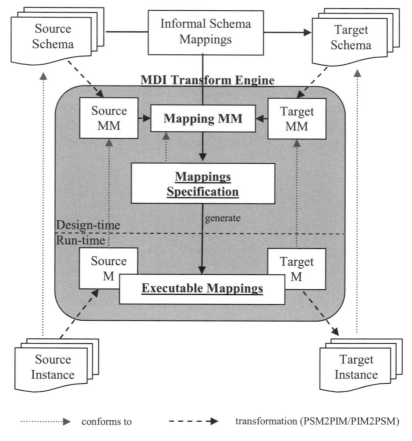

Figure 2. *Model-driven data exchange approach – overview*

___

2 http://www.eclipse.org/modeling/emf/?project=emf.

At the heart of the transformation is a mapping metamodel (depicted by Mapping MM in the figure), which enables us to specify the schema mappings (Mappings Specifications in the figure) in an intuitive way at the platform-independent level, based on the informal schema mappings provided by the user. Furthermore, our framework provides support for automatic generation of executable mappings that are used at run-time to execute the transformation of the Source Model (source data instances) to the Target Model (target data instances). This way, the user needs to focus on the transformations at the platform-independent level, with the actual data exchange being fully automated.

Another way of looking at the framework is through its design- and run-time elements. The following process takes place when using the framework for data exchange.

At design-time:

1. The platform-specific Source and Target Schemas are abstracted into platform-independent source and target metamodels through a given transformation (PSM2PIM) specific to the concrete technologies used at the platform-specific level.

2. By using the mapping metamodel, the mappings between the source and target metamodels are specified, based on the informal mappings provided by the user.

3. Executable mappings are generated from the mappings specified in the previous step, and will be used during the run-time data exchange.

At run-time:

4. The platform-specific Source Instance is abstracted into a source model through a given transformation (PSM2PIM) specific to the concrete technologies used at the platform-specific level.

5. The executable mapping rules from step 2 are executed for the source model and a target model corresponding to the source model is generated.

6. The target model is serialized into a platform-specific instance target through a given transformation (PIM2PSM) specific to the concrete technologies used at the platform-specific level.

In the following two sections we will focus on the techniques behind the MDI Transform Engine by introducing the mapping metamodel, specifying mappings, and generating executable transformations.

3. Platform-independent specification of transformations

Platform-independent specification of transformations between a source and target metamodel relies on the existence of a mapping metamodel. In this section we introduce our proposed metamodel and exemplifies its use in a simple yet realistic use case.

The Mapping MM, depicted in Figure 3, is inspired by graph-based approaches (Grønmo *et al.*, 2009) and Aspect-Oriented Modeling approaches (Morin *et al.*, 2010). The basic idea is to describe mappings between model fragments (the Left-Hand-Side (LHS) and the Right-Hand-Side (RHS)), at the instance level yet in a platform-independent manner. Working at the instance level allows us to easily express constraints, filters or patterns on the mappings. The mapping framework comes with a set of default Mapping Operations, which implement default mapping behaviors. In addition to classic operators (e.g. copy, split, merge specific attributes) we also provide composite adaptations which allow us, for example, to copy all the similar attributes (same name, same type). The metamodel is easily extensible and users can customize it as needed:

- By defining generic adaptations that can be applied to any input and output metamodels. In this case, these extensions can directly be integrated into the generic framework, so that any subsequent derivation of the framework will benefit from these adaptations.

- By defining domain-specific adaptation that takes into account the specific semantics of the given input and output metamodels. In this case, these extensions will only be integrated into the specific framework.

Since the LHS can match multiple times, we complement mappings with instantiation strategies introduced in (Morin *et al.*, 2010). This allows designers to control the way the elements of the RHS should be instantiated: every time the LHS matches, once, etc. By default, all the elements of the RHS are instantiated every time the LHS matches. The *global instantiation* strategy allows the designer to specify that some elements of the RHS are global i.e. only one instance of these elements will be created, even if the LHS matches several times. The *scoped instantiation* allows designers to relate the instantiation of some RHS elements to some LHS elements. Typically, this strategy allows handling overlapping mappings: if a RHS element has already been created and associated to a LHS element in a previous mapping, then it will be reused and not duplicated.

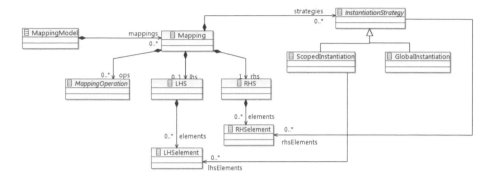

Figure 3. *Mapping metamodel*

Once the mapping framework has been automatically contextualized, designers can use it to define mappings. We adopt an interactive approach that guides the designer in defining mappings. The idea is to automatically infer some mappings that the user can validate, discard, or modify. We currently use simple string-based heuristics to identify potential mappings. However, since our approach is based on platform-independent models, it could easily benefit from the theory of model typing (Steel and Jézéquel, 2007), or bi-simulation (Nejati *et al.*, 2007), adapted to class diagrams. The idea would be to automatically identify fragments that would match in both metamodels, based on advanced heuristics.

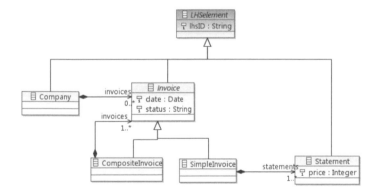

Figure 4. *Source MM linked to the Mapping MM (via LHSelement)*

To illustrate the use of the metamodel for specification of transformations consider the following example where invoices are sent from a source system to a target system. By a given transformation, the source invoice schema is abstracted in the ECore metamodel depicted in Figure 4. Invoices can be either simple or composite invoices. Simple invoices contain some statements (with the price), while composite invoices contain other invoices (simple or composite). Each invoice has a date and a status, modeled as a string.

By a given transformation, the target invoice schema is abstracted to the ECore metamodel depicted in Figure 5. Here, the invoices have a flat structure and contain some statements. Note that the date attribute is hold by the statements and not by the invoice. The state of the invoice is reified by the State abstract class, which has two concrete sub-classes: Paid or Waiting.

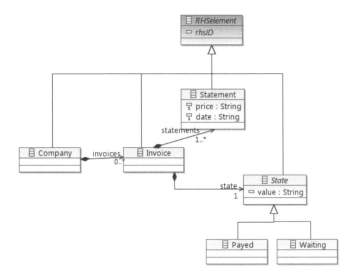

Figure 5. *Target MM linked to the Mapping MM (via RHSelement)*

The *informal mappings* between the source and the target schemas are as follows:

1. All the source invoices with an "OK" status are used to generate target invoices with *Paid* state.

2. All the source invoices with an "NOK" status are used to generate target invoices with *Waiting* state.

3. All the source simple invoices and their source statements are used to generate target invoices associated with target statements as follows: the price of the target statements should be copied from the corresponding source statements and the date of the target statements should be copied from the corresponding source invoices.

These informal mappings are captured in our framework by instantiating the mapping metamodel, as illustrated in Figure 6.

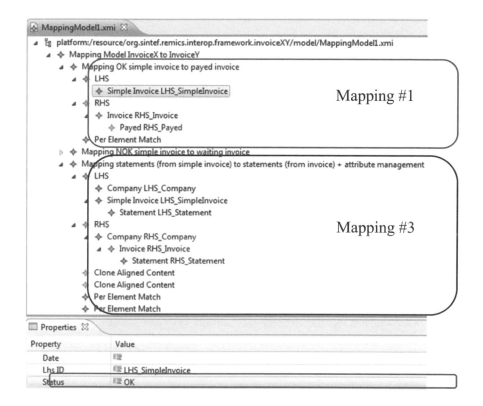

Figure 6. *Mapping specification*

In the first mapping the left-hand side is a simple invoice with its attribute status equal to "OK". This will basically match any simple invoice from the source data and filter these data according to the value of the status attribute. The second mapping is similar. The third mapping uses two "Clone aligned content" adaptations, which will actually copy all the aligned attributes (same name, compatible types) of the source into the target. The engine currently provides a limited support (based on the name of the classes) to infer these adaptations. Since the mappings are overlapping, the use of "Per Element Match" strategies makes it possible to reuse some elements that have been created by a previous mapping, in order to avoid inconsistent duplication of data.

4. Generation of executable mappings and run-time data exchange

For the platform-independent mappings specifications (such as those in Figure 6) to be usable at run-time for data exchange, executable transformations need to be generated. Our framework has been designed to automatically compile executable code (Java and Drools Expert[3]) from the specifications of mappings, using a 2-pass visitor implemented in Kermeta (Muller *et al.*, 2005). The first pass declares model-elements and manages their attributes, while the second pass is responsible for managing (potentially cyclic) references among elements. This generated code directly manipulates graph of objects (Source M and Target M) in memory. We use the persistency API of the source and target systems to load and save data from/to different sources, e.g., EMF models saved into XMI, XML files, databases, etc.

The following script illustrates the result of the first mapping described in the previous section. The *when* clause corresponds to the LHS. We use Drools Expert to automatically identify the pattern defined in the LHS of the mappings. Drools implements and extends the Rete algorithm with object-oriented optimizations. We can generate Drools code from any arbitrary pattern. The more precise the pattern is, the more reduced the set of matched places will be. This could be useful to migrate a precise sub-set of the input data. The first line of this clause specifies that the rule is looking for any simple invoice, which has a status equal to "OK". The second line of this clause is not actually used for this mapping. It re-declares the simple invoice variable and links it to the former declaration (*this ==...*). In more complex mappings including references among elements (such as the 3rd mapping presented above), this second declaration is responsible for handling references among elements. Since Drools (similarly to Java) does not allow referring to variables which are declared after a given statement, this two-staged declaration of variables makes it possible to handle (potentially cyclic) references.

```
rule "OK_simple_invoice_to_paid_invoice"
when
    LHS__SimpleInvoiceDecl: SimpleInvoice(status == "OK")
    LHS__SimpleInvoice: SimpleInvoice(this == LHS__SimpleInvoiceDecl)
then
    Invoice RHS__Invoice = null;
    Payed RHS__Paid = null;

    //Code dealing with the instantiation of the elements,
    //depending on the strategy. See Morin et al. MODELS 2010.

    RHS__Invoice.setState(RHS__Payed);
end
```

The *then* clause of the script corresponds to the RHS. All the elements of the RHS are first declared and set to null. Then that are properly instantiated according

---

3 http://www.jboss.org/drools/drools-expert.html.

to their associated strategy, as described in (Morin *et al.*, 2010). Finally, the mapping operations are compiled into *set* primitives that properly manage the attribute and references of the RHS elements.

This script is finally executed on source data such as the one illustrated on the left side of Figure 6.[4] By applying the script, we obtain the data depicted on the right of Figure 6. In particular, the composite structure of the invoices has been flattened, and the string-based status has been transformed into explicit states. The overall execution takes about 5 seconds for mapping 2000 statements (serialized in around 5000 lines of XMI) on an Intel Core i7-620M@2.67GHz, 8Gb RAM, Win7 64 bits.

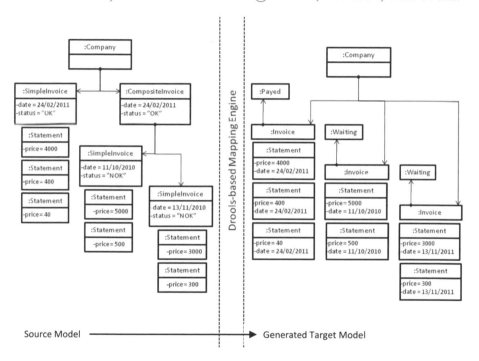

Figure 6. *Runtime Data Exchange*

5. Related work, conclusions, and outlook

Although the problem of mapping between data structures has been extensively studied for many years now, with schema mapping being a well established research

---

4 The relationships between instances of *SimpleInvoice* and instances of *Statement* have been omitted for clarity purpose. The simple invoices contain the statements located in the same column.

field (Bernstein and Melnik, 2007; Smith *et al.*, 2009), the use of OMG MDA for data mapping/exchange has not yet been widely investigated in the community. With this paper we provided a preliminary solution to the data exchange problem based on the use of OMG MDA as a mechanism for platform-independent specification of schemas and mappings between them, and generation of executable mappings to be used at run-time for data exchange. Our approach allows the mappings creator to focus on the platform-independent models behind the platform-specific schemas and specify the mappings at a more abstract, semantic level, rather than having to deal with technicalities of platform-specific schemas. With the use of automatic generation of executable mappings, the proposed framework allows both specification and execution of data mappings (i.e. design- and run-time mapping) in a single, unifying framework.

Our approach is inspired by the SmartAdapters aspect model weaver (Morin *et al.*, 2010). While Aspect-Oriented Modeling approaches (Whittle *et al.*, 2009; Reddy *et al.*, 2006) are usually concerned with endogeneous weaving, our approach is focused on the interoperability of exogeneous (yet, with some similarities) data. An aspect-model weaver basically takes two models conforming to the same metamodel and produces a third model, also conforming to the same metamodel. Our model-driven mapping engine takes a model conforming to a given metamodel and produces a model conforming to another metamodel. Despite this difference, we were able to reuse the SmartAdapters tool-chain in our framework (especially the Drools+Java code generator) with minor modifications.

Our approach to Model-Driven Interoperability is based on the definition of mappings at the instance level. More precisely, we define mappings between patterns (fragments of model). This allows designers to easily filter data based on patterns or on the values of attributes in order to identify different sub-sets in the source data that should be migrated according to different strategies. However, one of the main drawbacks of working at the instance level is that dedicated tools (such as advanced graphical editors) should be implemented or adapted for each source/target metamodels. Different from our approach, ModMap (Clavreul *et al.*, 2010) proposes to define mappings at the metamodel level. Mappings are defined in a graphical way by defining links between classes defined in ECore diagrams. These tools and the mappings have been used to generate some AspectJ code in order to align APIs of legacy systems (written in Java) and enable their interoperability. It could however be possible to generate other types of code, e.g. the code we generate to enable the interoperability of data. While this tool is very useful and easy to use to define mappings between classes, it is very cumbersome to define mappings among patterns (classes and references).

The work presented in this paper can be considered in the wider context of MDE model transformation techniques and languages (Czarnecki and Helsen, 2003; Mens and Van Gorp, 2006) such as ATL Transformation Languages (ATL).[5] ATL also relies on graph-based transformations, similar to our approach. However, our approach provides high-level constructs (such as the strategies) and mapping operators to control and ease the definition, which should be coded by the designers in ATL to achieve the same result. Another difference is that ATL, as well as most of the model transformation languages, focuses on the manipulation of EMF-based models. Our approach intends to manipulate data coming from different sources such as XML files or databases.

The recent work in (Liao *et al.*, 2010) provides a solution (FloraMap) to the data exchange problem with a focus on XML data exchange. It proposes the uses a logical rule language (Frame Logic) for formalization of schemas, instances, and transformations. Whereas it addresses the same problem and goes in the same direction of using a platform-independent approach for specification and execution of mapping, the approach presented in this paper strives to be more general through the use of well established OMG MDA technologies.

To summarize, in this paper we provided a preliminary report on the development of the data exchange framework. The preliminary experimental results indicate that the approach presented here is doable in practice. Nevertheless, there are various directions that can be considered to further enhance the framework presented in this paper:

1. Extensions for handling end-to-end n-m data exchanges, where multiple sources and multiple targets can exchange data.

2. (Semi-)Automated generation of platform-independent mapping rules, where techniques from e.g. ontology alignment techniques could be reused.

3. Address the issue of incompleteness of mappings by a coverage analysis which will ensure that all mandatory attributes are mapped.

4. Investigate possible synergies between instance-level mappings and metamodel-level mappings in order to mitigate respective drawbacks and combine respective advantages.

5. Systematic validation – whereas we performed some initial experimental results for the scalability of our framework, our approach need to be analyzed in a more systematic way (e.g. analyze the complexity of the specification of mapping rules, etc).

---

5 http://www.eclipse.org/atl.

6. Acknowledgements

This work is partly funded by the EU projects "A Semantic Service-oriented Private Adaptation Layer Enabling the Next Generation, Interoperable and Easy-to-Integrate Software Products of European Software SMEs (EMPOWER)" and "Reuse and Migration of legacy applications to Interoperable Cloud Services (REMICS)."

7. References

Bernstein P A, and Melnik S, "Model management 2.0: manipulating richer mappings", in *Proceedings of the 2007 ACM SIGMOD International Conference on Management of Data* (Beijing, China, June 11 - 14, 2007).

Bussler C, *B2B Integration.*, Springer, 2003.

Clavreul M, Barais O, and Jézéquel J-M. "Integrating legacy systems with MDE", in *ICSE'10: Proceedings of the 32nd ACM/IEEE International Conference on Software Engineering and ICSE Workshops*, volume 2, pages 69-78, Cape Town, South Africa, May 2010.

Czarnecki K and Helsen S, "Classification of Model Transformation Approaches", in *Proceedings of the OOPSLA'03 Workshop on the Generative Techniques in the Context of Model-Driven Architecture*, Anaheim, California, USA.

Grønmo R, Krogdahl S, and Møller-Pedersen B, "A Collection Operator for Graph Transformation", in *ICMT'09: 2nd International Conference on Theory and Practice of Model Transformations*, pages 67–82, Berlin, Heidelberg, Springer-Verlag, 2009.

Liao Y, Roman D, and Berre A-J, "Model-driven Rule-based Mediation in XML Data Exchange", in *Proceedings of the First International Workshop on Model-Driven Interoperability*. MDI 2010, Oslo, Norway, ACM, 89–97, 2010.

Mens T and Van Gorp P, "A Taxonomy of Model Transformation", *Electronic Notes in Theoretical Computer Science*, Volume 152, Pages 125-142, 27 March 2006.

Morin B, Klein J, Kienzle J, and Jézéquel J-M, "Flexible model element introduction policies for aspect-oriented modeling", in *Proceedings of ACM/IEEE 13th International Conference on Model Driven Engineering Languages and Systems (MoDELS 2010)*, Oslo, Norway, October 2010.

Muller P A, Fleurey F, and Jézéquel J M, "Weaving Executability into Object-Oriented Meta-languages", in *MoDELS'05: 8th Int. Conf. on Model Driven Engineering Languages and Systems*, Montego Bay, Jamaica, October 2005.

Nejati S, Sabetzadeh M, Chechik M, Easterbrook S M, Zave P, *Matching and Merging of State charts Specifications*. ICSE 2007: 54-64.

Reddy Y R, Ghosh S, France R B, Straw G, Bieman J M, McEachen N, Song E, and Georg G., "Directives for Composing Aspect-Oriented Design Class Models", in Awais Rashid and Mehmet Aksit, (eds) *Transaction on Aspect-Oriented Software Development*, volume 3880 of Lecture Notes in Computer Science, pages 75–105. Springer, 2006.

Smith K, Mork P, Seligman L, *et al.*, *The Role of Schema Matching in Large Enterprises*, CIDR Perspectives 2009.

Steel J and Jézéquel J-M. "On model typing", *Journal of Software and Systems Modeling (SoSyM)*, 6(4):401–414, December 2007.

Whittle J, Jayaraman P K, Elkhodary A M, Moreira A, and Araújo J., *Mata: A Unified Approach for Composing UML Aspect Models based on Graph Transformation*. T. Aspect-Oriented Software Development VI, 6:191–237, 2009.

MDI for SOA Management of a Crisis

Anne-Marie Barthe* – Frédérick Bénaben* – Sébastien Truptil* – Jean-Pierre Lorré** – Hervé Pingaud*

*University of Toulouse – Mines ALBI
Campus Jarlard – Route de Teillet
81000 ALBI - FRANCE
{first.last}@mines-albi.fr

** PETALS Link
4, rue Amélie
31000 Toulouse
{first.last}@petalslink.com

ABSTRACT: *This article aims at presenting a whole approach of Information Systems interoperability management in a crisis management cell. The main objective is to introduce model-driven steps (and tools) dedicated to providing a business model (CIM for Computer Independent Model), logical model (PIM for Platform Independent Model) and technical model (PSM for Platform Specific Model) of the interoperable structure in charge of orchestrating the collaborative behavior inside the crisis management cell. Due to the fact that this research work is articulated in two phases (phase 1 is over and phase 2 is still running) for each step of the model-driven approach, MDI results and tools are presented (from phase 1), as well as improvements targeted, current and future work (from phase 2).*

KEYWORDS: *Model transformation, Interoperability, BPM, Web-Services, Agility.*

1. Introduction

Nowadays, organizations (enterprises, institutions, administrations or others) have to work together and take part into collaborations to be able to face an unstable environment, such as a crisis situation. The efficiency of the answer to the crisis situation is determined by the speed and accuracy with which information can be managed and exchanged among the partners (i.e. the organizations involved into the collaboration). Considering the fact that an Information System (IS) is the visible part of an organization, our point is to tackle organizations' collaboration issue through ISs interoperability satisfying the business requirements. According to the European Network of excellence InterOp, **interoperability** is "the ability of a system or a product to work with other systems or products without special effort from the customer or user" (Konstantas *et al.*, 2005). It is also defined in (Pingaud, 2009a) as "the ability of systems, natively independent, to interact in order to build harmonious and intentional collaborative behaviors without deeply modifying their individual structure or behavior".

The main hypothesis of this article concerns the partners' IS that are supposed to follow the same conceptual logical architectural philosophy, i.e. Service Oriented Architecture (SOA) (Vernadat, 2007). According to (Morley *et al.*, 2002), IS can be seen as a set of interacting workflows, services and data. As it seems that the partners' ISs cannot natively assume the functions of data transfer and translation, services management and collaborative workflows orchestration (except with high constraints of technical standardization which do not fit the given definition of interoperability), a mediation approach is proposed (Wiederhold, 1992). A Mediation Information System (MIS), based on SOA principles, is a third-part system in charge of the coordination of the partners' activities by imposing a control structure dictated by collaborative processes, that must be run with compliance: it is a credible and pertinent way to support the ISs interoperability (Bénaben *et al.*, 2008). This MIS should meet the three requirements identified below among a set of SOA partners' ISs. It should handle (i) knowledge about partners' data, (ii) a repository of partners' services and (iii) a collaborative process model that should be run and a workflow engine that enables to run it. The Mediation Information System Engineering (MISE) 1.0 project (2004-2008) was launched in the Industrial Engineering Center of Ecole des Mines d'Albi-Carmaux and has been successfully developed. Its aim was to design and develop a MIS, which is based on model-driven engineering and on the associated model transformation concepts, i.e. a dive across several abstractions levels (business, logical and technological layers). This MIS was used in the French funded project (ANR-2006-SECU-006) ISyCri Project (ISyCri stands for Interoperability of Systems in Crisis situation), whose one objective was to design an IS for several partners who have to solve, or at least to reduce, a crisis into which they are involved. However, MISE 1.0 was predicated on several assumptions (that will be detailed in the article). In order to solve some limits and assumptions of MISE 1.0, the MISE 2.0 project was started in September 2009.

In this article, we first propose a brief description of a crisis situation management and of our use case, then to detail each layer of the Model-Driven Engineering (MDE) approach used in MISE 1.0 and MISE 2.0. We will also show the enhancements that MISE 2.0 provides to solve some limits of MISE 1.0.

2. Brief description of a crisis situation and of the use-case

A crisis can be political, military, economical, humanitarian, social, technological, environmental or sanitary (Devlin, 2006). Whatever its nature, according to (Lagadec, 1992) and (Devlin, 2006), a crisis is an abnormal situation which is the result of an instability impacting a subpart of the world (called ecosystem or system) with unacceptable consequences. This situation implies to deal with the crisis management through a dedicated set of stakeholders in charge of the crisis response. As stated by (Atlay et al., 2006) and (Beamon et al., 2004), the crisis management lifecycle is composed of four main steps:

1. Mitigation: this step aims at addressing the proactive social component of emergencies. This includes laws and mechanisms which reduce the vulnerability of the population and increases their resilience.

2. Preparedness: it aims at defining the actors' abilities thanks to the analysis of past experience/previous crisis situations and to prepare the means for the crisis response.

3. Response: once the crisis breaks out, several heterogeneous stakeholders have to work simultaneously in a hurry to reduce the crisis.

4. Recovery: this is the restoration of the impacted part of the ecosystem after the crisis (e.g. rebuild roads, houses, railways, etc.).

Both the ISyCri project (Truptil et al., 2008) and MISE 1.0/2.0 projects focus on the response step in the lifecycle of the crisis management, as their main objective is to help the stakeholders in charge of this situation (called "crisis cell" in the article) to deduce, via the preparedness step results, and to give the crisis a response.

In order to illustrate our MIS design approach of the MISE project, this article will propose examples extracted from a Chemical Biological Radiological and Nuclear (CBRN) use-case (Truptil, 2010) which is inspired by a CBRN exercise, realized in 2004 by French authorities. It took place on a railroad crossing, near the railway station of a village, where a tanker collided with a passenger train. Moreover, the product contained in the tanker was unknown, and a cloud of products escaped and the people of the railway station started feeling sick.

Policemen were informed of that accident. Once on site, they saw that the truck motor was on fire. This is the beginning of the crisis response.

3. Mediation Information System Engineering: business deduction

To be useful for the crisis response, the MIS has to be perfectly relevant for the crisis situation. That is the reason why the MIS deduction approach starts by deducing a collaborative process from the crisis information and the description of each stakeholder. This step is based on the metamodel of the crisis (Truptil, 2010) which is represented by the Unified Modeling Language (UML): it contains three main parts concerning the studied system (part of the world impacted by the crisis situation), the crisis characterization (specific elements of the crisis) and the treatment system (actors and resources that can be mobilized). Once this knowledge about the crisis situation is gathered, it is injected into an ontology (which embeds the information about partners' abilities). Secondly, the deduction rules, detailed in (Truptil *et al.*, 2010) are run to extract the actors' abilities, which could be used to reduce one/several issue(s) of the crisis. Afterwards, the order of stakeholders' abilities execution is deduced through data provided by the crisis cell: the priority ranking of identified issues (e.g. (1) Explosion risk, (2) Contamination risk, (3) Sick people, (4) Panic risk) and their selection among the set of selected abilities for example (e.g. *Explosion risk = FightExplosion by Firemen + SetSecurityPerimeter by Policemen*). This set of services and priority ranking are the basic elements of the collaborative process deduction, as detailed in (Truptil *et al.*, 2010), and represented by Business Process Model Notation (BPMN) (Figure 1). Each partner and the MIS are represented by a pool.

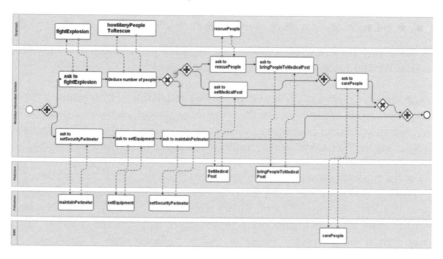

Figure 1. *The BPMN model of the collaborative process (CBRN exercise)*

Even if these mechanisms are powerful and have been positively checked on use-cases (including real-size exercises), there are some limitations that are currently improved through research works. Actually, only a single collaborative process is deduced, which mainly covers operational activities (such as fight fire or care injured people). However, such a collaborative situation should be managed through a more covering process cartography. For instance, decisional processes and support processes should also be deduced, including all their connections. The deduction of such a collaborative process cartography, instead of a single collaborative process, would definitely improve the business level of the proposed crisis management approach. In order to obtain such a cartography, the proposed approach is based on a three dimension characterization framework: enterprise modeling (with four levels: organizational, informational, functional and processes), management (with three levels: decisional, operational and support) and lifecycle (with four levels inherited from MDA: CIM, PIM, PSM and run-time). The global purpose is to gather the knowledge about the collaborative situation and to store it into models covering several areas of the framework (organizational, informational and functional knowledge at the CIM level) in order to deduce (by applying model transformations based on the structure of the framework) models from other areas of the framework (decisional, operational and support processes at the PIM level).

The deduced BPMN collaborative process (or the future process cartography) can be used at the next stage in order (i) to extract the executable workflows and (ii) to deploy the SOA infrastructure able to orchestrate the behavior of the crisis management cell (by running BPEL workflows among web services).

4. Mediation Information System Engineering: workflow execution

Once the model of the collaborative process is deduced at the business level, it is necessary to build the technical architecture model in order to obtain an executable workflow. Based on the technical architecture metamodel defined in Figure 2 (Touzi, 2007), the previous BPMN model is transformed into an UML model, with additional knowledge. The technical architecture metamodel is composed of three views. The service view describes the partners' services and MIS' services involved. The information view describes the data involved in the collaboration and managed by the several services (the data is exchanged as messages between the services). The process view describes the orchestration of services and the interactions between several services. The necessary additional knowledge is composed of the full description of the Web services (as we chose SOA architecture) like the Web Service Language Description (WSDL) files for each service, the format of the exchanged messages between the services, and the message transformation models (as services ask for defined input/output message formats, and these formats are not necessary the same for the whole services).

Through another transformation detailed in (Truptil, 2010), we obtain the workflow, represented by Business Process Execution Language (BPEL), and a set of configuration files (that are linked to the server used to run the workflow). In both MISE and ISyCri projects, the workflow is run on an Enterprise Service Bus (ESB), which is PETALS, developed by the French editor PETALS Link. This ESB is compliant with the JBI standard (also based on JSR208 standard (JSR, 2005)). The JBI standard implies the use of Services Unit (SU) and Services Assembly (SA) that compose the configuration of the services on the ESB. The several SUs and SAs are automatically generated for all the services of the collaborative process. They are necessary to use both partners' services (which can be real web services or just interfaces that make the link between the SOA architecture and a manual/technical operation) and the mediation service (the BPEL orchestrator which runs the collaborative process described into the BPEL file).

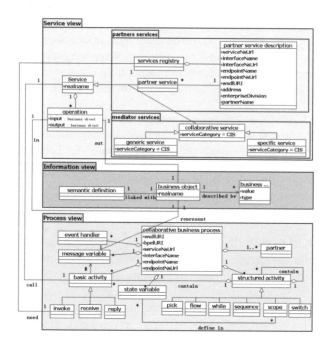

Figure 2. *Technical architecture metamodel*

This transformation from the BPMN model into a set of JBI deployment files including SA, SU (describing web services and BPEL) is feasible because of one strong hypothesis: the business characterization of the situation and the BPMN deduction are based on the fact that business abilities of partners are defined above the deduction mechanism. Furthermore, we assume that each of these business abilities exactly match with one technical web service. For instance, the business ability fight fire will be supported by a technical web service showing an interface in charge of informing the firemen representative (within the crisis cell) that it is time to start the business activity of fight fire. One major current improvement concerns the separation of business activities and technical web services: first the granularity level could be very different (business activities might be very high-leveled while web services could be very low leveled) and second, the matching might be one-to-many or even many-to-many. To tackle this issue, the adopted solution embeds (i) semantic annotation of business activities and technical web-services (describing inputs, outputs and operations) and (ii) semantic reconciliation mechanisms in order to manage automated matching between a set of business activities (deduced at the business level in the BPMN file) and a set of technical web services (deduced at the workflow level in the BPEL file). Furthermore, this semantic reconciliation is also dedicated to ensure "on the fly" translation of inputs and outputs in order to obtain a runnable workflow.

5. Mediation Information System Engineering: agility and monitoring

As a crisis is intrinsically an evolutionary phenomenon, the system shall remain compliant with the expectations of the actors. This implies to measure the efficiency of the response, to be able to take in account the changes of the crisis or in the crisis cell. According to (Pingaud, 2009b), two kinds of evolutions of such collaborative situations exist:

– the evolution of the crisis situation itself: the perceived characteristics of the crisis, in particular the issues to solve, are not the same at the beginning of the crisis and need a new response to the crisis;

– the evolution of the response to the crisis: the management of the response to the crisis situation may evolve due to (i) an evolution of the structure of the crisis cell (e.g. arrival, leaving of stakeholders), (ii) a dysfunction of the execution of a service (leading to the interruption of the workflow of the response), or (iii) due to a partial initial definition of the process of the response.

Depending on the kind of evolution, the MIS does not evolve the same way. If the situation itself evolves, then the characterization of the crisis has to be modified and the whole deduction process should be done again. If the response evolves, the design of the MIS may be restarted at the level of (i) the set of available services, (ii) the selection of the chosen services to solve the issue (i.e. identified risks or facts), (iii) the natively incomplete definition. Finally, for some dysfunction cases, it is possible to keep the same process model but asking a partner to redo some of his activities. According to some authors like (Badot, 1998), agility is a reconfiguration of the system to satisfy a need of adaptation. For (Kidd, 1994), (Lindberg 1990) agility is a need of flexibility and reactivity. Concerning our field of study (information system), reactivity is provided by the automated MDE approach while flexibility needs may require an evolution of the process (Truptil, 2010). We consider that reactivity is linked with time and we suppose that this time is short, implying the fact that updates can only be done on the configuration of the MIS. Then, we consider that flexibility is the ability of the MIS to start relevant evolutions, whatever the distances between its initial behavior (i.e. before the triggering event that implies an evolution) and the expected behavior (i.e. after the update of the MIS) are. To apply the mechanisms of agility, it is critical to detect the significant events of a consequent evolution of the situation. A tool, named control panel, was developed by Truptil (Truptil, 2010) to track the evolution of the crisis characteristics, the evolution of the course of the collaborative process (including the activities provided by the called services), and the evolution of the set of the collaboration partners. This tool is a kind of business activity monitoring. It is made of four tables, as shown in the screenshot of Figure 3.

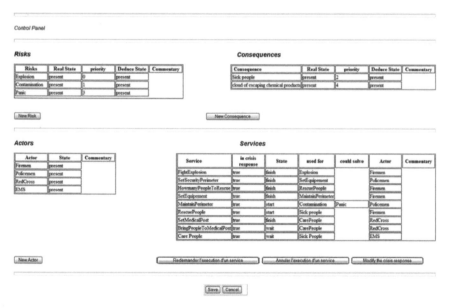

Figure 3. *The control panel allows the tracking of events or evolutions*

Two tables (*Risks* and *Consequences*) summarize the information about the crisis characterization. Other tables (*Partners* and their *Services*) describe the execution of the process. For all these tables, several statuses were defined to qualify the risks, the consequences, the actors and the services. For example, the status of a risk may be "being solved" or "not taken in account". Therefore, when an evolution occurs, the MIS design process can be restarted at several levels to obtain a MIS, specifically dedicated to the current situation. Nevertheless, it is necessary to ensure that what has already been done is taken into account. For this task, another tool has been added: the mediation services. Moreover, the need of flexibility of the MIS design process is satisfied by the implementation of the whole design-time workflow on an ESB. This implies that all the functionalities used in the several steps of the process design exist as web services (which are implemented on the ESB). We can notice that the design workflow is set on the same ESB as the one used to run the workflow to solve (or at least reduce) the crisis (see Figure 4). If the detection of changes is then based on human diagnosis (stored in the control panel), current research work is dedicated on event-based and cloud architecture in order to allow web services to send automatically their own events in run-time. These events are managed in the clouds, through complex-event processing tools in order to produce new events that can fill automatically the control panel.

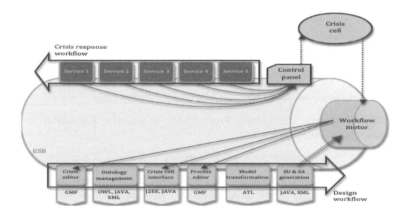

Figure 4. *Design-time workflow and crisis response workflow on the ESB*

6. Conclusion

This paper presents a theoretical overview of a model-driven approach dedicated to build an SOA mediation IS dedicated to support the crisis management. The approach allows the crisis cell to **reactively** deduce this MIS and to keep it **flexibly** adapted to the evolving crisis situation. The SOA structure of the deduction tools allow to remove the frontier between design-time and run-time. However, two main features are currently being implemented concerning (i) the deduction of a process cartography (instead of a single collaborative process), (ii) the semantic reconciliation between business and technical levels (instead of assuming a one-to-one matching between activities and web services) and (iii) the automated detection of significant evolutions through event-based cloud architecture (instead of manual filling of the control panel). Furthermore, another point concerning non-functional aspects (quality of services, governance, monitoring) is also studied in order to bring robustness and credibility to the MIS. All this research work is supported by several national projects (ANR/ISyCri, ANR/SocEDA, FUI/ISTA3), a European one (PLAY), and seven PhD students (J. Touzi, V. Rajsiri, S. Truptil, N. Boissel-Dallier, W. Mu, A.-M. Barthe and S. Zribi).

7. References

Atlay N., Green W. III, "OR/MS research in disaster operations management", *European Journal of Operational Research 175*, 2006, pp. 475–493

Badot O., *Théorie de l'entreprise agile*, Harmattan, 1998

Beamon B.M., Kotleba S.A., "Inventory modelling for complex emergencies in humanitarian relief operations", *International Journal of Logistics: Research and Applications 9*, 2004, pp.1–18

Bénaben F., Touzi J., Rajsiri V., Lorré J.-P., Pingaud H., "Mediation Information System Design in a collaborative SOA Context through a MDD Approach", *Proceeding of MDISIS'08 (Special workshop of CAISE'08)*, 2008, Montpellier, France

Devlin E., *Crisis Management Planning and Execution*, 2006, p.528

JSR, JSR208: The Java Community Process(SM) Program – JSRs :Java Specification Requests – detail JSR#208, 2005

Kidd P. T., *Agile Manufacturing: Forging New Frontiers*, Addison-Wesley, 1994, London

Konstantas D., Bourrières J.-P., Léonard M., Boudjilida N., "Preface of: Interoperability of Enterprise Software and Applications", *I-ESA'05 Interoperability of Enterprise Software and Applications*, pp. v-vi. Springer, Geneva, 2005

Lagadec P., "La gestion des crises", *Ediscience International*, 1992, p. 326

Lindberg P., "Strategic Manufacturing Management : A Proactive Approach", *International Journal of Operations & Production Management*, 10 (2), 1990, pp.94-106

Morley C., Hugues J., Leblanc B., *UML pour l'analyse d'un système d'information*, 2nd Edition, Dunod, 2002, France

Pingaud H, "Prospectives de recherches en interoperabilité: vers un art de la mediation", *Plenary Lecture, 8th International Congress on Industrial Engineering (CIGI)*, 2009, Tarbes

Pingaud H., "Rationalité du développement de l'interopérabilité dans les organisations", *Management des technologies organisationnelles*, pp. 19–30. Presses de l'Ecole des Mines de Paris, 2009, France

Touzi J., Aide à la conception d'un Système d'Information Collaboratif, support de l'interopérabilité des entreprises, PhD thesis, 2007, Institut National Polytechnique, Toulouse

Truptil S., Bénaben F., Couget P., Lauras M., Chapurlat V., Pingaud H, "Interoperability of Information Systems in Crisis Management: Crisis Modeling and Metamodeling", *IESA 2008*, 2008, Springer, Germany

Truptil S., Bénaben F., Pingaud H., "Collaborative process deduction to help the crisis cell emerging ecosystem to coordinate the crisis response", *IEEE DEST 2010*, 2010, Dubai

Truptil S., Etude de l'approche de l'intéropérabilité par médiation dans le cadre d'une dynamique de collaboration appliquée à la gestion de crise, PhD thesis, 2011, Institut National Polytechnique, Toulouse

Vernadat F., "Interoperable enterprise systems : Principles, concepts, and methods", *Annual Reviews in Control*, vol.31, no.1, 2007, pp 137—145

Wiederhold G., "Mediators in the architecture of future information systems", *IEEE Computer Magazine*, 1992, vol. 25-3

Workshop W4

Standards Ensuring Enterprise Interoperability and Collaboration, the State of the Art and Perspectives

Standards and Initiatives for Service Modeling – The Case of OMG SoaML

Dumitru Roman – Cyril Carrez – Brian Elvesæter – Arne-J. Berre

SINTEF, P. O. Box 124 Blindern, N-0314 Oslo, Norway
dumitru.roman@sintef.no
cyril.carrez@sintef.no
brian.elvesater@sintef.no
arne.j.berre@sintef.no

ABSTRACT: *Service modeling is a key element of any service-oriented system. It is the foundation on which core service-related tasks such as service discovery, composition, and mediation rely. During recent years standardization bodies such as W3C, OMG and OASIS have been working on standardizing various aspects of services such as service functionalities, behavior, quality of services, etc. At the same time, initiatives from academia focused on developing ontologies and formal languages for specifying services. In this paper we give a brief overview of relevant initiatives and standardization activities in the area of service modeling, and, as an example of the use of such standards, guide the reader through the use of the OMG Service oriented architecture Modeling Language (SoaML) in a concrete service-oriented scenario in the manufacturing domain.*

KEYWORDS: *service modeling, standards, SoaML*

1. Introduction

The *service-orientation* paradigm has emerged during the last decade for distributed computing and e-business processing. It utilizes *services* – autonomous, platform-independent computational elements that can be described, published, discovered, composed, and accessed over the Internet using standard protocols – as fundamental elements for developing applications/solutions. In recent years, various forms of service-oriented metaphors have appeared, the most important being Web services, e-Services, Grid and Cloud services, and Semantic Web Services. With the IBM's introduction of *service science* (Spohrer *et al.*, 2007) as an interdisciplinary approach to the study, design, and implement services systems (complex systems in which specific arrangements of people and technologies take actions that provide value for others) the service-orientation paradigm received new dimensions in supporting the service innovation process. Irrespective of such dimensions, being able to describe and model services is a key requirement for all service-related tasks.

There exists a plethora of service description efforts[1] that mainly differ on the information they capture about services. This can be related to IT or business aspects of services, or the whole service ecosystem. With this paper, we focus primarily on standardization efforts for service descriptions and provide a brief survey of the most relevant initiatives in this area. We then use the OMG Service-oriented architecture Modeling Language (SoaML) to provide a concrete example in the manufacturing domain for service modeling using a standardized approach.

The remaining of this paper is organized as follows. Section 2 provides an overview of activities of the most relevant standardization bodies in the area of service modeling. Section 3 provides an example of using the OMG SoaML, and section 4 provides a summary of this paper.

2. Service modeling – overview of standards and initiatives

The World Wide Web Consortium (W3C)[2] develops standards to "ensure the long-term growth of the Web." W3C has been actively involved in standardization activities related to service descriptions[3]. W3C sees service descriptions as an important part of accessing a service, and therefore the W3C standards in this area focus on the access aspect of services. Probably the most important standards for service description proposed by W3C are WSDL and SAWSDL:

---

1 A comprehensive list, albeit incomplete, of service description efforts is available at
http://www.w3.org/2005/Incubator/usdl/wiki/D1.
2 http://www.w3.org.
3 http://www.w3.org/standards/webofservices/description.

- *Web Services Description Language (WSDL)* (Chinnici *et al.*, 2007) provides a model and an XML format for describing Web services by separating the description of the abstract functionality offered by a service from concrete details (e.g. binding, concrete transport protocols) of a service description such as "how" and "where" that functionality is offered. The number of publicly deployed WSDL services is estimated to around 28000[4].

- *Semantic Annotations for WSDL and XML Schema (SAWSDL)* (Farrell and Lausen, 2007) defines set of extension attributes for the WSDL and XML Schema definition language that allows description of additional semantics of WSDL components. It provides mechanisms through which concepts from semantic models (e.g. ontologies), typically defined outside the WSDL document, can be referenced from within WSDL and XML Schema components using annotations.

W3C is presently active in standardization of service descriptions through the Unified Service Description Language (UDL) Incubator Group[5] which aims to define a language for describing general and generic parts of technical and business services.

The Object Management Group (OMG)[6] develops enterprise integration standards. Its core standardization activity in the area of service descriptions is the *Service oriented architecture Modeling Language (SoaML)* (OMG SoaML, 2009). SoaML defines a UML profile and a metamodel for the design of services within a service-oriented architecture. It supports a wide range of modeling requirements for service-oriented architectures such as specification of systems of services, service contracts, individual service interfaces, service implementations, etc. Section 2 provides further details on the elements of SoaML in a concrete application scenario.

Organization for the Advancement of Structured Information Standards (OASIS)[7] produces standards for the information society in a variety of areas such as security, Web services, conformance, business transactions, supply chain, etc. In the area of service descriptions OASIS has developed two specifications that, although do not prescribe a concrete language for representing aspects of services, clarifies the elements of service-oriented architecture and their relationships:

---

4 http://webservices.seekda.com/browse.
5 http://www.w3.org/2005/Incubator/usdl.
6 http://www.omg.org.
7 http://www.oasis-open.org.

- *Reference Model for Service Oriented Architecture* (MacKenzie *et al.*, 2006) provides an abstract framework for understanding significant entities and relationships between them within a service-oriented environment

- *Reference Architecture Foundation for Service Oriented Architecture* (Estefan *et al.*, 2009) provides an architecture that follows from the concepts and relationships defined in the OASIS Reference Model for Service Oriented Architecture. The architecture describes a possible template upon which a SOA concrete architecture can be built.

OASIS has been active in standardizing various aspect of SOA[8] in areas such as business processes (e.g. WSBPEL).

The Open Group[9] develops standards in the enterprise integration domain. Relevant to service descriptions, The Open Group has developed *SOA Ontology*[10] which contains a formal definition of the concepts, terminology, and semantics of SOA in both business and technical terms. The ontology is expressed in the Web Ontology Language (OWL), but with explanatory text including UML diagrams and examples. It covers aspects such as actors and tasks, services, contracts, service interfaces, compositions, policies, events.

The Open Geospatial Consortium (OGC)[11] is developing standards for geospatial and location-based services. Although its focus is on geospatial aspects of services, some of its specifications such as WFS and WPS are generally applicable to services:

- *Web Feature Service (WFS)*[12] provides a standardized interface allowing requests for (geographical) features across the Web using platform-independent calls. It provides generic operations such as query and retrieval of features based on spatial and non-spatial constraints, or creation and deletion of new feature instances.

- Web Processing Service (WPS)[13] provides standardized interfaces that facilitates the publishing of geospatial processes and clients' discovery of and binding to those processes. It defines WPS operations for returning service-level metadata, description of a process including its inputs and outputs, and executing the process.

---

8 http://www.oasis-open.org/committees/tc_cat.php?cat=soa.
9 http://www.opengroup.org.
10 http://www.opengroup.org/soa/standards/ontology.htm#_The_Open_Group_2.
11 http://www.opengeospatial.org.
12 http://www.opengeospatial.org/standards/wfs.
13 http://www.opengeospatial.org/standards/wps.

Service Ontologies. Several service ontologies in the area of semantic Web services have been developed by the research community and were submitted for standardization primarily at W3C. These include:

- *OWL-S*[14] is an OWL ontology for service and contains three main parts: the service *profile* for advertising and discovering services; the *process model*, which gives a detailed description of a service's operation; and the *grounding*, which provides details on how to interoperate with a service, via messages.

- *Web Service Modeling Ontology (WSMO)*[15] is a conceptual framework and a formal language for semantically describing relevant aspects of Web services in order to facilitate the automation of discovering, combining and invoking electronic services over the Web. It includes Ontologies, Web services, Goals, and Mediators as core elements.

- *Lightweight Semantic Descriptions for Services on the Web (WSMO-Lite)*[16] provides a lightweight set of semantic service descriptions in RDFS that can be used for annotations of various WSDL elements using the SAWSDL annotation mechanism. These annotations cover functional, behavioral, non-functional and information semantics of Web services.

Although such ontologies for services have not been standardized, research for the development of ontologies is ongoing. An analysis of some of the service ontologies that have been developed primarily by the research community can be found in (Sorathia *et al.*, 2010).

3. Service modeling with SoaML

The SoaML specification provides UML extensions to support the modeling of services as required in SOA. The main extensions are the following. *Participants* are components that play the role of service providers or service consumers (or both) through their ports. *Service Architectures* define how the Participants work together by providing and using services between them. *Service Contracts* describe interaction patterns between two or more service entities. *Service Interfaces* define the operations provided and required by a service. *Service data* specify the information exchanged between service consumers and service providers. Finally, *Capabilities* specify a cohesive set of functions or resources provided by a service.

---

14 http://www.w3.org/Submission/OWL-S.
15 http://www.w3.org/Submission/WSMO.
16 http://www.w3.org/Submission/WSMO-Lite.

The rest of the section focuses mainly on Service Architectures and Service Contracts. We will exemplify our presentation with a case study in the domain of Manufacturing. A Boom Dealer is selling crane boom trucks, but uses the services of a Manufacturer. The Manufacturer will create the necessary metal pieces from raw material and assemble them on site. Raw material (i.e. steel plates) and the coating of metal pieces are provided by third parties. Moreover, it is possible that some pieces are too big for the Manufacturer to build (because of a lack of adequate equipment for instance). In that case a third party will create the metal piece for the Manufacturer.

We follow the SoaML methodology developed during the SHAPE project (Elvesæter *et al.* 2011), and which provides guidelines for using BPMN and SoaML to specify an SOA, both from the business and the IT perspective. We concentrate here only on some aspects of SoaML.

A top-down approach for specifying SOA and using SoaML will start with Service Architectures. A Service Architecture is a high level specification of how Participants work together by providing and consuming services. It is modeled as a UML Collaboration, stereotyped <<ServicesArchitecture>>. It specifies the different Participants that take part in the service, and the relations between them. Those relations are expressed through collaboration uses. For instance, Figure 1 shows the Service Architecture for the *BoomManufacturing*, with the following Participants: *BoomDealer*, *Manufacturer*, *PartManufacturer*, *Coater* and *SteelProvider*. Those Participants interact with each other through the services identified by a number of collaboration uses. Each of those collaboration uses is in turn typed by a Service Contract.

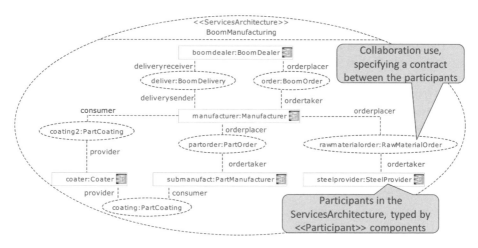

Figure 1. *Services Architecture for Boom Manufacturing*

The next step of the methodology is to specify the Service Contracts. They specify how the service is to be consumed and provided, by defining the role each Participant will play in the interaction, with interfaces and behavior. A Service Contract is modeled by a UML Collaboration stereotyped <<ServiceContract>>. It specifies the interfaces each Participant must implement in order to abide the service contract. A UML behavior can also be specified, as state machine or message sequence chart. Figure 1 shows the two Service Contracts used between two Participants. The *BoomDealer* will play the role *orderPlacer* in the *BoomOrder* service, while the *Manufacturer* will play the role *orderTaker*.

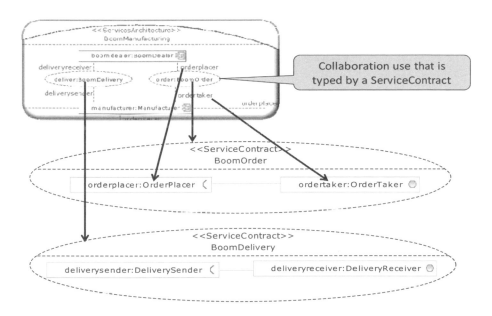

Figure 1. *Collaboration uses and Service Contracts*

The Service Contracts are further refined by specifying the provided and consumed interfaces. The interfaces are respectively stereotyped <<Provider>> and <<Consumer>>, and define the operations and service data associated with them. For instance, Figure 2 shows the two interfaces specified with the *BoomOrder*. The role *orderTaker* is typed by a <<Provider>> interface, and defines the operations *quote* and *orderConfirmation*.

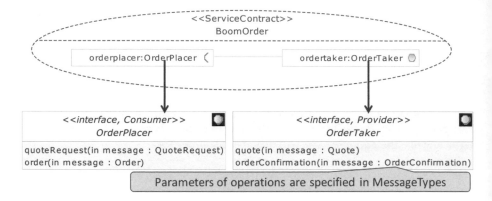

Figure 2. *Service Contracts and Interfaces*

The parameters of the operations are specified as Message Types, which is a document-centric service specification[17]. This means that XML documents will be exchanged between participants of a service. In SoaML this is modeled using a classes stereotyped <<MessageType>>. Figure 3 shows the service data to the interfaces presented earlier, with the corresponding Message Types.

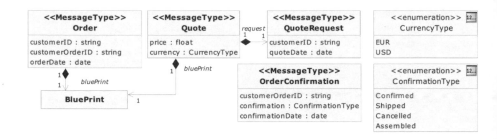

Figure 3. *Service Data*

For more details on the elements of SoaML and their use we refer the reader to the SoaML specification at http://www.omg.org/spec/SoaML/.

---

17 SoaML supports as well RPC-centric service specifications, but are not tackled in this article.

4. Summary and outlook

A variety of initiatives and standards for service description have emerged during the past decade focusing on providing means for capturing information about services. This can be related to IT or business aspects of services, or the whole service ecosystem. In this paper we have given a brief overview of standardization efforts for service descriptions and provided a brief survey of the most relevant initiatives in this area. We used the OMG Service-oriented architecture Modeling Language (SoaML) to provide a concrete example in the manufacturing domain for service modeling using a standardized approach.

There is no doubt that standards in the area of service modeling will continue to develop, with some of the existing standards currently being revised and new standards being proposed. With the emergence of the service science discipline, service modeling is seen as a key requirement for all service-related tasks and will therefore animate the service science landscape during the coming years. In the short term, it would be interesting to follow the development of the Unified Service Description Language (UDL) in the context of W3C, and investigate and harmonize the various ontologies proposed for modeling services.

5. Acknowledgements

This work is partly funded by the EU projects "A Semantic Service-oriented Private Adaptation Layer Enabling the Next Generation, Interoperable and Easy-to-Integrate Software Products of European Software SMEs (EMPOWER)", "Networked Enterprise transFormation and resource management in Future internet enabled Innovation CloudS (NEFFICS)", and "Reuse and Migration of legacy applications to Interoperable Cloud Services (REMICS)."

6. References

Chinnici R, Moreau J J, Ryman A, Weerawarana S. Web Services Description Language (WSDL) Version 2.0 Part 1: Core Language. W3C Recommendation 26 June 2007. Available at http://www.w3.org/TR/wsdl20/.

Elvesæter B, Carrez C, Mohagheghi P, Berre A J, Johnsen S G, Solberg A. "Model-driven Service Engineering with SoaML", in: *Service Engineering*, pp25-54. S. Dustdar, F. Li (Eds). Springer, 2011.

Farrell J and Lausen H. Semantic Annotations for WSDL and XML Schema. W3C Recommendation 28 August 2007. Available at http://www.w3.org/TR/sawsdl/.

MacKenzie C M, Laskey K, McCabe F, Brown P F, Metz R. Reference Model for Service Oriented Architecture 1.0. OASIS Standard, 12 October 2006. Available at http://docs.oasis-open.org/soa-rm/v1.0/soa-rm.pdf.

OMG SoaML. Service oriented architecture Modeling Language (SoaML) - Specification for the UML Profile and Metamodel for Services (UPMS). OMG Adopted Specification Finalisation Task Force Beta 2 document (FTF Beta 2), 2009. Available at http://www.omg.org/spec/SoaML/.

Sorathia V, Ferreira P L, and van Sinderen M. "An Analysis of Service Ontologies", *Pacific Asia Journal of the Association for Information Systems*, 2 (1). pp. 17-46, 2010,ISSN 1943-7544.

Spohrer J, Maglio P P, Bailey J, Gruhl D. "Steps Toward a Science of Service Systems", *Computer*, vol. 40, no. 1, pp. 71-77, Jan. 2007.

Estefan J A, Laskey K, McCabe F, Thornton D. Reference Architecture Foundation for Service Oriented Architecture Version 1.0 14 October 2009. Available at http://docs.oasis-open.org/soa-rm/soa-ra/v1.0/soa-ra-cd-02.pdf.

Standard for eBusiness in SMEs Networks: the Increasing Role of Customization Rules and Conformance Testing Tools to Achieve Interoperability

Arianna Brutti – Piero De Sabbata – Angelo Frascella – Cristiano Novelli – Nicola Gessa

ENEA
Via Martiri di Monte Sole, 4
40129 Bologna
Italy
arianna.brutti@enea.it
piero.desabbata@enea.it
angelo.frascella@enea.it
cristiano.novelli@enea.it
nicola.gessa@enea.it

ABSTRACT: *The adoption of a public standard at application domain level enables systems to interoperate, with a positive impact for eBusiness adoption, especially towards SMEs networks. Nevertheless conformance to standard specification is not enough to guarantee interoperability between different implementations.*

If we consider interoperability based on three levels (technical, semantic and organizational) not all the standard specifications aim to cover all the three levels. One of the key enablers of a "service based economy" is the interchangeability of the service providers that requires that all the three levels of interoperability are effectively achieved.

This paper analyzes first these critical factors in adopting technical standardized specifications for data exchange in eBusiness; then analyzes one of the possible countermeasures: domain specific use profiling and related conformance testing tools based on customization rules.

KEYWORDS: *interoperability, standard, conformance testing tool, customization rules, eBusiness, UBL, Schematron, SMEs business.*

1. Introduction

Lack of interoperability is often observed between different implementations in data exchange for eBusiness, even when the systems implement the same standard specification. This paper tries to analyses the reasons of the problem and focuses on **customization** and **testing** as critical factors to tackle this matter.

The problem is relevant in the present eBusiness applications but, in a "Future Internet" perspective, it could increasingly hamper a *"plug and play"* interoperability between applications and services.

Firstly this paper investigates the gap between the conformance to the specifications of Information Technology (IT) systems and the achievement of interoperability between different systems with the aim to identify the potential causes.

Secondly, customization being the first action to improve interoperability, two cases based on UBL (Universal Business Language, Bosak *et al.*, 2006) towards different domains are considered:

– eBIZ-TCF[1], a project funded by the European Commission (EC) in order to Harmonize eBusiness in the Textile, Clothing and Footwear industry, produced a set of specifications based on UBL for its vertical domain;

– PEPPOL[2], another project funded by the EC to establish guidelines and specifications for the European public eProcurement, entirely based on UBL document formats.

Thirdly, further possible countermeasures are analyzed in order to reduce the problem, with a specific focus on the role of business rules adopted in the use profiles in order to enable automatic tools to discover contents that prevent the achievement of interoperability.

2. The problem and the state of the art

The adoption of public standards for business data exchange enables systems to interoperate, with a positive impact for eBusiness adoption, especially towards Small and Medium Enterprises (SME) networks.

These networks, indeed are, potentially, the greatest beneficiary of the application level standard adoption: they have not enough resources and skills to define by themselves complex specifications and are far from being able to impose their solution on their commercial partners.

---

1 www.ebiz-tcf.eu.
2 www.peppol.eu.

The drawback is that, presently, the implementation of really interoperable systems sometimes is perceived more as a black art rather than the rational application of a technical specification. That is exactly the opposite of a *"plug-and-play"* approach that is what is needed by the SMEs networks to be interoperable.

The point is that conformance to standard specification is not enough to guarantee interoperability between real IT systems, due to different implementations of the specifications. Different ways are in fact possible to express documental specifications for a domain.

The most common representation of specifications is XML Schema[3] to represent the templates of the different types of business documents. They are used both for automatic conformance test of an instance document and for documentation.

In the past, EDI (Electronic Data Interchange) applications were less sensitive to the problem: they were based on a one-to-one approach between large companies (that had resources to tune the EDI systems exactly to their needs) or on a hub-spoke approach where, again, the large company was able to define the implementation and impose it (a black box, usually with a private EDI dialect) to its partner.

In the present eBusiness scenarios, the communication infrastructure is "commoditized" and XML-based tools allow a more diffused adoption of eBusiness (for example lightweight EDI solutions but also new service-based solutions) to the industry in a real *many-to-many* networked approach where private dialects are less effective and acceptable.

If the problem is relevant today, it could become fatal in the Future Internet perspective (Hourcade *et al.*, 2009, Papadimitriou *et al.*, 2009) by preventing the creation of an "Internet of Services" where services should be clearly defined, available and interchangeable (for example the interchangeability of the service providers must be assured).

Thus it is relevant to identify different causes of the lack of interoperability between systems implementing the same specification:

Firstly in order to have interoperability among real systems on all the three levels of interoperability (**technical**, **semantic** and **organizational**) should be effectively achieved (EIF 1.0, 2004). In some cases a fourth level, the **legal** level (EIF 2.0, 2010), also has to be considered, like in PEPPOL project. On the contrary not all the specifications cover all the levels.

Secondly there is a dichotomy between the need for **generality** and the need for **specialization**: supporting as much as possible scenarios (or requirements) against maintaining an acceptable level of complexity of the specifications.

---

3 www.w3.org/TR/xmlschema11-1.

The *80/20* Pareto's principle is largely applied to standardization: satisfying the 20% of the requirements, *usually* leads to supporting 80% of the cases. In fact there are always unsupported cases that lead to misrepresent specifications, and innovative or niche services (that are a pillar in the Internet diffusion) are the most periled to this risk.

Thirdly, despite many specifications that deal with the semantic aspects of interoperability, very often they do not achieve complete semantic interoperability but leave some degrees of freedom to the implementer that causes **uncertainty** and **redundancy** in the exchanged data; in the first case. For example, we can have different containers or representations for the same information; in the second case much information has to be managed to be compliant while it should not be necessary for a specific case (De Sabbata P. *et al.*, 2010).

This problem led us to define restrictions of the specifications that are related to a domain or a sub-domain (namely *customizations*).

Fourthly, we observe that a specification defines some *static* constraints for a document model, like the *OrderResponse*, through XML Schema representation that are always valid but that, in some circumstances have to be restricted, depending on a **dynamically** changing context (due, for example, to the progression in a workflow). This case could be considered as a sub-case of the previous one but here we report it separately to put the case in evidence.

This could be considered as a short list of the potential sources producing lack of interoperability between systems implementing the same documental specification. The possible countermeasures are many and different according to the given requirements and policies adopted by the standard developers.

3. Documental formats and their limits, role of customizations

Documental specifications for eBusiness can be reduced to two different macro-categories: **vertical standards** and **horizontal standards**[4]. In the first case, vocabularies define a lot of domain-specific terms (*patient record, textile darning commission, vehicle certificate insurance, hotel availability request*, etc.), in the second case terms are defined to be understood and used in any domain (*order, catalog,* etc.). In the second case the constraints are less compulsory and the risk of non interoperable implementations is higher.

A good approach to understand the effectiveness of a specification in order to assure interoperability is to identify a list of the requisites that are related to the

---

4 Examples of vertical standards are HL7, ACORD, CIDX; examples of horizontal standards are EDIFACT, UBL, GS1 XML, etc.

domain. Each requisite that cannot be satisfied by the original specification should be translated in (or related to) a **customization rule** (Bausà, 2010).

The result of the application of customization rules to a specification is a *use profile* that modifies some characteristics in order to reduce the uncertainty and redundancy in its implementation on a given domain; this approach is applied, for example, to horizontal specifications to achieve the same performance of a vertical one as described in (De Sabbata P. *et al.*, 2010).

What is important to observe is that this approach is usually based on human readable user guides or, in the best cases, on XML Schemas that restrict the general Schemas to a subset; they are valid for all the transactions of the domain and are usually the only weapon available for automatic (low cost) conformance testing.

In the next section we will analyze two different customizations of the same horizontal standard to put in evidence that further tools can be used beyond XML Schemas. Furthermore, we will observe that interoperability achievement is also jeopardized by requirements that change dynamically in the context domain (for example, according to the workflow progression).

The standard specification we analyze is UBL: produced by OASIS, based on XML, it is a good example of horizontal specification for eBusiness; it defines a library of terms and a set of generic business document models, not tailored for a domain.

UBL has been customized within two European projects, eBIZ-TCF and PEPPOL, to implement flows of data in two relevant domains.

The projects appear to have extremely different contexts although they based their implementations on the same common UBL specification.

A short summary of the two projects features is given in Tables 1 and 2.

Context	eBIZ-TCF	PEPPOL
Geopolitical	Europe	Europe
Industry	Textile, clothing, footwear industry	All
Official constraints	None	European directive
Business process	Product supply and production	Public procurement (Publication, Tendering, Sourcing, Ordering, Billing)

Table 1. *The contexts of eBIZ-TCF and PEPPOL according to the classification proposed by the Core Component Technical Specification (CCTS, 2003) adopted by UBL*

Requirements	eBIZ-TCF	PEPPOL
Actors	SME networks	Public administration towards SMEs as well as large firms
Article identification	GS1 GTIN is required	No restriction; GS1 GTIN is suggested.
Party identification	GS1 GLN is required	Code issued by agencies listed in ISO 6523
National localization	no	yes
Invoice has legal value	no	yes

Table 2. *Other features of eBIZ-TCF and PEPPOL domains*

4. Different types of customization rules

Customization rules are applied upon the specification (UBL in this case) to be customized that supplies a syntax that cannot be broken; the customization rules can be grouped according with the different origin of the constraints they express:

A **first group** of customization rules is dedicated to identify the subset of information elements that must be supported in the domain.

For example, the product identification is supported by UBL with different structures (*Buyers Item Identification, Sellers Item Identification, Manufacturers Item Identification, Standard Item Identification, Catalogue Item Identification, Additional Item Identification*) and both eBIZ-TCF and PEPPOL choose the same pair of elements (*Sellers Item Identification* and *Standard Item Identification*) discarding the others. This means that, although humans could understand the discarded structures, they have been excluded by the scope of the IT systems in order to keep the implementations cheaper and simpler.

A **second group** of rules define coding and ranges of allowed values for the information. For example, for product identification, eBIZ-TCF exclusively accepts GS1 GTIN (Global Trade Item Number[5]) coding while PEPPOL does not make restrictions (GS1 GTIN is "suggested" only).

A **third group** of rules declares some optional data structures as mandatory in the domain. For example, to satisfy legal requirements, PEPPOL eInvoice always requires the full name and address of the taxable person and of the customer, on the

---

5 www.gs1.com.

contrary in eBIZ-TCF they are not allowed. In this case the two customizations, although UBL conformant, express opposite and incompatible requirements.

A **fourth group** declares co-constraints, constraints arising from dependencies between data in the same document (Jelliffe, 2001), that must **always be satisfied** in the domain. For example in *Invoice, invoice total amount* must equal the sum of the line *totals.*

Finally, there are two last groups related to constraints depending on dynamic execution of the data exchange:

A **fifth** group of rules declares constraints related to the context or the roles of the actors involved in the transaction. An example comes, in PEPPOL, from national requirements: some information must be provided depending on the country of the issuer.

A **sixth group** of rules declares constraints related to the position of the current transaction in the running business process. For example in eBIZ-TCF the *dispatch advise* can adopt a "delivery-based" structure or a "package-based" structure according to the current workflow.

5. Conformance test tools: Schematron-based implementation

In order to reach a good level of interoperability between the systems adopting customized specifications, it is important to make available, to all the involved parties (developer and users), conformance test tools that can provide an objective and unbiased verification of the conformance of the electronic documents being exchanged (CEN BII WG3, 2010).

Conformance tests are relevant in two distinct situations having different objectives and actors:

– at **development/implementation time**, to help software vendors and implementers to test whether software components are able to generate, manage and understand conformant document instances;

– the actors performing *test* are the software developers/vendors.

– at **run-time**, to give the final users a way to check the goodness of the exchanged instances;

– the actors performing the *validation* are the final users of systems.

Test tools are implementations of the customization rules that can automatically check if document instances satisfy them. Usually the tools are based on two kinds of elements: a software engine for document validation and the rules that can be represented through different syntaxes: the most diffused are XML Schema and Schematron[6].

The approach followed by eBIZ-TCF is based on:

- XML Schemas representing subsets of information elements from UBL that supply the basic data structure; one XML Schema for each document model plus a library of common terms;
- Schematron rules expressing all the other types of customization rules;
- a web application as software engine that is public, available for any user and embedding the XML Schemas and Schematrons (that are not public).

The main functionalities of the Web application[7] are uploading an instance of XML document of the user, choosing the reference transaction to be supported, applying the corresponding XML Schemas and Schematron set of rules and producing a response. The answer of the system is related to syntactic conformance (towards UBL) and conformance towards the customization rules.

In this approach the developers and users have at their disposal the Web application as a black-box for manual testing of XML document instances. Since the eBIZ-TCF systems implement a complete automation of the document flows, it follows that the tool is addressing mainly "test" rather than "validation" activities.

Differently, PEPPOL bases its approach on:

- original UBL XML Schemas that supplies the basic data structure;
- public Schematron rules expressing all the customization rules;
- a set of Web applications as software engine that are public, available to any user and based on the XML Schemas and Schematrons.

The main functionalities of the reference Web application[8] are uploading XML code of the user representing the document instance, choosing the couple reference transaction/set of rules to be applied (they can refer to different countries), applying the corresponding Schematron set of rules and producing a response. The answer of the system is only about conformance towards the customization rules.

The developers and users have the possibility to develop their own tools using the public Schematrons as well as to rely on the public ones. The approach is to supply artifacts that can be used to perform both test at development time as well as run-time validation on the real data flows.

---

6 www.schematron.com.
7 winter.bologna.enea.it/eBiz-TCFValidator.
8 www.invinet.org/recursos/conformance/invoice-validation.html.

To obtain some figures about the customization rules that are necessary to implement a "real" customization, the *eInvoice* document model has been examined both in PEPPOL and eBIZ-TCF and classified according with the kinds of rules identified in section 4 (Table 3).

In PEPPOL, excluding national requirements, rules related to the *Invoice*, are more than 450[9], in eBIZ-TCF they are more than 120[10], the largest part belongs to the first type of customization rules (400 and 90 respectively).

These figures point out the complexity of the development and maintenance of the customizations: the number of rules is very high and represents still an open challenge.

Type of rules	PEPPOL	eBIZ-TCF
1. data structure	80% (the "core" of the data structure)	75%
2. coding and ranges	4% (75% expressed as code lists)	6%
3. mandatory elements	5%	8,2%
4. content (co-) constraints always true	8.4%	10%
5. (co-)constraints depending on role or content	2.4% (according to the different countries)	-
6. rules related to the workflow	0.2%	0,8%

Table 3. *A compared classification of the different types of rules involved in the customization of a sample business document model, the Invoice*

6. Conclusions

Causes of the lack of interoperability that can be found even between applications that are conformant to a common documental specification have been analyzed. The scope and the different types of customization rules have been presented with the conclusion that they can play a relevant role to improve interoperability. These rules are the basis for automatic tools aiming to check the conformance of an implementation to a specific customization.

Nevertheless the analysis has shown two problems:

---

9 www.peppol.eu/work_in_progress/wp5-einvoicing/results,
10 www.moda-ml.net/ebiz-retail/repository/TCF-UseProfile/v2008-1/en/default.asp?nomenu=1

- different customizations of the same specification could result in non-interoperable applications;
- in some cases the validity of a document against a customization rule cannot be assessed only by examining the single document instance, because aspects related to the external context must be evaluated.

Two different cases of customization, eBIZ-TCF and PEPPOL, have been compared, their different approaches have been evidenced as well as their common root in UBL. The complexity of the construction of such a set of rules, like in the examined cases, put in evidence that a huge effort is required to set up the testing tools and some kind of automatic support will be necessary to reduce it.

7. References

Bausà O., Kingstetd A., Forsberg M., Frade J., Birgisson G., Fromyr J., Rasmussen S., "Conformance and interoperability testing", in *CWA 16073-3, Annex B on Conformance Testing*, from CEN WS BII, Brussels, 2010, www.cen.eu/cwa/bii/specs/Tools/documents/BII3-B-ConformanceTesting_d09.doc.

Bosak J., McGrath T., Holman G.K., Universal Business Language v2.0, Standard, OASIS Open, December 2006; docs.oasis-open.org/ubl/os-UBL-2.0.

CCTS, UN/CEFACT "Core Components Technical Specification, Part 8" of *the ebXML Framework in Version 2.01*, UN/CEFACT, November 2003 www.unece.org/cefact/ebxml/CCTS_V2-01_Final.pdf.

CEN BII WG3, "Business Interoperability Interfaces for Public procurement in Europe - Part 3: Toolbox Requirements", in *CWA 16073-3: Toolbox Requirements* from CEN WS BII, Brussels, 2010, www.cen.eu/cwa/bii/specs/Tools/documents/CWA_CEN_ISSS_BII_Part3.pdf.

De Sabbata P., Gessa N., Brutti A., Novelli C., Frascella A., D'Agosta G., "Standard creation and adoption for SME networks", in *Interoperability for Enterprise Software and Applications*, pp. 41-51, Hervé Panetto, Nacer Boudjlida (eds), ISTE, London and John Wiley & Sons, New York, June 2010.

EIF 1.0, European Interoperability Framework for pan-European eGovernment Services IDABC project, 2004, Belgium, ec.europa.eu/idabc/servlets/ Docd552.pdf?id=19529.

EIF 2.0, Annex II - EIF (European Interoperability Framework) of the Communication "Towards interoperability for European public services" on the 16th of December 2010, European Commission, 2010.

Hourcade J-C., Neuvo Y., Posch R., Saracco R., Wahlster W., Sharpe M., Future Internet 2020, Vision of an industry expert group, report for DG Information Society and Media, May 2009

Jelliffe R., "The Current State of the Art of Schema Languages for XML". 2001, www.planetpublish.com/pdfs/RickJelliffe.pdf.

Papadimitriou D., Future Internet, the Cross ETP vision document, white paper, January 2009, Future Internet portal, www.future-internet.eu.

CEN/ISO 11354 - Framework and Maturity Model for Enterprise Interoperability

David Chen

IMS – University of Bordeaux
351, cours de la liberation, 33405 Talence
France

david.chen@ims-bordeaux.fr

ABSTRACT: *This paper presents the CEN/ISO 11354 standard which is an on-going international standardization initiative jointly carried out by CEN TC310/WG1 and ISO TC184 SC5/WG1. It aims at defining a standard Framework for Enterprise Interoperability (FEI) and a Maturity Model for Enterprise Interoperability (MMEI). The standard provides a common understanding of the enterprise interoperability and defines metrics for measuring enterprise interoperability maturity.*

KEYWORDS: *Interoperability, Framework, Maturity Model, standard, Enterprise system.*

1. Introduction

This standard considers interoperability as a generic concept, and it is therefore assumed that common problems of interoperability failure and solutions to overcome them can be identified and developed for any particular enterprise. Therefore, CEN/ISO 11354 considers enterprise interoperability to be an engineering discipline, separating it from business-related issues. Interoperability is seen as a necessary support to allow business collaboration to happen, but interoperability is not the business collaboration itself (CEN/ISO, 11354).

The motivation and main reason of elaborating this standard is based on the fact that the concept of enterprise interoperability is not precisely defined. Enterprise interoperability still means many things to many people and it is often interpreted in many different ways with different expectations. Without a clear and shared understanding on the concept of interoperability, research and development efforts cannot be efficiently carried out and coordinated (Interop, 2006). Consequently the purpose of this standard is to define a Framework for Enterprise Interoperability which defines the domain of enterprise interoperability, i.e. its problem space and solution space.

This standard is based on the main input from the initial research works carried out in LAPS of University of Bordeaux 1 under the INTEROP NoE (Chen & Daclin, 2006) (Interop, 2006). It has also taken into account the state of the art on existing works on interoperability frameworks reported in (Chen, Doumeingts and Vernadat, 2008) and maturity models presented in (Guédria et al., 2008) (Ford, 2008). It has been considered that the IDEAS Interoperability framework (IDEAS, 2003), ATHENA interoperability framework (ATHENA, 2003), European Interoperability Framework (EIF, 2004) do not address explicitly interoperability problems, and do not allow structuring interoperability knowledge according to the problems. The maturity Model for Enterprise Interoperability (MMEI) is based on the standard framework but influenced by some existing maturity models: LISI (Levels of Information Systems Interoperability) (C4ISR, 1998) (Kasunic, 2004), OIM (Organizational Interoperability Model) (Clark et al., 1999), OIAM (Organisation Interoperability Agility Model) (Kingston et al., 2004), LCIM (Levels of Conceptual Interoperability Model) (Tolk et al., 2003), EIMM (Enterprise Interoperability Maturity Model) (Athena, 2003) and ISO/15504 (SPICE) and CMMI (2010). Existing maturity models focus, in most cases on one simple facet of interoperability (data, technology, conceptual, Enterprise modeling, etc.). They are complementary rather than contradictory. Consequently MMEI aims at structuring the different approaches into one single interoperability maturity model to avoid redundancy and ensure consistency.

CEN/ISO 11354 applies to manufacturing enterprises, but can also apply to other kinds of enterprises. It is intended for use by stakeholders who are concerned with developing and deploying solutions based on information and communication technology for manufacturing enterprise process interoperability. It focuses on, but is not restricted to, enterprise (manufacturing or service) interoperability (CEN/ISO, 11354).

The paper is structured as follow: section 2 presents basic concepts of enterprise interoperability and the Framework for Enterprise Interoperability (FEI). In section 3 the Maturity Model for Enterprise Interoperability (MMEI) is outlined. A Kiviat graph is used to represent the result of an interoperability assessment. Finally, section 4 concludes the paper.

2. Framework for Enterprise Interoperability (FEI)

The Framework for Enterprise Interoperability (FEI) has been specified in CEN/ISO 11354-1. It aims at structuring basic enterprise interoperability concepts and issues. The framework has three basic dimensions: (i) *interoperability concerns* that define the content of interoperation that may take place at various levels of the enterprise (data, service, process, business); (ii) *interoperability barriers* that identify various obstacles to interoperability in three categories (conceptual, technological, organisational), (iii) *interoperability approaches* that represent the different ways in which barriers can be removed (integrated, unified, and federated).

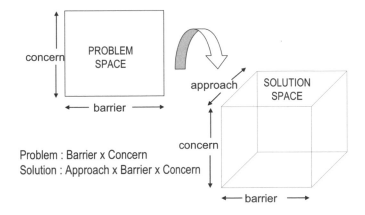

Figure 1. *Problem space vs. Solution space*

The first two dimensions: interoperability concerns and interoperability barriers constitute the problem space of enterprise interoperability (see Figure 1). The intersection of an interoperability barrier and an interoperability concern is the set of interoperability problems having the same barrier and concern. The three dimensions of the framework constitute the solution space of enterprise interoperability (see also Figure 1). The intersection of an interoperability barrier, an interoperability concern and an interoperability approach is the set of solutions to the breakdown of that interoperability barrier existing for the particular concern and using the selected approach.

2.1 Dimension "interoperability barrier"

By the term "barrier" we mean an "incompatibility" or "mismatch" which obstructs the sharing and exchanging of information. Three categories of barriers are identified: conceptual, technological and organisational.

The conceptual barriers are concerned with the syntactic and semantic incompatibilities of information to be exchanged. These problems concern the modeling at the high level of abstraction (such as for example the enterprise models of a company) as well as the level of the programming (for example low capacity of semantic representation of XML).

The technological barriers are concerned with the use of computer or ICT (Information and Communication Technology) to communicate and exchange information.

The organizational barriers are concerned with the incompatibilities of organization structure and management techniques implemented in two enterprises.

2.2. Dimension "interoperability concern"

This standard addresses the interoperations that can take place from the various concerns (or viewpoints) of the enterprise. Although the definitions are mainly given from a point of view of IT-based applications, they apply to non-computerized systems as well.

The interoperability of data is concerned with finding and sharing information coming from heterogeneous data bases, and which can moreover reside on different machines with different operating systems and data bases management systems.

The interoperability of services is concerned with identifying, composing and operating together various applications (designed and implemented independently) by solving the syntactic and semantic differences as well as finding the connections to the various heterogeneous databases.

The interoperability of processes aims to make various processes work together, for example to build collaborative process between two companies.

The interoperability of business refers to work in a harmonized way at the levels of organization and company in spite of for example, the different modes of decision-making, methods of work, legislations, culture of the company and commercial approaches etc. so that business can be developed and shared between companies.

2.3. Dimension "interoperability approach"

Establishing interoperability requires relating entities together in some way. According to ISO 14258 (Concepts and rules for enterprise models) (ISO 14258, 1999), there are three basic ways to relate entities together: integrated, unified, and federated.

Developing interoperability through an *Integrated Approach* means that there exists a common format for all models. Diverse models are built and interpreted using/against the common template. This format must be as detailed as the models themselves. The common format is not necessarily an international standard but must be agreed by all parties to elaborate models and build systems.

Interoperability can also be established using a *Unified Approach*. It means there is a common format but it only exists at the meta-level. This format is not an executable entity as is the case in integrated approach. Instead it provides a mean for semantic equivalence to allow mapping between models and applications.

In the case of using a *Federated approach*, there is no common format at all. To establish interoperability, parties must accommodate and adjust "on the fly". Using the federated approach implies that no partner imposes their models, languages and methods of work.

The graphical representation of the Framework for Enterprise Interoperability is shown Figure 2. The FEI defines the domain of enterprise interoperability. It allows us to capture and structure interoperability knowledge and solutions according to their ability to remove interoperability barriers. For example, PSL (Process Specification Language) is a standard solution (ISO 18629) that contributes to the removal of *conceptual* barriers (both syntax and semantics) concerning *process* interoperability using a *unified* approach.

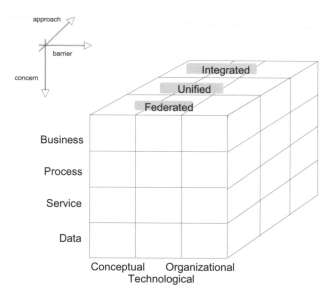

Figure 2. *Enterprise interoperability framework*

3. Maturity Model for Enterprise Interoperability (MMEI)

Maturity Model for Enterprise Interoperability (MMEI) has been specified in CEN/ISO 11354-2 which is a New Work Item Proposal (NWIP). The maturity model will enable an assessment of an enterprises capability to interoperate with another enterprise. MMEI is built on the FEI described above and covers the whole problem space of the FEI (four interoperability concerns and three kinds of interoperability barriers). Five levels of interoperability maturity are defined as shown in Table 1. Each level identifies a certain degree of capability to interoperate with another enterprise.

Maturity Level	Maturity assessment
Level 4 - Adaptive	Capable of negotiating and dynamically accommodating with any heterogeneous partner
Level 3 - Organized	Capable of meta modeling for mapping in order to interoperate with multiple heterogeneous partners
Level 2 - Aligned	Capable of making necessary changes to align to common formats or standards
Level 1 - Defined	Capability of properly modeling and describing systems to prepare interoperability
Level 0 - Unprepared	Not relevant: there is no capability for interoperation

Table 1. *Interoperability maturity levels*

The maturity levels are defined according to the interoperability approach dimension of Framework for Enterprise Interoperability (see section 2 and Figure 2). Levels 0 and 1 are not covered by the framework because they correspond to the situation where there are no or only some capabilities for ad hoc interoperations. From levels 2 to 4, three levels of maturity are defined that correspond to the three Interoperability Approaches of the FEI (Integrated, Unified and Federated). Table 2 shows the mapping between maturity levels and interoperation environments.

Maturity Level	Interoperation environments
Level 4 - Adaptive	Federated: No pre-defined format or meta-models. Dynamically adjust and accommodate
Level 3 - Organized	Unified: Use of meta-models allowing heterogeneous systems to map one to others
Level 2 - Aligned	Integrated: Common format (or standard) for all partners to build their systems (components)
Level 1 - Defined	Connected: Simple electronic exchange of information, messaging, etc.
Level 0 - Unprepared	Isolated: Occasional and manual exchange of information (document, fax,..)

Table 2. *Maturity levels vs. interoperation environments*

Each level of maturity also corresponds to a degree of interoperability ranging from no interoperability to full interoperability as shown in Table 3.

Maturity Level	Interoperability degree
Level 4 - Adaptive	Generalized (full interoperability to any potential partner)
Level 3 - Organized	Extended (many-to-many multiple heterogeneous partners)
Level 2 - Aligned	Restricted (Peer-to-peer, to use common format/standard)
Level 1 - Defined	Limited (with only some ad hoc interoperations)
Level 0 - Unprepared	Nonexistent

Table 3. *Maturity levels and interoperability degree*

Table 4 gives a high level view of MMEI and shows the main focus for each combination of each maturity level and for each interoperability barrier category. These interoperability barriers are already defined in the framework (FEI) by its interoperability barrier dimension (conceptual, technological, organizational).

Maturity Levels/ Barriers	Conceptual	Technological	Organizational
Level 4 - Adaptive	Accommodated	Reconfigurable	Agile
Level 3 - Organized	Mapped	Open-architecture	Trained
Level 2 - Aligned	Adhered	Arranged	Flexible
Level 1 - Defined	Modeled	Connectable	Specified
Level 0 - Unprepared	Incomplete	Inaccessible	Inexplicit

Table 4. *Focus of concerns in MMEI*

Table 5 shows how a particular maturity is defined. Each maturity level is described in detail based on the FEI (dimensions of interoperability concerns and interoperability barriers). Each cell defines requirements (or criteria to meet) which are necessary to reach that interoperability maturity level. The transition from one level to a higher one corresponds generally to a removal of interoperability barriers and satisfaction of requirements. An example of these tables is shown in Table 5, which shows the details of level 0.

		Conceptual	Technological	Organizational
Level 0	Business	Visions, strategies, politics not described	No IT infrastructure /platform in place	Undefined organization structure
	Process	Processes not formally described	Manual processes	Undefined /undocumented methods of work
	Service	Services not formally defined	Stand-alone services	Responsibilities /authorities for services not known
	Data	Heterogeneous data representation, not completely modeled	Closed data storage devices, manual exchange	Responsibilities /authorities for data not defined

Table 5. *Description of the maturity level 0*

The initial level of interoperability maturity is characterized by proprietary (heterogeneous) nature of systems. All the systems resources are not meant to be shared with other systems. Systems modeling and description are not complete or even not existent. The organization is not explicitly specified. There is in general no capability for interoperation with other companies. Communication remains on the level of manual exchange. Systems run stand-alone and are not prepared for interoperability (Guédria *et al.*, 2009).

The proposed MMEI is inspired from and influenced by some existing known maturity models in the following ways:

– LISI: technology aspect at all levels of concern (data, service, process and business) and all five maturity levels;

– OIM/OIAM: organizational aspect at all levels of concern (data, service, process and business) and all five maturity levels;

– LCIM: conceptual aspect, mainly at the level of data concerning data interoperability;

– EIMM: conceptual aspect mainly from enterprise modeling and models elaboration points of view;

– SPICE/CMMI: all maturity levels, to define and model explicitly processes in particular.

The interoperability assessment results of an enterprise can be represented in different ways. Figure 3[1] shows one such representation as a Kiviat graph (radar plot) that allows one to represent the 5 maturity levels in relation to the 4 concerns and 3 barrier types identified in the FEI.

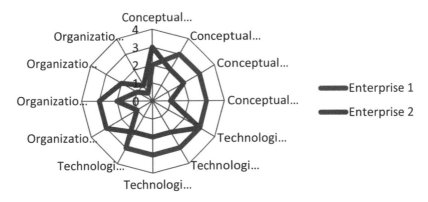

Figure 3. *Interoperability maturity assessment (kinds of barrier and concern)*

Figure 3 also shows an illustrative example of an assessment of two enterprises' interoperability capabilities. Depending on the enterprise goal to reach a particular capability level being 1, 2, 3 or 4, the sufficient and missing capabilities can be identified. In the example, for the blue enterprise the organizational capabilities of the business maturity level do not even reach level 1 whereas the conceptual and technological capabilities reach up to the maturity level 3 for process and service

---

1 Originally proposed by K. Kosanke and D. Shorter.

and data, respectively. If the level 2 were the desired one for the intended cooperation between two enterprises, improvements would have to be made in technological capabilities on the business concern and in organizational capabilities on the three concerns: business, process and data.

It is the objective of this standard to define levels of enterprise interoperability maturity and their associated criteria and accomplishments that must be met to achieve a given maturity level. However it is not the objective of the standard to standardize a methodology for collecting required data to evaluate a particular enterprise. The reason is for a given maturity model there might exist different ways to use to carry out an evaluation process. In other words, how to formally assess an enterprise to define its maturity level depends on its industrial sector, the size of the company and many other factors. However the standard will provide an example of such a methodology in its annex.

4. Conclusions

This paper presented a CEN/ISO 11354 standardization initiative to define Enterprise Interoperability Framework and Maturity Model. Prior to this initiative, basic concepts and approaches have been surveyed and identified from existing frameworks and maturity models.

With respect to existing frameworks (ATHENA, IDEAS, EIF, etc.), the proposed FEI is barrier-driven. If a problem or a solution cannot find its place in the framework, it is not related to an interoperability concern per se. Incompatibility is the fundamental concept used in FEI. The concept "incompatibility" has a broad sense and is not only limited to "technical" aspect as usually considered in the IT domain, but also includes "information" and "organization", and concerns all levels of the enterprise.

MMEI is defined on the basis of the FEI and consistent to it. It is to note that a lower interoperability maturity for a company does not mean a systematic dysfunction at all levels and for all functions of the company. A high level degree of interoperability cannot be achieved for free. It is generally costly and time consuming. Each enterprise must define its interoperability requirements and maturity level to be reached. It is not recommended to look for the highest interoperability level regardless of their needs.

5. Acknowledgements

The author acknowledges members of CEN TC310/WG1 and ISO TC184/SC5 WG1 for their contributions to this standard.

6. References

ATHENA, (2003) Advanced Technologies for Interoperability of Heterogeneous Enterprise Networks and their Applications, FP6-2002-IST-1, Integrated Project.

C4ISR (1998) Architecture Working Group (AWG), Levels of Information Systems Interoperability (LISI).

D. Chen, G. Doumeingts, F. Vernadat (2008), "Architectures for Enterprise Integration and Interoperability: Past, Present and Future", *Computers In Industry*, Vol 59, Issue n°5.

CEN/ISO 11354-1 (2009), Part 1: Framework for enterprise interoperability, Draft International Standard ISO/DIS 11354-1.

CEN/ISO 11354-2 (2011), Part 2: Maturity model for assessing enterprise interoperability, Draft for proposed activation of WI 00310094, document N270.

Clark, T., Jones, R. (1999), "Organizational interoperability maturity model for c2", in: *Proc. of the Command and Control Research and Technology Symposium*, Washington.

CMMI for Development. CMMI-DEV (Version 1.3) (2010). Carnegie Mellon University Software Engineering Institute.

EIF, CompTIA: European Industry Association (2004), European Interoperability Framework white paper - ICT Industry Recommendations, http://www.comptia.org.

W. Guédria, Y. Naudet, D. Chen (2008), "Interoperability Maturity Models - Survey and Comparison", in *EI2N'2008*, November 12-13, Monterrey, Mexico.

W Guédria, D. Chen and Y. Naudet (2009), "A Maturity Model for Enterprise Interoperability", *IFAC/IFIP Workshop* (EI2N2009), Vilamoura (Portugal), November 3-4.

M. Kasunic, W. Anderson (2004), Measuring systems interoperability: challenges and opportunities, Software Engineering Measurement and Analysis Initiative, Technical note, cmu/sei-2004-tn-003, Carnegie Mellon University.

G. Kingston, S. Fewell, & W. Richer (2004) "An Organisational Interoperability Agility Model", *Proc. 10th ICCRTS*.

IDEAS (2002) Consortium, Thematic Network, IDEAS: Interoperability Development for Enterprise Application and Software – Roadmaps, Annex1 – Description of Work.

IEEE, (1990) IEEE standard computer dictionary: a compilation of IEEE standard computer glossaries.

INTEROP, (2003) Interoperability Research for Networked Enterprises Applications and Software, Network of Excellence, Proposal Part B.

INTEROP (2006), Enterprise Interoperability – Framework and knowledge corpus, INTEROP DI Deliverable DI 1.2.

ISO/IEC 15504 (2001), Software Process Improvement and Capability Determination Model (SPICE).

C. Thomas Ford (2008), Interoperability Measurement – PhD thesis Dissertation, AFIT/DSE/ENV/08-S01, Air Force Institute of Technology, Air University.

A. Tolk, J.A. Muguira (2003), The levels of conceptual interoperability model, *In: 2003 Fall Simulation Interoperability Workshop*, USA.

A. Tolk (2003), "Beyond Technical Interoperability - Introducing a Reference Model forMeasures of Merit for Coalition Interoperability", *Proc. 8th ICCRTS*.

Standards Ensuring Enterprise Interoperability and Collaboration, Challenges and Opportunities

Martin Forsberg

Ecru Consulting
Holländargatan 11
11120 Stockholm
Sweden

martin.forsberg@ecru.se

ABSTRACT: *This article describes how standards for electronic business from particularly UN/CEFACT and OASIS Universal Business Language address different levels of interoperability. It is often underestimated how much effort is needed to make the standards implementable by end users and software providers. The process of detailing and refining a standard is called contextualization – to customize it to meet requirements for a particular context. There are many ways to communicate and document the refinements. Words like superset, subset and core are used to describe different approaches.*

KEYWORDS: *UN/CEFACT, UBL, XML-standard, context, electronic business.*

1. Introduction

The standards and methodologies that will be discussed in this paper primarily come from UN/CEFACT and OASIS Universal Business Language (UBL). Standards from these groups cover several domains but with emphasis on electronic trade facilitation. UBL has currently standardized 31 XML messages covering both transport processes and procurement, such as product catalog, order, invoice and reminder. A new version is planned to be published in 2011 which adds over 30 new business messages including e-tendering and Collaborative Planning, Forecasting and Replenishment (CPFR).

UN/CEFACT has a number of domain groups covering supply chain, tourism, e-government, agriculture, insurance and many more. The domain group for supply chain (TBG1) has the biggest overlap with OASIS UBL in terms of coverage. During the last years UN/CEFACT has published XML standards for Invoice, Order, Catalogue and other typical supply chain messages.

A lot of effort has been invested during the last 4 years in converging the two standards. The convergence work has been successful in many areas, especially related to harmonization of business requirements, but less successful on the more technical side (the use of XML). The standards development process can be described (in simplified terms) to consist of the following steps: 1. Gathering of business requirements; 2. Development/mapping against a data model; 3. Binding to XML-syntax. To add more or harmonize requirements is easy, but to change the underlying design rules of how the binding to XML should be done is harder. The XML Naming and Design rules are also standards themselves (OASIS UBL NDR and UN/CEFACT XML NDR).

Both standardization groups have in common that the standards being developed support a wide range of use cases. Both standardization groups also consider that their respective standards will be implemented in many-to-many relation scenarios. The requirements that they are built from come from both the public and the private sector and from a wide range of industries.

It should be noted that the issues of contextualization and customization also applies for other types of standards besides the e-business domain, such as those used for financial transactions (ISO20022, SWIFT), energy data exchange (eBIX) and more.

2. Many levels of interoperability

These standards address the well-known interoperability levels as described in the European Interoperability Framework (EIF). And by implementing international standards, added value can be created. It is however important to understand that the benefits offered by these standards, are limited unless they are further specialized and detailed. This is something that often is overlooked in the discussions throughout Europe (especially in relation to e-invoices). The choice of standard receives much more common interest and is regarded as much more important than the choice of implementation group. As described in this article, two implementations of the same standard can very well be non-interoperable on many levels.

The separation of issues that relates to different aspects/levels of interoperability helps to understand where they impact. The European Interoperability Framework describes the four levels like this:

Legal interoperability - Sometimes, incompatibilities between legislation in different Member States make working together more complex or even impossible, even where such legislation is the result of transposing European directives into national law.

Organizational interoperability - This aspect of interoperability is concerned with how organizations, such as public administrations in different Member States, cooperate to achieve their mutually agreed goals. In practice, organizational interoperability implies integrating business processes and related data exchange.

Semantic interoperability - Semantic interoperability enables organizations to process information from external sources in a meaningful manner. It ensures that the precise meaning of exchanged information is understood and preserved throughout exchanges between parties.

Technical interoperability - This covers the technical aspects of linking information systems. It includes aspects such as interface specifications, interconnection services, data integration services, data presentation and exchange, etc.

Interoperability Level	How it is addressed by standards organizations	What is necessary for implementation
Legal Interoperability	Limited added value. UN/CEFACT Business Requirement Specifications can in some cases give some guidance on for example VAT usage.	More detailed guidance and specification of the legal and fiscal rules.
Organizational Interoperability	Some added value. The standards normally describe the choreography of message exchange. The choreography is not normative but should be considered as a default or a best	Restrictions and specifications of possible design choices in choreography. Possibly limitation in roles that the trading partner takes in the business process.

Interoperability Level	How it is addressed by standards organizations	What is necessary for implementation
	practice. The choreography also includes the parties involved and their main responsibilities.	
Semantic Interoperability	The standards definitely support the semantic interoperability to a certain degree. There is however a tendency to generalize the names of business terms, definitions and business rules. The semantic building blocks therefore often need to be refined and clarified. The standards setting groups often prefer to be generic rather than specific and by being generic hoping to be useful for a more general purpose.	Refinements/restrictions of code lists, guidance and usage rules for data elements that are usually too generic which opens for multiple interpretations. Adjustments of cardinality (making optional information entities mandatory or marking entities as not used) based on the intended context of use.
Technical Interoperability	The syntax realizations (XML-schemas) provide a good possibility to check and verify conformance against structure, data types and formats. It is however very complicated to implement 100% of a standard due to the large and complex structures. There is a need for bilateral or multilateral agreements on what part/subset of the standard to actually use.	Development of artefacts that can be used to enforce and validate the context specific adjustment of the semantic model of the message. For XML-syntaxes, profiled schemas or schematron rules are often used.

Table 1. *Interoperability levels and how they are addressed by standards*

3. Context is everything

The key to interoperable solutions is context. Any level of interoperability is impossible to reach if the trading partners do not share a common understanding of the context. The most common context drivers that we encounter in the standardization of trading documents come from:

- business process, choreography, overall goals;
- geopolitical peculiarities;
- official constraints – legal or fiscal rules;
- industry-specific needs.

There have been long discussions within UN/CEFACT and OASIS UBL related to how context specific the standards should be. Two extreme viewpoints can be observed:

Extreme 1: All standards (and XML-messages) should be fully contextualized so that they can be used directly, out of the box, by the trading partners. This also means that we will e.g. have several invoice standards, one for metered utility invoices, one for direct material in the automotive industry, one for transportation services and so on.

Extreme 2: The other extreme says that the standard should only have one generic business message used for all transactions like order, order response, despatch advice, quote and so on. This message is reused everywhere but the context is indicated with a code value or a set of code values. Different business rules are applied depending on the context. It is up to someone else than the standardization group to define the details of these business rules.

The first extreme viewpoint would help the implementers in that the standard will have very little complexity that stems from other, out of scope, situations. From a semantic point of view, the standard would be precise. The drawback is that (using the current mechanism for how XML-structures/messages are created – Naming and Design Rules for XML) each contextualized business message would end up with a unique XML-schema, non-interoperable, on a technical level, with other variants of the same business message. The reason for this is the way context currently is conveyed using the XML-namespace.

The other extreme would support the providers of mapping tools and other actors that are helped by a reusable superset that all variants of a message can be contained within. So the software that consumes a Request for Quote and Order only has one XML-schema to implement. The drawback of this approach is that the semantic interoperability will be hard to achieve since the standard most likely would have to be very generic and un-precise.

The approach taken by both UN/CEFACT and OASIS UBL is to target something in between the two extremes. The business message should have a clear business function but also be possible to use in slightly different variations. But even this approach results in complex models, especially over time as more and more requirements are identified and expected to be supported (it is easy to add a new data element, but it is almost impossible to take one out).

4. New standards under development

The Technology and Methodology group within UN/CEFACT runs a project called UN/CEFACT Context Methodology (UCM). The purpose is to develop a methodology and technical specification for developing, registering and using context drivers in a more unified approach. The lack of standardized ways of marking and communicating the context/usage rules for a business message leads to proprietary and non-reusable solutions. To document the business context for each business term in a data model offers guidance on how a message should be assembled. The context information can also be used to customize a business process as it tells in what circumstances a business term or transaction should be used. A common methodology for business context will provide a more predictable and machine processable option to the proprietary tools and solutions available today.

5. Current European contextualization initiatives

The European Committee for Standardization (CEN) is hosting several workshops (which can be compared to projects) related to implementation guidelines for e-business or e-invoicing. The CEN workshops offer a platform and working procedure that is fairly agile and well suited for implementation guidelines. There is currently a lot of debate about how the implementation guides should be developed. The aforementioned context methodology (UCM) from UN/CEFACT is still not a published standard so there is yet no formal methodology to support the work.

There are many examples of situations where two implementations of the same standard result in non-interoperable solutions. It takes many small and big decisions in order to customize a standard. Code lists may be restricted to only contain the values relevant for the business context, business terms not relevant are removed or indicated as not used, cardinalities may be restricted (optional elements made mandatory) and data types may be restricted. The monetary amount elements do not always have mandated calculation rules and dependencies. On the contrary, this is often specified during the customization work.

The likelihood of two groups, working independently, developing two interoperable solutions is almost non-existent.

Two approaches are being discussed to address this situation. Either will the workshops create a *subset* of a standard, containing all data elements that are considered useful for especially European e-business, or alternatively a *core* is created to expose just the minimum content, shared by all participants in the work.

The subset alternative has the benefit that other groups can then further contextualize, and derive new implementation guidelines based on the subset. The challenge is that the standards are extremely comprehensive with many thousands of possible data elements. A subset supporting all European e-business requirements will likely be so large that it will offer very limited guidance and therefore will not support interoperability. The core concept would, instead of encompassing everything useful, only contain everything shared – the common denominator for a certain context. The core would probably be quite small and in itself not very useful. But the idea is that having something truly in common will support interoperability better than just having the outer boundaries of a subset in common. Future national or regional standards could then derive their implementation guidelines from the core and by that, share something in common. An area where this is considered to be useful is the data elements necessary for VAT compliance for invoices, including calculation rules and code lists.

The demand for standards for e-business, and especially for public e-procurement, is growing. Projects like PEPPOL (Pan-European Public Procurement On-Line) on a European level, Single Face To Industry in Sweden or OIO in Denmark all implement the same international standards. It is of great importance that the possibility to create interoperable solutions is not lost, just because the contextualization/customization is done in silos, with different methodologies. CEN may be the vehicle to create a common base, but the development approach is vital for the success.

6. References

OASIS UBL, http://www.oasis-open.org/committees/tc_home.php?wg_abbrev=ubl.

UN/CEFACT, http://www.unece.org/cefact.

ISO20022, http://www.iso20022.org.

eBIX, http://ebix.org.

European Interoperability Framework, http://ec.europa.eu/isa/strategy/doc/annex_ii_eif_en.pdf.

UN/CEFACT Context Methodology (UCM),
http://ec.europa.eu/isa/strategy/doc/annex_ii_eif_en.pdf.

PEPPOL (Pan-European Public Procurement On-Line), http://www.peppol.eu.

Single Face To Industry, http://www.sfti.se.

OIO, http://digitaliser.dk/katalog/2.

Modeling Enterprise Architecture Transformations

Sabine Buckl* — Florian Matthes* — Ivan Monahov* — Christian M. Schweda*

*Chair for Software Engineering for Business Information Systems
Technische Universität München, 85748 Garching, Germany
sabine.buckl@in.tum.de, matthes@in.tum.de,
ivan.monahov@in.tum.de, schweda@in.tum.de

ABSTRACT: *A rapidly changing business environment, regulatory development, and technological advancements constantly impose changes on the modern enterprise. Thus, the ability to perform EA transformations in a timely manner has attracted growing attention recently within the field of EA planning. Based on the different EA planning perspectives, numerous models and modeling techniques have been developed and examined over the last few years. Yet, the question "How do these perspectives of EA planning interrelate?" remains unanswered. This paper focuses on the ways in which different perspectives of EA transformation – activities, replacements, and lifecycles – can be modeled as add-ons for EA models and the ways they interrelate.*

KEYWORDS: *Enterprise architecture, EA transformation, EA transformation modeling*

1. Motivation

Challenging economic, regulatory, and technical environments force modern enterprises to continuously change and adapt themselves in order to reshape the foundation of their business execution (see Ross *et al.*, 2006). This need for constant change especially pertains to what is called the *enterprise architecture* (EA), i.e. pertains to the "fundamental organization of the enterprise embodied in its components, their relationships to each other and to the environment as well as the principles guiding its design and evolution". This definition of the EA, based on the ISO Std. 42010 (ISO, 2007) gives an indication on the complexity of the subject of change. According to Wagter *et al.* (Wagter *et al.*, 2005) this subject has to be made *dynamic* in order to react to environmental changes or to proactively realize potential for optimization.

The above requirements lead to the discipline of EA management in general and the activity of *EA planning* in particular. EA planning provides an embracing and holistic perspective on organizational change and facilitates enterprise transformation, thereby seeking to maintain and foster the alignment between the different parts of the enterprise. Especially, ensuring and strengthening the mutual alignment of business and IT is, according to Luftman *et al.* (Luftman *et al.*, 1993), a key objective of enterprise transformations and hence of EA planning.

Reflecting the ongoing interest in the field of EA management, the area of EA planning has received particular attention in recent years. Different methods and modeling techniques aim to cover the intricate topic of guiding and describing EA change in a way that is applicable to enterprise architects in transforming organizations. The works of Buckl *et al.* (Buckl *et al.*, 2009a and 2009b) or of Aier and Gleichauf (Aier *et al.*, 2010a and 2010b) make excellent examples of recent contributions to the field. These and other approaches, as we show in section 2, provide punctiform solutions to distinct problems in EA planning. In particular, each approach puts emphasis on a dedicated relevant aspect of transformation planning, with each aspect reflecting a specific perspective on changing EAs. These perspectives complementarily lead to different ways of modeling EA transformations. This motivates the first research question of this article, which reads as follows:

Which different perspectives on EA planning exist in literature and how do they interrelate?

Foreclosing the answer to the first question, we state that four perspectives exist, of which one – namely that of *temporality* – is fundamental to all other perspectives. These three perspectives in turn do not have much in common and are described in approaches largely unrelated to each other. With the missing linkage between the approaches, a user willing to establish EA planning in a practice-relevant way on a rigorous basis, is faced with a situation that he or she has to decide which of the aspects is most important, being able only to select one aspect for implementation. Rephrasing these considerations to the impact of EA transformation planning on EA modeling, which this article is dedicated to, this means the following: an organization that wants to plan its EA's transformation has to select one of four different ways of modeling transformation. Having selected not only the basic solution of temporality, there is indeed no predefined way to add other perspectives to the selected one. This situation yields the second research questions of this article, which can be described as follows:

How can different perspectives on EA transformation be modeled as add-ons for EA models? How do the add-ons interrelate?

With the first research question being answered at the end of section 2, section 3 is dedicated to a concise representation of EA transformation perspectives. Preparing this, we discuss some liabilities of object-oriented modeling and present a slightly enhanced form in order to capture the "true" ontological nature of the different perspectives. As our presented solution is well-grounded in existing literature on the field, we abstain from giving a virtual case for evaluating the findings. Instead, we head for a critical reflection in section 4 summarizing questions that arise from the article's findings and give an outlook on how to incorporate our solution into a comprehensive method for EA transformation planning.

2. Literature review

Schönherr showed that a plurality of literature on EA management currently exists, thus mirroring the continuing interest in the subject (Schönherr, 2008). This situation nevertheless particularly aggravates a comprehensive coverage of the topic. Against that background, we opt to build the subsequent review of literature on the analysis (Buckl and Schweda, 2011). This general analysis gives an overview on the prescriptions made by individual EA management-related approaches. Based on the analysis, we select The Open Group Architecture Framework (TOGAF) (The Open Group, 2009), the approach presented by Buckl *et al.* (Buckl *et al.*, 2009a and 2009b), and that of Aier and Gleichauf (Aier *et al.*, 2010a and 2010b), as these approaches are mentioned to provide good coverage of EA planning related aspects. The review is complemented by the approach of Brückmann *et al.* which presents a practitioner's perspective on modeling lifecycles of EA elements. During the review of these approaches, we specifically focus on the modeling techniques provided and in particular on the *underlying information models*, if present.

The most basic way of modeling temporal aspects of EA elements is to assign a period of validity to each individual element. TOGAF (The Open Group, 2009) applies this way of modeling onto different concepts in its "content metamodel", as the information model is called in the framework. Key architectural concepts such as "process", "service", "information system", and "application component" are equipped with an attribute "retire date". According to the metamodel's documentation, this attribute is used to delineate the end of life for an element of that type. For the "physical application component" in particular TOGAF not only provides a retirement date, but complementarily introduces an "initial live date", used to denote the day of that actual component going into production. Regarding the utilization of the corresponding attributes, TOGAF does not make specific prescriptions, abstaining from giving consistency constraints. Lifecycle modeling is also alluded to in the content metamodel, but receives limited attention with regard to the fact that only the current lifecycle status for physical application components may be modeled, ranging from "proposed" over "live" to "retired". With this kind of lifecycle modeling, we can again exemplify the omission of consistency constraints, such that a component may be in a "proposed" state even at a point in time where its "retire date" has long passed.

Buckl et al. take a different perspective on EA planning, emphasizing the role of projects as drivers of enterprise transformation (Buckl et al., 2009a and 2009b). They commit to the principle that any change at an enterprise level is the consequence of execution of a project or a similar activity. Exemplifying this with the subject of business support provided by the enterprise's business applications, Buckl et al. devise a way of modeling that introduces an intermediary concept "business support" that links business applications with the supported business processes when using organizational units. This intermediary concept is therein regarded as reification of the ternary relationship between the three concepts and is equipped with attributes to denote the relationship's period of validity. The period of validity is nevertheless not defined for each particular business support element, but is derived from the activities (named "work packages" there) that may be linked to elements committing to this concept. More precisely, Buckl et al. define three different types of relationships between work package and business support, namely "introduces", "changes", and "retires". The first and last relationship in particular supply the periods of validity for the associated element, such that a business support is valid once the introducing work package has finished and the retiring work package has not yet been started. Different work packages are in turn composed of the projects changing the make-up of the overall EA. Due to the means of modeling introduced, it is not only possible to relate the business support to the drivers of its change (Buckl et al., 2009a and 2009b). Buckl et al. discuss this fact, introducing a specific stereotype **«projectDependency»** that may be used to indicate that a specific concept in the EA has a period of validity derived from the corresponding projects. This thinking on the one hand lays the groundwork for the mechanism to be discussed in section 3, but remains limited when it comes to the interplay between different project-dependent concepts. Specifically, Buckl *et al.* do not discuss consistency constraints between concepts and their linking relationships.

Aier and Gleichauf discuss how the transformation nature of EA planning may be reflected in the corresponding management methods (Aier *et al.*, 2010a and 2010b). The central aspect of their discussions is a so-called "transformation model" that describes which EA element from a previous state is replaced by which element in a subsequent state of the EA. As part of their considerations, Aier and Gleichauf introduce different types of EA states, namely the "as-is" and the "to-be" states that are considered during transformation planning. A transformation model describes the replacement relationships linking models of two different EA states (Aier *et al.*, 2010b). This may in particular be an as-is and a to-be state, or two to-be states targeting different points of time in the future. Complementarily, Aier and Gleichauf further introduce the notion of the "will-be" state, reflecting that the actual transformation may proceed differently from the planned one. Such a "will-be" state is used as the basis for subsequent planning steps instead of the to-be state actually intended to hold for the specific point in time. Building on the transformation models, Aier and Gleichauf describe a set of analysis techniques that may be used to understand the EA transformation plan in more detail. One analysis technique leverages the "classical" critical path analyses on an EA level, seeking to find which series of transformations is critical for the evolution of the overall EA. The analysis techniques nevertheless do not account for consistency constraints in the transformation model or the models of the different states. With no dedicated information model given, it is further not easy to judge which concepts in an EA may be considered as subjects of transformation. The general terms in which the topic of EA planning is discussed nevertheless support the assumption that the transformation of EA elements committing to arbitrary EA concepts may be modeled (Aier *et al.*, 2010a and 2010b).

Brückmann *et al.* present a lifecycle model of EA elements, and define the following five lifecycle states: "proposed", "test", "productive", "standard", and "retired" (Brückmann *et al.*, 2009). The "proposed" state suggests that an existing EA element either does not fully meet the requirements or that a new EA element promises advantages to existing ones. Following the proposal's approval, the EA element enters the "test" state. Depending on the test results, the EA element can change its state to either "productive" or "retired". Once an approved EA element is in use, it automatically enters the "productive" state. If an EA "productive" element fits into the long-term IT strategy, it obtains the status "standard", otherwise "retired". The benefits of a particular EA element in the "standard" state and its alignment with the IT strategy are proven in production by the EA management. "Retired" EA elements are not to be used in future scenarios. New versions of the "retired" EA elements should be created and proposed instead.

3. Modeling EA transformation

In the existing literature of the field as revisited above, we can discover four different principles for approaching the modeling of EA transformations. The most simplistic, but fundamental approach assigns a period of validity to any object that participates in a transformation. Speaking more precisely, any EA concept, whose transformation should be modeled, is reflected in a model type that supplies properties for specifying an associated instance's period of validity. By making distinct instances of that type valid in different periods of time, a change in the EA may be described. The aforementioned principle is nevertheless only the most basic way to represent EA transformations. In particular, the three following aspects of EA transformation are not accounted for by this modeling principle:

- **EA elements do not change accidentally.** An element of the EA is change by some sort of activity, e.g. a project, and does not change on its own. In order to manage the EA transformation it may be necessary to know which activity is changing which EA element.

- **EA elements may replace each other.** An element may supersede a previously existing one, taking over some or all of this element's responsibilities. On the contrary, an element may also be retired without having a replacement or may be newly introduced.

- **EA elements have a lifecycle.** Quite a number of EA elements undergo a change of lifecycle phase as well, e.g. being "proposed" at a certain point in time, whereas being "retired" at the end of their life.

Any of the above aspects adds a specific perspective on EA transformation that refines the basic principle of the period of validity, with a driving activity (**A**), a replacement relationship (**R**), and lifecycle information (**L**), respectively. As the literature review in section 2 showed, each of the aspects may occur independently, but in particular the work of Buckl *et al.* provided an indication that different perspectives may be applied simultaneously, if needed (Buckl *et al.*, 2010a). Exploring this idea in more detail, we subsequently elaborate on the interplay of the different principles and show how this is reflected in corresponding EA information models. Figure 1 provides a conceptual framework for these elaborations introducing the different types of modeling that we would expect.

Before nevertheless starting with the elaborations on the modeling techniques specific for the perspectives, we have to add a side-note on two ontological principles in conceptual modeling that are employed in the subsequent considerations. To do so, we follow the exposition of the principle as provided by Guarino and Welti (Guarino *et al.*, 2000a) further calling on the terminology of Guizzardi (Guizzardi, 2005). The first principle is the one of identity. A concept can carry the identity of the associated elements or may dispersive, i.e. not relevant with respect to the elements' identities. Put in a slightly different way, we may say that an identity-carrying concept supplies a sort of equivalence relation which the model users employ to differentiate between elements covered by the concept. An example for this would be the concept "website" which carries the identity of corresponding elements in turns of the property of the "url" or the concept "book" identifying the elements with the property "isbn". A dispersive concept does not provide that kind of equivalence relation to identify corresponding elements and can hence be thought of as some kind of categorizing concept. Continuing the above example, possible categorizations may be "English", "Swedish" or "German". These categorizations may apply both to books and to websites, thus not being sub-concepts thereof. These concepts on the contrary would name "English book" or "Swedish website". As both books and websites may be categorized by concepts as "English"[1], this shows a particular difference between dispersive and non-dispersive concepts. As Guizzardi delineates, this distinction with respect to the ontological nature of a concept is not well reflected in today's conceptual modeling languages (Guizzardi, 2005). In these languages each concept, either dispersive or not, is mapped to a type or class, neglecting a potentially important difference. Seeking to explore the true ontological nature of EA transformation modeling, we do not prematurely commit ourselves to the simplified point of view taken in most modeling languages. On the contrary, we employ a technique inspired by Guizzardi denoting dispersive types with a stereotype in order to distinguish them from their non-dispersive counterparts.

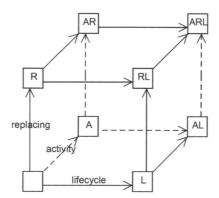

Figure 1. *Aspects of EA transformation modeling*

The second principle of interest is the principle of rigidity. Put in short, it asks whether an element commits over its entire lifetime to the same concept or, if different concepts cover different phases of the element's life. While elements of

1 More precisely the categorizing concept should be called "English content".

rigid concepts stay committed to the concept of their entire existence, non-rigid concepts are applicable only for a limited period of time. Quickly calling on an example we think of the concept "human" which applies to the corresponding elements over their entire lifetime, thus being a rigid concept. In contrast, the concept "teenager" is non-rigid, as a teen has previously been a "kid" and (hopefully) matures to an "adult". Thinking again of how concepts are represented as types and classes in today's prevalent languages for conceptual modeling, one comes to a similar finding that non-rigid typing is not well-supported in these languages (Guizzardi, 2005). Repeating the statement on dispersive types, we call on a technique inspired by Guizzardi and will use stereotypes in the subsequent models to denote that a type actually is non-rigid. Equipped with this ontological groundwork, we are ready to proceed to modeling the first perspective as follows.

3.1. Activity modeling

Refraining the perspective taken by Buckl *et al.*, the first perspective introduces the notion of the "transformation activity" (Buckl *et al.*, 2009a and 2009b). Such activities may be identified with transformation projects or, more precisely, a part thereof, e.g. a work-package. In particular, an activity may introduce or retire an element of the EA, as represented in an instance of an EA type. Conversely, any such element may be introduced or retired by a maximum of one of such activities. Reflecting the ontological nature of this kind of activity modeling, the model fragment presented in Figure 2 introduces the dispersive type of the **ActivityAffectable**. An organization may decide to subtype this type to indicate that a specific EA type is subject to transformation.

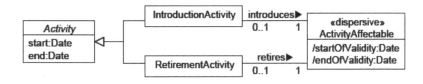

Figure 2. *Activity modeling*

In order to ensure conceptual consistency of models committing to the activity modeling fragment, the following constraints apply:

```
ctx Activity: start < end
ctx ActivityAffectable:
startOfValidity = (introduces==null)?null:introduces.end
endOfValidity = (retires==null)?null:retires.start
```

The former constraint ensures that any activity ends after it has started, where the latter activity is used to derive the period of validity of an EA element from the corresponding introducing and retiring activities. If no such activities exist, then no actual limits for the period of validity of the corresponding element are assumed.

3.2. *Replacement modeling*

Aier and Gleichauf introduce the concept of the transformation model linking models of different EA states (Aier *et al.*, 2010a and 2010b). The transformation model describes which EA element from an older state is replaced by which EA element from a newer state. While Aier and Gleichauf do not provide an explicit information model, they give a graphical indication on the true nature of a transformation model. This indication mirrors the conception as shown in Figure 3, where a general dispersive type **Changing** is introduced. Each EA element instantiating a subtype of **Changing** participates in an acyclic predecessor-successor relationship. This relationship denotes which preceding EA elements are superseded by the EA element in consideration and conversely denotes the EA elements that replace the particular element.

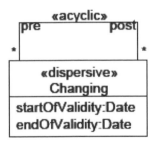

Figure 3. *Replacement modeling*

The predecessor-successor relationship complements the mechanisms of the period of validity in the sense that a superseding EA element must exist "later":

```
ctx Changing:
forall p in pre: p.endOfValidity < endOfValidity
forall p in pre: p.startOfValidity < startOfValidity
forall p in post: p.endOfValidity > endOfValidity
forall p in post: p.startOfValidity > startOfValidity
```

3.3. *Lifecycle modeling*

The topic of lifecycle modeling is already sketched in TOGAF as discussed in section 2 (The Open Group, 2009). A lifecycle thereby denotes that a single element of the EA evolves over different phases, of which most notably "development", "production", and "retirement" are used. Also the EA management pattern catalog (Chair for Software Engineering of Business Information Systems, 2010) supports lifecycle modeling for different EA concepts, such as business applications or the services provided thereby. The corresponding information model nevertheless is simplistic and introduces dedicated properties for delimiting the periods of validity for the individual phases. With the ontological primitive of non-rigid typing in mind, we can express the true nature of lifecycled EA elements in a more concise manner. The information model fragment shown in Figure 4 provides such an ontologically well-founded method of describing element lifecycle, by subtyping the abstract base type into distinct phases, i.e. non-rigid, subtypes. An actually lifecycled concept may in turn apply the fragment by adding the fragment's base type to the type representing the concept, thus inheriting the different phases.

When it comes to the question of corresponding constraints, the rich semantics of phased types allows any additional constraints (Guizzardi, 2005) to be omitted. In particular, Guizzardi not only considers phases as non-rigid types, but also demands them to be disjoint with respect to a given state of affairs. Thereby, he demands that exactly one of the phases applies at a particular point in time.

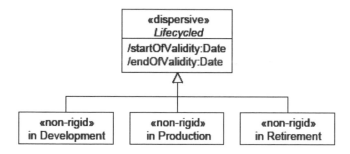

Figure 4. *Lifecycle modeling*

3.4. *Modeling activities, replacement, and lifecycle*

Superimposing the three types of EA transformation modeling as described above, we result in a modeling fragment as shown in Figure 5. In this fragment the simplistic replacement relationship is mediated via the relating concept of an activity. An activity in turn does not introduce or retire an EA element completely, but refrains the notion of the non-rigid type. This means that an activity describes that an EA element is put into production or into retirement, whereas the identity of that particular element remains unchanged.

With the embracing way of modeling activities, replacement, and EA element lifecycle described above, different constraints also apply. With the help of these constraints, we ensure that an EA information model using the corresponding modeling fragment is bound to describe ontologically consistent states of the universe of discourse. In particular, constraints on the periods of validity apply such that any phase is only valid for a period of time bounded by the corresponding starting or ending activities. An additional constraint applies with respect to the predecessor-successor relationship in a way that a superseded version must have at least one lifecycle phase starting earlier than the superseding version. A converse constraint holds for the end of one lifecycle phase. In particular the former rule calls for the phases' "development" and "retirement", respectively.

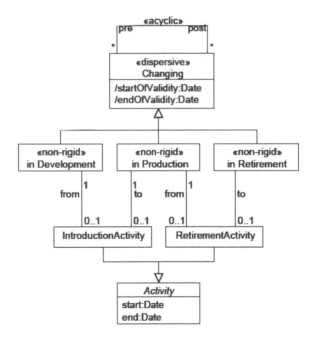

Figure 5. *Modeling activities, replacement, and lifecycle*

Revisiting the diffcrent ways for modeling EA transformation, we conclude with a critical perspective on the role of constraints. In the above model fragments, only the constraints that apply within the specific fragment are alluded to. Contrariwise constraints in the overall EA model also arise from the need to model EA transformation, especially, when different types in the EA are subject to transformation. Exemplifying this, we may investigate an EA model, where transformation planning should be applied to both business applications and infrastructure components. It is sensible to assume that in such a model the business applications are further linked to the infrastructure components on which they rely. With the two related types being subject to transformation, an additional constraint has to be applied to ensure temporal consistency of the model: each business application can only rely on infrastructure components with an appropriate period of validity. From a more general perspective, each relationship between two transformable types may be subject to an additional constraint demanding that the related instances are valid at the same time. Nevertheless, such constraints do not necessarily hold for any kind of relationship, as exemplified above with the "replacement" relationship. This yields a critical distinction between two kinds of relationship with respect to their temporal qualities (Guarino and Welti, 2000b):

- **synchronic relationships** that are only valid relating EA elements whose periods of validity intersect. In particular, relationships of that kind only hold for the intersecting period;

- **diachronic relationships** that may validly relate EA elements with non-intersecting periods of validity and hold independently of the elements' periods of validity.

Within typical EA information models such as the one presented by TOGAF (The Open Group, 2009), Lankhorst et al. (Lankhorst et al., 2009) or in the EAM pattern catalog (Chair for Software Engineering of Business Information Systems, 2010), the majority of relationships are synchronic in nature. Against this background, it is sensible to assume that any relationship is synchronic by default, whereas an additional stereotype "diachronic" may be used to denote this nature. We shall further assume that all instances of an EA type that do not participate in transformation modeling have an unlimited period of validity such that the constraint of synchronicity may natively be fulfilled.

Another interesting topic applies in the former information models, especially when they shall be used as "model fragments" for building an organization-specific and transformation-aware information model. The dispersive types and their subtypes used throughout the information models then gain additional semantics, in which they act as "type templates". This in particular becomes obvious with the example of the different lifecycle phases. The three phased types themselves represent an abstract understanding of lifecycle, which may generically be applied ("added") to a particular type in the EA information model. In fact, the phases actually become semantically meaningful with this application, while they themselves may only be regarded as placeholders for a real world type. This type is indeed not actually modeled, but results from the augmentation of the EA type under consideration. We nevertheless abstain from delving into the details of templating types, which may be regarded as a technical issue of formalistic model composition of fragments. With the paper's focus on different perspectives on modeling EA transformations, we call for an intuitive understanding of the presented fragments rather than a formal one.

4. Outlook

This paper is devoted to the topic of modeling EA transformation, whose importance reverberates through a multitude of different EA management approaches as shown in section 1. The state of the art in this field, as revisited in section 2, presents four different perspectives on transformation modeling, of which one – validity modeling – builds the common basis. In section 3, we showed how the different perspectives relate to each other and presented re-usable fragments for adding transformation modeling to arbitrary EA information models.

Complementing these discussions, we briefly revisited how transformation modeling influences the understanding of relationships in information models, hence devising the notions of synchronicity and diachronicity, respectively.

A key finding of this paper is the framework that displays the orthogonality of the different types of EA transformation modeling. This framework may be helpful not only for practitioners to understand the different ways of modeling transformations, which they may select from; but the framework also allows positioning and analyzing specific EA information models with respect to their coverage of the topic. Having complemented the different perspectives with fragments that implement the specific understanding of transformation in the particular perspective, the article further provides easy to use building-blocks for EA information model design. The distinction between synchronic and diachronic relationships finally provides a contribution to the ongoing question on the appropriate meta-language for EA information modeling (Buckl *et al.*, 2010b).

This latter point nevertheless deserves more research in the future. Synchronic relationships may not exist for the full period of validity of their corresponding relationship participants, but may have a more limited period of validity on their own. Refraining the example from section 3, we may assume that over its lifetime one business application relies on different infrastructure components without either the components or the application being retired in that time. In this context, the relationship itself becomes a subject of EA transformation being valid for a shorter period than its participants. At this point, one may enter a discussion, if it is really the *same* business application or if the application has significantly changed with the infrastructural relationship being revised. Whereas from a philosophic point of view, there may be good arguments for the latter, i.e. for the business application not being "the same", we see no benefit in such understanding. Instead, we would expect that future research in this field re-assesses the understanding of identity that underlies typical models and information models of the EA. The work of Guarino and Welti (Guarino *et al.*, 2002a and 2002b) seems to us to be a valuable starting point for further investigations. Complementary, Guizzardi's notion of the "relator universal" (Guizzardi, 2005) may be beneficially applied to resolve the issue of a relationship's period of validity. Nevertheless, the ontological aspects conveyed in the works of Guarino and Welti as well as of Guizzardi must always be mirrored against the pragmatic quality of the EA models, as those models are to be used by enterprise architects and to be implemented in EA management tools. Future solutions in this area should hence do their best in covering the true ontologic nature of the subject, but should also present re-usable building-blocks for EA information modeling, accessible and comprehensible for their future application.

5. References

Aier, S., Gleichauf, B., "Application of enterprise models for engineering enterprise transformation". *Enterprise Modelling and Information System Architectures*, vol. 5, 2010, pages 56–72.

Aier, S., Gleichauf, B., "Applying design research artifacts for building design research artifacts: A process model for enterprise architecture planning", *DESRIST*. Lecture Notes in Computer Science, vol. 6105, 2010, pages 333–348.

Brückmann, M., Schöne, K.M., Junginger, S., Boudinova, D., "Evaluating enterprise architecture management initiatives – how to measure and control the degree of standardization of an IT landscape", *Enterprise Modelling and Information Systems Architectures*, 2009, pages 155–168, Ulm, Germany.

Buckl, S., Ernst, A.M., Matthes, F., Schweda, C.M., "An information model for managed application landscape evolution", *Journal of Enterprise Architecture (JEA)* vol. 5, no. 1, 2009, pages 12–26.

Buckl, S., Ernst, A.M., Matthes, F., Schweda, C.M., "Visual roadmaps for enterprise architecture evolution", *The 1st International Workshop on Enterprise Architecture Challenges and Responses*. 2009, Deagu, Korea.

Buckl, S., Matthes, F., Schweda, C.M., "Conceptual models for cross-cutting aspects in enterprise architecture modeling", *5th International Workshop on Vocabularies, Ontologies, and Rules for the Enterprise (VORTE 2010)*, 2010, Victoria, Brazil.

Buckl, S., Matthes, F., Schweda, C.M., "A meta-language for EA information modeling – state-of-the-art and requirements elicitation", *Enterprise, Business-Process and Information Systems Modeling*, Lecture Notes in Business Information Systems, 2010, pages 169–181, Springer.

Buckl, S., Schweda, C.M., "On the state-of-the-art in EA management literature", Technical report, Chair for Informatics 19 (sebis), 2011, TU München, Germany.

Chair for Software Engineering of Business Information Systems (SEBIS), TU München, "EAM pattern catalog wiki", 2010, http://eampc-wiki.systemcartography.info (cited 2010-07-01).

Guarino, N., Welty, C.A., "A formal ontology of properties". *12th International Conference on Knowledge Acquisition, Modeling and Management*, Juan-les-Pins, France, 2000, pages 97–112, Springer.

Guarino, N., Welty, C.A., "Identity, unity, and individuality: Towards a formal toolkit for ontological analysis". *14th European Conference on Artificial Intelligence*, Berlin, Germany, 2000, pages 219–223, IOS Press.

Guizzardi, G., "Ontological foundations for structural conceptual models". Ph.D. Thesis, CTIT, Centre for Telematics and Information Technology, 2005, Enschede.

International Organization for Standardization, "ISO/IEC 42010:2007 Systems and software engineering – Recommended practice for architectural description of software-intensive systems", 2007.

Lau, A., Fischer, T., Buckl, S., Ernst, A.M., Matthes, F., Schweda, C.M., "EA management patterns for smart networks". *SE 2009 – Workshopband*, 2009, pages 79–90, Gesellschaft für Informatik, Heidelberg, Germany.

Luftman, J.N., Lewis, P.R., Oldach, S.H., "Transforming the enterprise: The alignment of business and information technology strategies". *IBM Systems Journal*, vol. 32, no. 1, 1993, pages 198–221.

Ross, J.W., Weill, P., Robertson, D.C., *Enterprise Architecture as Strategy*, Harvard Business School Press, Boston, MA, USA, 2006.

Schönherr, M., "Towards a common terminology in the discipline of enterprise architecture", Pre-Proceedings of the *3rd Workshop on Trends in Enterprise Architecture Research*. 2008, pages 107–123, Sydney, Australia.

The Open Group, "TOGAF ''Enterprise Edition'' Version 9", 2009, http://www.togaf.org (cited 2010-02-25).

Wagter, R., van den Berg, M., Luijpers, J., van Steenbergen, M., *Dynamic Enterprise Architecture: How to Make IT Work*. John Wiley, 2005.

Lexical, Syntactic and Semantic Comparison of Business Vocabulary and Rules

Iker Martínez de Soria* – Xabier Larrucea* – Naiara Esteban**

*Parque Tecnológico de Zamudio 202
48170 Zamudio
Spain
iker.martinezdesoria@tecnalia.com
xabier.larrucea@tecnalia.com

** Ribera de Axpe, nº 11, 211
48950 Erandio
Spain
nesteban@datinet.net

ABSTRACT: *The purpose of this paper is to present a process for comparing business vocabulary and rules written according to SBVR standard from a lexical, syntactic and semantic point of view. It involves the transformation of the SBVR vocabulary expressed in the SBVR XML Schema, the creation of an Abstract Syntax Tree that represents the SBVR vocabulary using the ANTLR language and the application of algebraic formulas in order to measure how close two set of business vocabulary and rules are. Furthermore, this paper presents a use case where an ICT company uses this process to compare its Project Management area defined according to SBVR standard with one process area of the ECMM Maturity Model.*

KEYWORDS: *Business Vocabulary and Rules Comparison, SBVR, ANTLR, Abstract Syntax Tree, ECMM.*

1. Introduction

The Semantics of Business Vocabulary and Rules (SBVR) was published as an Object Management Group (OMG) available specification in February 2008 (Object Management Group 08) and this specification was the first step in providing standard support for the "business vocabulary management" and "business rules management" tools that have recently appeared in the marketplace. These tools capture the business concepts and business rules in languages that are close enough to ordinary language so that business experts can read and write them, and at the same time formal enough to capture the intended semantics and present it in a form that is suitable for engineering the automation of rules (Raventós, 2009).

Unfortunately, these tools do not include a mechanism to compare automatically business rules[1] that are written according to SBVR standard, with other business rules also defined with the SBVR standard. The contribution of this paper is to present a comparison process between different business rules that have been specified regarding the SBVR standard. The paper focuses on the complete comparison process based on the creation of an Abstract Syntax Tree as a result of using the ANTLR tool for natural language recognition, which represents each SBVR vocabulary[2], and the application of algebraic formulas to measure how close the two SBVR vocabularies are. Furthermore, this paper presents a use case where an ICT company has proved the comparison process though the definition of its Project Management process area with the SBVR standard so as to compare it with a process area of the ECMM Maturity Model, which also has been written according to SBVR standard.

The next section provides an overview of the SBVR specification and the ANTLR language tool and section 3 describes the complete comparison process. Section 4 presents the use case and the final section provides a conclusion and discussion on future research.

2. Background

2.1. *SBVR*

The Semantics of Business Vocabulary and Business Rules (SBVR) is a new standard for business modeling of the OMG. The standard provides a number of conceptual vocabularies for modeling a business domain in the form of a vocabulary and a set of rules. The SBVR specification defines a structured, English vocabulary

---

1 From now on, business rules include the concept of business vocabulary.
2 SBVR vocabulary means business vocabulary and rules written according to SBVR standard.

for describing vocabularies and verbalizing rules, called SBVR Structured English. One of the techniques used by SBVR structured English are font styles to designate statements with formal meaning. In particular:

- the **term** font (normally green) is used to designate a noun concept;

- the *name* font (normally green) designates an individual concept;

- the *verb* font (normally blue) is used for designation for a verb concept;

- the keyword font (normally red) is used for linguistic particles that are used to construct statements.

The basic mantra of SBVR is *"Rules are built of fact types and fact types are built of terms"* which is clearly described in (Object Management Group 08).

2.2. *ANTLR (ANother Tool for Language Recognition)*

ANTLR, ANother Tool for Language Recognition, is a language tool that provides a framework for constructing recognizers, compilers and translators from grammatical descriptions containing actions in a variety of target languages such as C, Java, Python, C# and Objective C. In computer-based language recognition, ANTLR is the name of a parser generator that uses LL(*) parsing. ANTLR is the successor to the Purdue Compiler Construction Tool Set (PCCTS), first developed in 1989, and is under active development thanks to Professor Terence Parr of the University of San Francisco.

ANTLR allows for generation of parsers, lexers, tree parsers and combined lexer parsers. Furthermore, parsers can automatically generate Abstract Syntax Trees which can be further processed with tree parsers. From a formal grammar, ANTLR generates a program that determines whether sentences conform to that language. In other words, it is a program that writes other programs. By adding code snippets to the grammar, the recognizer becomes a translator or interpreter. ANTLR provides excellent support for intermediate-form tree construction, tree walking, translation and provides sophisticated automatic error recovery and reporting (Parr 07).

3. Business vocabulary and rules comparison process

This section presents the process followed to compare business vocabulary and rules according to SBVR standard. Next, a brief description of each stage is introduced:

- **XML Transformation**. The SBVR vocabulary is received in XML based on the SBVR XML Schema and this information is transformed into a text format, which satisfies the general text structures explained in section 3.1 of this paper, in order to make the analysis easier to the SBVR analyzer.

– **SBVR Analyzer**. The main goal of this stage is based on the treatment of the SBVR vocabulary received by the previous stage to create an Abstract Syntax Tree. The SBVR analyzer is composed of the following subcomponents:

- *Lexical Analyzer*. Once the XML has been transformed, the lexical analyzer breaks up the input stream of characters that belongs to the previous stage so as to put in order the vocabulary in representative tokens which are based on the SBVR specification.

- *Syntactic Analyzer*. Once the tokens have been identified and classified, the syntactic analyzer creates the first Abstract Syntax Tree based on the structure of the SBVR vocabulary.

- *Semantic Analyzer*. Once the Abstract Syntax Tree is created, the semantic analyzer, on one side, defines an iterator of this tree and, on the other side, creates another Abstract Syntax Tree that contains semantic equivalent meanings.

– **Abstract SBVR Tree Comparator**. This stage of the process works with two Abstract Syntax Trees applying some algebraic formulas in order to assess how similar both SBVR vocabularies are.

– **Final Results**. The process ends with a percentage taking into account three different levels: lexical, syntactic and semantic.

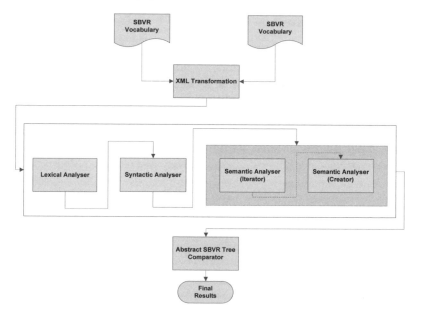

Figure 1. *Stages of the business vocabulary and rule comparison process*

3.1. First stage: XML transformation

The SBVR defines the vocabulary and rules for documenting the semantics of business vocabularies, facts and business rules as well as an XMI schema for the interchange of business vocabularies and business rules among organizations and between software tools (Object Management Group 08).

The comparison process presented in this paper is based on the idea that the vocabulary is expressed in terms of SBVR using XML documents that conform to an XMI-based XML schema created from the SBVR Metamodel since this provides a standard way of modeling the SBVR vocabulary and makes the interoperability between different systems easier. For example, considering the following XML:

```
<sbvr:designation xmi:id="rental" signifier="rental-t" meaning="rental-c"/>
<sbvr:objectType xmi:id="rental-c"/>
<sbvr:text xmi:id="rental-t" value="rental"/>
<sbvr:preferredDesignation xmi:id="charge"/>
<sbvr:thing1IsThing2 thing1="charge" thing2="rental/>
```

Figure 2. *XML of a noun concept*

The XML transformation stage generates this code: *"rental"_charge_;*

So the general text structure[3] for noun concepts is: *"TERM"_SYNONYM$_1$,SYNONYM$_2$,...,SYNONYM$_N$_;*

Regarding fact types and taking into account the next example[4]:

rental *has* **rental duration**
Synonym: **rental duration** *is in* **rental**

The XML transformation stage generates the following code: *"rental" #has# "rental duration"_"rental duration" #is in# "rental"_;*

So the general text structure[5] for fact types is: *"TERM$_1$" #VERB# "TERM$_2$"_SYNONYM$_1$,SYNONYM$_2$,...,SYNONYM$_N$_;*

---

3 Synonyms may not appear.
4 XML has not been included because the code is extensive.
5 SYNONYMN has the structure "TERM1" #VERB# "TERM2" and "TERM2" may not appear.

Finally, this example[6] shows a business rule written according to SBVR standard: It is obligatory that the **rental duration** *of* each **rental** *is at most **90 rental days***. Thus, the XML transformation turns the business rule into the following code:

<it is obligatory that> <the> "rental duration" #of# <each> "rental" #is at most# '90 rental days';

The transformation of business rules is more complex than the transformation of noun concepts and fact types. Therefore, Table 1 shows the general text structure related to SBVR rules that the XML Transformation stage may find.

Element	Example	Transformation
Term	**rental**	"TERM"→"rental"
Name	*90 rental days*	'NAME'→'90 rental days'
Verb	*has, is qualified*	#VERB# → #has#, #is qualified#
keyword (quantification)	each, some, more than one etc.	<KEYWORD> → <each>, <some>, <more than one> etc.
keyword (logical operations)	and, or, if, then etc.	<KEYWORD> → <and>, <or>, <if>, <then> etc.
keyword (modal operations)	it is obligatory that, it is necessary that etc.	<KEYWORD> → <it is obligatory that>, <it is necessary that> etc.
keyword (verb complexes)	must, always, never, may etc.	<KEYWORD> → <must>, <always>, <never>, <may> etc.
keyword (other keywords)	the, a, an, that, who etc.	<KEYWORD> → <the>, <a>, <an>, <that>, <who> etc.

Table 1. *Relationship between business rule elements and the XML transformation*

3.2. Second stage: SBVR Analyzer

This section presents the design of the three subcomponents which compose the SBVR analyzer. The principal aim of this stage is to create an Abstract Syntax Tree as a representation of the SBVR vocabulary that is desired to be compared.

---

6 XML has not been included because the code is also very extensive.

3.2.1. *Lexical Analyzer*

The main goal of the lexical analyzer is to break up the input stream of characters received by the XML Transformation stage into vocabulary symbols for the syntactic analyzer, which will apply the SBVR grammatical structure to that symbol stream. Firstly, the lexical analyzer defines a collection of tokens that contain all the keywords of the Annex C in (Object Management Group 08). Table 2 shows the type of keywords as well as examples[7] of ANTLR code.

Type of Key Words	ANTLR Code Example	SBVR Specification
Quantification	QUANTIFICATION_EACH = "each" ;	C.1.1.1
Logical Operations	LOGICAL_OP_AND = "and" ;	C.1.1.2
Modal Operations	MODAL_OBLIGATION = "it is obligatory that" ;	C.1.1.3
Verb Complexes	AUX_VERB_MUST = "must";	C.1.1.3
Other Key Words	OTHER_THE = "the" ;	C.1.2

Table 2. *Keywords defined in the lexical analyzer and some ANTLR code examples*

On the other side, the lexical analyzer also defines a set of rules to manage the text received by the XML Transformation stage. Table 3 shows some of the rules defined by this component even though there are also some other rules related to blank spaces, semicolons, underscores, types of returns, etc.

Rule Name	Algorithm
MEANING_KEYWORD	'<' ! (~('<'|'>'|'\n'|'\r'|'\t'))* '>' !
MEANING_TERM	'"' ! (~('"'|'\n'|'\r'|'\t'))* '"' !
MEANING_NAME	'\"' ! (~('\"'|'\n'|'\r'|'\t'))* '\"' !
MEANING_VERB	'#' ! (~('#'|'\n'|'\r'|'\t'))* '#' !
LETTER	'a'..'z' | 'A'..'Z'
IDENT	(LETTER)*

Table 3. *Some rules of the lexical analyzer*

---

7 Table 2 only shows one example of each type of keyword defined in the lexical analyzer and its ANTLR code, but really the lexical analyzer has implemented all the keywords of Annex C of the SBVR specification.

Considering the following example of SBVR vocabulary generated by the XML transformation stage:

"rental"; "rental" #has# "requested car group"; <it is necessary that> <each> "rental" #has# <exactly one> "requested car group";

Figure 3 a) shows the result of the lexical analyzer as a console output. Tokens of the SBVR vocabulary of this example are classified taking into account the type of keywords defined in Table 2 and also other unimportant symbols such as a semicolon even though it is necessary to recognize them. Numbers near the tokens represent an internal code used by the ANTLR classes to identify them. Finally, this result serves as an entry to the syntactic analyzer.

3.2.2. Syntactic Analyzer

The main goal of the syntactic analyzer is to create an Abstract Syntax Tree with tokens generated by the lexical analyzer. Therefore, it defines a collection of ANTLR rules so as to detect the likely combinations of noun concepts, fact types and business rules of the SBVR vocabulary mantra as well as the creation of tree nodes based on the lexical structures of the previous stage.

Firstly, Table 4 shows the ANTLR rules applied to create the arboreal structure of noun concepts taking into account the possible synonyms that may appear.

Rule Name	Algorithm
vocabulary	initVocabulary {##=#(#[NOUN_CONCEPT, "NOUN_CONCEPT"] ,##);}
initVocabulary	rule1V SEMICOLON!
rule1V	MEANING_TERM (rule2V)? {## = #(#[TERM, "TERM"] ,##);}
rule2V	UNDERSCORE! (IDENT (COMMA!)?)+ UNDERSCORE!{## = #(#[SYNONYMOUS, "SYNONYMOUS"] ,##);}

Table 4. *Noun concept rules*

Secondly, Table 5 shows the ANTLR rules applied to create the arboreal structure of fact types taking into consideration the possible synonyms that may appear.

Rule Name	Algorithm
fact	initFact {## = #(#[FACT_TYPE, "FACT_TYPE"] ,##);}
initFact	rule1F (rule4F)* SEMICOLON!
rule1F	MEANING_TERM rule2F
rule2F	MEANING_VERB rule3F
rule3F	MEANING_TERM
rule4F	UNDERSCORE! (rule5F)+ UNDERSCORE! {## = #(#[SYNONYMOUS, "SYNONYMOUS"] ,##);}
rule5F	rule1F (COMMA!)? {## = #(#[SYNONYMOUS_FORM, "SYNONYMOUS_FORM"] ,##)

Table 5. *Fact type rules*

Finally, the set of ANTLR rules applied to create the arboreal structure of business rules represent a very complex collection[8] of algorithms since this part of the syntactic analyzer must recognize all the possible structures of sentences that could appear. This means identifying a huge number of syntax combinations which is mostly solved thanks to the recursivity applied to many of the ANTLR rules.

Due to the complexity of this issue, this collection of ANTLR rules has been tested with business rules defined in the Annex E in (Object Management Group 08) in order to train them but not limited to other examples.

Figure 3b shows the resulting Abstract Syntax Tree of the syntactic analyzer. As can be seen, tokens of the previous stage are classified again but this time an arboreal structure is created. Once the SBVR vocabulary is divided into three groups (noun concepts, fact types and rules), the tree is formed by pairs of nodes where the father node contains the text of the type of keyword and its child describes the real content of the SBVR vocabulary, i.e. the text of business vocabulary and rules.

3.2.3. *Semantic analyzer*

The iterator function of the semantic analyzer is used to provide the creator part of this stage with a mechanism for covering all the nodes of the Abstract Syntax Tree. From a software design point of view, this component can be considered an elegant way of managing the ANTLR code since it can easily be reused by other analyzers. As well as the lexical analyzer, the iterator does not create an Abstract Syntax Tree but also defines many rules that are very similar to the syntactic analyzer.

---

8 More than 13 rules have been defined.

The creator function of the semantic analyzer extends the previous iterator and creates the final Abstract Syntax Tree, which provides the equivalent meanings of the SBVR rules. Furthermore, the creator invokes three different functions in order to establish equivalent meanings depending on the composition of the SBVR rule. The first function, which is called *addEquivalentRuleMeaning(...,....)*, is used each time a new rule is discovered by the creator and checks if an equivalent rule meaning can be done. For example, as is indicated in Annex C in (Object Management Group 08):

it is permitted that q only if p is equivalent to it is obligatory that not q if not p
it is possible that q only if p is equivalent to it is necessary that not q if not p
... may...only if p is equivalent to ...must not...if not p

Once this function has done the checking and depending on a great number of possibilities[9] regarding equivalent meanings, the creator adds a new rule to the Abstract Syntax Tree with the tag "EQUIVALENT_RULE_MEANING". Therefore, this component needs to create an Abstract Syntax Tree.

The second function, which is called *addEquivalentQuantifierMeaning(...,....)*, is used in the beginning of the rule in order to check the equivalent meanings related to quantifiers. For example, as is defined in Annex C in (Object Management Group 08):

at least (n) is equivalent to more than (n-1)
the is equivalent to a or an

In this case, the creator adds a new node to the Abstract Syntax Tree with the tag "EQUIVALENT_QUANTIFIER_MEANING". Finally, the last function, which is called *addEquivalentModalMeaning(...,....)*, is used in the beginning of the rule so as to check the equivalent meanings related to modal operations. For example, as is described in section 10.1.1 of (Object Management Group 08):

it is forbidden that p is equivalent to it is obligatory that not q
it is possible but not necessary that p is equivalent to it is neither impossible nor necessary that p

In this case, the creator adds a new node to the Abstract Syntax Tree with the tag "EQUIVALENT_MODAL_MEANING".

Figure 3c shows one possible resulting Abstract Syntax Tree of the semantic analyzer. As it can be appreciated, an equivalent rule and modal meaning is added to the original rule[10]. Thus, this stage generates the most complex arboreal structure

---

9 All these possibilities come from the SBVR specification.
10 This rule is different from the lexical and syntactic analyzer example (Figures 3a and b).

due to the great number of possible equivalences that (Object Management Group 08) defines in its sections.

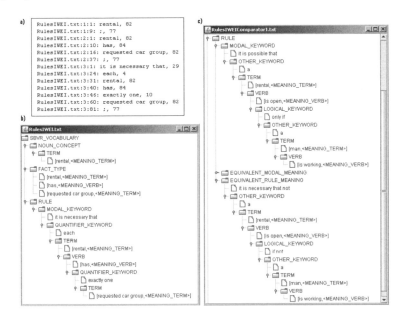

Figure 3. *Results of the SBVR analyzer*

3.3. *Third stage: abstract SBVR tree comparator*

This stage receives two Abstract Syntax Trees corresponding to the two SBVR vocabularies that want to be assessed. The comparison between them is done taking into account (Alloca *et al.*, 2009), where a method to compare two ontologies through the application of the three algebraic formulas shown below has been defined. The variable T is the threshold and the variables X_1 and X_2 are the ontologies given.

lexicographicallySimilarTo(X_1, X_2)
$$\frac{\left|Voc(X_1)\bigcap Voc(X_2)\right|}{\max\left(\left|Voc(X_1)\right|,\left|Voc(X_2)\right|\right)} \geq T \qquad [1]$$

syntacticallySimilarTo(X_1, X_2)
$$\frac{\left|X_1\bigcap X_2\right|}{\max\left(\left|X_1\right|,\left|X_2\right|\right)} \geq T \qquad [2]$$

semanticallySimilarTo(X_1,X_2)
$$\frac{\left|LC(X_1,X_2)\bigcap LC(X_2,X_1)\right|}{\max\left(\left|X_1\right|,\left|X_2\right|\right)} \geq T \qquad [3]$$

Due to the fact that SBVR is also related to the Ontology Definition Metamodel (ODM) as such it is indicated in Annex K in (Object Management Group 08), and even though there are appreciable differences between them it has been considered a good choice to apply the algebraic formulas of (Alloca *et al.*, 2009) since it provides a mathematic method that can be applied to the SBVR vocabularies in order to measure how similar the Abstract Syntax Trees created by the previous stage at a lexical, syntactic and semantic level are.

3.3.1. *Lexical similarity*

The application of the first algebraic formula (see formula [1]) is used to compare noun concepts and fact types where Voc(Xi) represents the text of a node of one Abstract Syntax Tree regarding a noun concept or a fact type and taking into account the synonyms that can appear (see Figure 4 as an example).

3.3.2. *Syntactic similarity*

The application of the second algebraic formula (see formula [2]) is used to compare business rules where X_i represents the sequence of type of keywords (see Table 2 and Figure 4 as an example). Owing to the complexity of the comparison at the syntactic level, it was decided to carry out a cross comparison (see formula [6]) and a lineal comparison (see formula [7]) in order to offer information that is complete as possible related to the similarity of business rules.

$$R_n \longrightarrow R_M \qquad \frac{|X_n \cap X_M|}{\max(|X_n|, |X_m|)} = C \qquad [4]$$

$$R_1 \longrightarrow \{R'_1, R'_2, \ldots, R'_n\} \qquad \frac{\sum (C_1 + C_2 + \ldots + C_n)}{N} = C' \qquad [5]$$

$$R_1 \longrightarrow \{R'_1, R'_2, \ldots, R'_n\} \qquad R_2 \longrightarrow \{R'_1, R'_2, \ldots, R'_n\} \qquad \ldots \qquad R_m \longrightarrow \{R'_1, R'_2, \ldots, R'_n\}$$

$$\frac{\sum (C'_1 + C'_2 + \ldots + C'_n)}{M} = T \qquad [6]$$

$$R_1 \longrightarrow R'_1 \qquad R_2 \longrightarrow R'_2 \qquad \ldots \qquad R_m \longrightarrow R'_n$$

$$\frac{\sum (C_1 + C_2 + \ldots + C_n)}{M} = T \qquad N \leq M \qquad [7]$$

3.3.3. *Semantic similarity*

The application of the third algebraic formula (see formula [3]) is used to compare business rules where $LC(X_n, X_m)$ represents the possible equivalences found by the semantic analyzer (see the *Semantic Analyzer* section and Figure 3c as an example). As well as in the syntactic similarity, the same concept of cross and lineal comparison is applied in this case with the exception of variable C of the formula below:

$$R_n \longrightarrow R_M \qquad \frac{\left|LC(X_n, X_m) \bigcap LC(X_n, X_m)\right|}{\max(|X_n|, |X_m|)} = C \qquad [8]$$

3.4. *Final stage: final results*

The final results present an overview of the business rules' similarity as an outcome of the application of the algebraic formulas described in the previous stage through a percentage representation of the threshold (T). Figure 4 in the next section shows the final results of a use case in an ICT company as an example of this stage.

4. Use case

The use case is oriented to the performance of a Process Area that belongs to a Maturity Model, which is being currently developed in the context of the COIN IP Project (COIN 07): the Enterprise and Collaboration Maturity Model (ECMM) (Martínez de Soria *et al.*, 2009).

The Collaborative Project Management Process Area of ECMM has been written according to SBVR standard in order to allow an enterprise to compare its process of project management, which has also been written according to SBVR standard, with the SBVR vocabulary of the ECMM process area through the comparison process presented in the section 3 of this paper. The final goal of the comparison is to check if the company satisfies the specific goals and practices of the ECMM process area.

The company that has participated in this use case is called Datinet and it has great experience not only in the implementation of quality standards such as CMMI Dev v1.2, ISO 9.001, ISO 20.000 and ISO 14.001 but also in the collaboration with other companies in order to develop software applications for important customers. Datinet is an ICT company located in the north of Spain with great expertise in different sectors such as Public and Local Administration, Public Health, Industry, Banking and Insurance and which represents its total commitment to quality in Services and Project Management.

Table 6 shows the number of noun concepts, fact types and business rules of the SBVR vocabulary that has been used to carry out this use case both for ECMM Process Area and Datinet.

SBVR Vocabulary	Noun Concept	Fact Type	Business Rules
ECMM Process Area	46	38	63
Datinet Project Management	35	23	52

Table 6. *Size of SBVR vocabulary used for the ECMM and Datinet process area*

Finally, Figure 4 shows the final results of the comparison process taking into account a part of the Abstract Syntax Trees[11] of ECMM and Datinet process area.

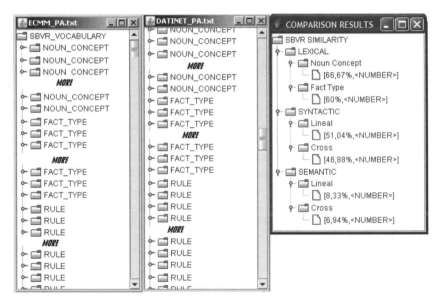

Figure 4. *Use case results*

5. Conclusions and future work

This paper brought into discussion the comparison of business vocabulary and rules written according to SBVR standard. The approach is based on the concepts of using an interpreter of natural language as ANTLR and the application of algebraic

11 Due to the great number of elements, only a part of the image is shown.

formulas in order to measure the similarity between two SBVR vocabularies. Furthermore, the comparison process presented in this paper also takes into account the XML transformation for the SBVR vocabulary defined through the SBVR XML Schema and final results based on different perspectives depending on a lineal or a cross comparison at the syntactic and semantic level. These points of view emerge from the idea of offering the most complete information possible related to the similarity of business rules. Besides, as a proof of concept for the proposed SBVR comparison process, a use case has been defined where an ICT company has written business rules of its Project Management process area in order to compare them with the Collaborative Project Management process area of the ECMM Maturity Model that also has been written according to SBVR specification. The results indicate that the concept, ideas and proposed SBVR comparison process are promising. However, there are still some challenges that deserve future research:

–   Development of more use cases with other companies in order to define the optimal threshold of the algebraic formulas and to train the comparison process.

–   Inclusion of a comparison process in the tools to allow other systems to decide if they want to interoperate because of the similarity of their business rules.

–   Enrich the Abstract Syntax Tree with special emphasis on the semantic equivalent meanings so as to have more comparison possibilities.

6. References

Alloca, C., Mathieu, A., Motta, E., *DOOR: Towards a Formalization of Ontology Relations*, 2009.

COIN Consortium (IP-216256), *Collaboration and Interoperability for Networked Enterprises.* Annex I – Description of Work, 2007.

Martínez de Soria, I., Alonso, J., Orue-Echevarria, L., Vergara, M., "Developing an Enterprise Collaboration Maturity Model: Research Challenges and Future Directions". *Proceedings of ICE Conference 2009*, Leiden – The Netherlands.

Object Management Group, *Semantics of Business Vocabulary and Rules Specification*, 2008.

Parr, T., *The Definitive Antlr Reference: Building Domain-Specific Languages.* Pragmatic Bookshelf, 2007.

Raventós, R., An Object-Oriented Approach to the Translation between MOF Metaschemas. Application to the Translation between UML and SBVR. Doctoral Thesis. Universitat Politécnica de Catalunya, 2009.

SA-Policy: Semantic Annotations for WS-Policy

Nicolas Boissel-Dallier*,** — **Jean-Pierre Lorré*** — **Frédérick Bénaben****

Petals Link, 4 rue Amélie
31000 Toulouse, France

{nicolas.boissel-dallier, jean-pierre.lorre}@petalslink.com

Industrial Engineering Center
Université de Toulouse   Mines d'Albi
Route de Teillet, 81013 Albi Cedex 9, France
{nicolas.boissel-dallier, frederick.benaben}@mines-albi.fr

ABSTRACT. *Web Services Policy is a machine-readable language for representing the capabilities and requirements of a Web service (Security, Quality of Service, etc.). Policies are about expressing behavioral qualities, so they can range dramatically in size or nature. In order to make Web service selection or ranking easier, it could be useful to add semantic concepts to policy descriptions. This paper presents an extension of WS-Policy specification which allows users to add semantic annotations into policy descriptions. This new specification, called SA-Policy, enables semantic reasoning on policies in order to compare customer requirements and provider capabilities or to consider user preferences.*

KEYWORDS: *SA-Policy, WS-Policy, Specification, Semantic Annotations, Semantic Matchmaking*

1. Introduction

Dynamic Web service discovery is one of the main purposes of SOA-based Information Systems. In order to find all the Web services which fit our needs, we have to match both functional and non-functional requirements/capabilities. Functional information is brought by WSDL description, while non-functional aspects are described by other standards such as Web Service Policy Framework (WS-Policy) [VED 07b]. Information from both description standards is only syntactic. Then, Web service search or comparison is limited to exact matching or similarity measures mechanisms.

[BER 01] was the first semantic Web initiative. It described methods and technologies to allow machines to understand the meaning (or semantics) of information on the Internet. Those mechanisms were quickly adated to semantically describe functional properties of services (such as OWL-S [MAR 05], WSMO [ROM 05], SAWSDL [FAR 07], WSMO-Lite [VIT 08]). Only a few ones focused on non-functional properties. This paper proposes a semantic annotation mechanism for WS-Policy description in order to make up for this deficiency.

First, this paper introduces WS-Policy, an available standard dedicated to the non-functional description of Web services (section 2). Then, section 3 presents SA-Policy, our semantic annotation mechanism for WS-Policy. Finally, after a survey on relative work (section 4), the last section concludes this paper.

2. WS-Policy overview

WS-Policy is a W3C recommendation made up of two main parts: (i) WS-Policy Framework which offers mechanisms to represent consistent combinations of non-functional capabilities and requirements [VED 07b] and (ii) WS-Policy attachment which allows users to name and reference policies and to associate them with Web service metadata constructs such as service, endpoint and operation [VED 07a]. This part presents this recommendation in order to point out the semantic lack of policy descriptions.

2.1. General structure

The WS-Policy vocabulary is relatively simple. It contains only four main elements and two attributes. However, policies introduce unique structural considerations that differ from the simple technical interface focus of WSDL and XML Schema. Because policies are about expressing behavioral qualities, they can range dramatically in size and in the nature of the policy content. Additionally, the flexibility and extensibility built in to the WS-Policy language allows its few elements and attributes to be combined into a variety of complex designs (see Figure 1). A policy expression can be comprised of one or more elements that express specific policy requirements or properties. Each of these is called a policy assertion. In order to group policy assertions, we use a set of features from the WS-Policy language known as policy operators. Policy expressions can optionally be isolated into a separate document, referred to as a WS-Policy definition.

2.2. *Policy assertions*

A policy assertion is a piece of service metadata, and it identifies a domain (such as messaging, security, reliability and transaction) specific behavior that is a requirement. WS-Policy only allows users to bind Web services with policy assertions defined in other specifications. Policy assertions are defined by several WS-* protocol specifications and applications: WS-Addressing Metadata, WS-Addressing WSDL Binding, WS-Atomic Transaction, WS-Business Activity, WS-Message Transmission Optimization Mechanism (MTOM) Serialization Policy, WS-Security Policy, WS-Reliable Messaging Policy, etc.

Each specification defines new assertions, its meaning as Policy uses and possible interactions/interweaving of assertions.

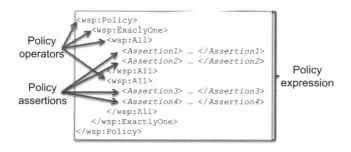

Figure 1. *WS-Policy information model*

2.3. *Assertion composition*

Policy assertions can be combined in different ways to express consistent combinations of behaviors (capabilities and requirements). There are three policy operators for combining policy assertions:

The wsp:Policy and wsp:All elements are similar. They allow the user to group policy assertions or expressions. These operators mean that all the behaviors represented by these assertions are required/provided. They can be seen as the Boolean operator AND.

The wsp:ExaclyOne element groups a set of policy assertions from which only one can be used. Using this element introduces the concept of policy alternatives as part of a policy expression. Each child element within this construct is considered as a distinct alternative in the overall policy expression. This element can be seen as the Boolean operator XOR (Exclusive OR).

Here is an example of Policy expression:

```
<wsp:Policy>
      <sp:TransportBinding>
            <wsp:All>
                  <sp:AlgorithmSuite>
                        <wsp:Policy>
                              <wsp:ExactlyOne>
                                    <sp:Basic256Rsa15/>
                                    <sp:TripleDesRsa15/>
                              </wsp:ExactlyOne>
                        </wsp:Policy>
                  </sp:AlgorithmSuite>
                  <sp:TransportToken>
                        <wsp:Policy>
                              <sp:HttpsToken/>
                        </wsp:Policy>
                  </sp:TransportToken>
            </wsp:All>
      </sp:TransportBinding>
</wsp:Policy>
```

Listing 1. *Security Policy example.*

In order to understand this last policy expression, we have to refer to [LAW 09]. In this case, we notice the Web service supports the HTTPS protocol in order to exchange messages. In addition, the precise user can encrypts messages using two algorithms: Basic256Rsa15 or TripleDesRsa15 (both define in WS-SecurityPolicy standard [LAW 06]).

There is more than one way to express the same policy. We could also switch Policy operators around in order to split transport binding policy in two smaller within each one possible algorithm.

2.4. *Policy attachment*

WS-Policy defines mechanisms for associating policies with various XML web service entities (WSDL part, Schema, etc.). On the one hand, it defines attributes that allow users to identify policies. Three similar attributes for wsp:Policy tag exist. They use absolute URI or Qualified name to identify resources uniquely. On the other hand, it makes available some policy reference mechanisms which enable us to bind XML Elements and identified Policies. (i) The first mechanism enables us to embed policy reference directly in the XML codes. The specification defines an attribute wsp:PolicyURIs and a tag wsp:PolicyReference, both used to add Policy references to any XML element. (ii) The second mechanism takes the opposite point of view and enables us to attach a list of targeted elements with the policy description. The wsp:PolicyAttachement tag embeds classical Policy Expressions and a new tag (named wsp:AppliesTo) which contains references to external documents. This mechanism allows the user to add Policy to any external element, without modifying targeted XML document.

3. SA-Policy specification

All assertions are fully defined in its specifications. Then, the lack of semantic is not a problem for the interpretation of unique assertions or for exact matching of consumer requirements and provider capabilities. As we saw in the previous part, there is more than one way to express policies and it could be hard to understand and compare them: (i) some assertions are functionally equivalent or close, (ii) policy expressions are not semantically defined... Even if the WS-Policy seems simple, there are a lot of possible assertions and combinations.

In order to make Web service selection/ranking easier, it could be useful to add semantic concepts to policy descriptions. This section defines the extension attribute for WS-Policy definition language that allows reference to semantic models.

3.1. SA-Policy model reference

In order to facilitate adoption and use of this new extension, we try to define our extension attribute staying close to the SAWSDL annotation mechanism [FAR 07] which is provided by W3C. SA-Policy Model reference can be used in every WS-Policy tag including assertions.

The SA-Policy modelReference owns the same XML Schema as SAWSDL modelReference with a difference namespace in order to use them at the same time:

```
< xs:attribute   name="modelReference" type="listOfAnyURI"/>
<xs:simpleType name="listOfAnyURI">
        < xs:list  itemType="xs:anyURI"/>
</xs:simpleType>
```

Listing 2. *SA-Policy* modelReference *XML schema.*

The value of sawsp:modelReference is a set of zeroes or more URIs, separated by whitespaces, that identify semantic concepts. Each URI is a pointer to a concept in a semantic model and is intended to provide semantic information about the Policy component being annotated. This specification does not define the logical relation between multiple URIs in the same modelReference attribute.

Pointed concepts could be written in any semantic representation languages such as RDF [MAN 04], RDF-S [BRI 04], OWL [BEC 03] or WSML [STE 08]. It only requires that the semantic concepts defined in it be identifiable via URI references.

3.2. Annotating policy description

There are many Policies assertions and future specifications that could define new ones in order to express new requirements or capabilities. With the help of these specifications, each assertion is clearly defined and users can refer to the assertion definition to understand it. Doubts about policy matching are mainly brought by policy expressions (groups of assertions) and by different ways to express one combination of policies.

The WS-Policy mechanism combines assertions surrounding them by only three different tags, which are in the middle of our target. So, the first use of `sawsp:modelReference` concerns those three tags:

```
<wsp:Policy (sawsp:modelReference="xs:anyURI*")?...>
    (<wsp:Policy (sawsp:modelReference="xs:anyURI*")?...>
        ...
    </wsp:Policy> |
    <wsp:ExactlyOne (sawsp:modelReference="xs:anyURI*")?...>
        ...
    </wsp:ExactlyOne> |
    <wsp:All (sawsp:modelReference="xs:anyURI*")?...>
        ...
    </wsp:All>)*
</wsp:Policy>
```

Listing 3. *Compact schema of embedded SA-Policy.*

If the policy description cannot be annotated (e.g. using an external policy file), the `sawsp:modelReference` can be extended to Policy reference mechanisms as follows:

```
<!-- Adding modelReference to wsp:PolicyReference -->
<wsp:PolicyReference URI="xs:anyURI"
                     sawsp:modelReference="xs:anyURI*".../>

<!-- Pairring modelReference with wsp:PolicyURIs -->
<XMLElement wsp:PolicyURIs="xs:anyURI*"
            sawsp:modelReference="xs:anyURI*".../>
```

Listing 4. *Compact schema for external WS-Policy annotation.*

In the last case, the `sawsp:modelReference` attribute has to be used at the same time. This case is problematic because of multiple possible URIs in both attributes. An XML Element can refer to many policies and each policy can be linked to many semantic concepts.

3.3. *Embedding semantic models in policies*

The URIs used in the `sawsp:modelReference` attribute typically refer to concepts in a semantic model that is external to the Policy description. However, the URIs can also refer to elements within the Policy description if semantic information is included in the document via the Policy extension element as shown in the following example:

```
<wsp:Policy>
    <rdf:RDF xml:base="http://example.com/onto">
        <owl:Class rdf:ID="MyClass"/>
    </rdf:RDF>
    <wsp:Policy sawsp:modelReference="http://example.com/onto#MyClass"/>
        ...
    </wsp:Policy>
</wsp:Policy>
```

Listing 5. *Example of embedded semantic in WS-Policy description.*

WS-Policy already allows extension elements within the `wsp:Policy` element so SA-Policy does not define an additional container. This example illustrates the adding of OWL/RDF-S description but any semantic language could be added in a new tag within `wsp:Policy`.

3.4. *Illustration*

In a classic case (without semantic annotation), we only could check if the provider's WS-Policy capabilities perfectly match with consumer requirements: assertions have to be equals. Thanks to semantic annotations and semantic tools (reasoners, matchmakers, etc.), it becomes possible to make service ranking according to expressed relations between assertions or other properties like user preferences.

Like other semantic annotation mechanisms (such as SAWSDL), SA-Policy allows us to affect ontology concepts or instances to technical description. The mechanism is simple in our case: both client and providers express their requirements or capabilities using specific ontologies, embedded or not in related service descriptions, as explained in section 3.3. Now, each provider can annotate policies with those concepts directly into policy descriptions, using SA-Policy (see section 3.2). Then, we are able to make service selection and ranking based on those semantic annotations and inferences on the ontologies, certifying interoperability between policy groups.

3.5. *Namespaces*

Table 1 lists XML Namespaces that are used in this document. The choice of any namespace prefix is arbitrary and not semantically significant.

4. Related work

SA-Policy focused on semantic integration in WS-Policy. Some previous work has already taken an interest in semantic policies. [PRU 04] compares XML and RDF for representing WS-Policy in order to encourage people to represent policies using RDF. It also presents an RDF schema for expressing WS-Policy directly in triples. That allows users to infer on policies but this approach is limited by RDF language capabilities. [PAR 05] proposes to express WS-Policy with OWL-DL ontology

Prefix	XML namespace	Ref.
owl	http://www.w3.org/2002/07/owl	[BEC 03]
rdf	http://www.w3.org/1999/02/22-rdf-syntax-ns	[MAN 04]
sawsp	http://www.petalslink.com/ns/2010/11/sa-policy	This
sp	http://docs.oasis-open.org/ws-sx/ws-securitypolicy/200702	[LAW 09]
wsp	http://www.w3.org/ns/ws-policy	[LAW 06]
xs	http://www.w3.org/2001/XMLSchema	[FAL 04]

Table 1. *Used XML namespaces*

language. This paper provides required mechanisms and tools to automatically translate policies from basic XML to OWL. This approach allows users to use full semantic policies but seems to avoid the link with described policies and web services.

Some other groups also worked on semantic policy matching (algorithms, matchmaking engines, complete frameworks). To support this, they usually propose means to add semantic into policy descriptions. [KAG 04] uses OWL-S semantic services coupled with a rule based engine in order to match policies. For support this, it extended OWL-S profiles and annotated it with semantic policies. In this paper, authors represent policies using Rei, an RDFS-based language for policy specification [KAG 03]. [USZ 04] developed the KAoS policy and domain services which is dedicated to specify, analyze and match policies. It proposes to represent policies using KAoS Policy Ontology, an OWL-based policy language, then use a specific rule language to infer on semantic policies. [VER 05] used a similar approach but replaced value-maps with SWRL rules. In order to express policies and to incorporate them into service description, it defines an URI-based mapping between assertion qualified names and semantic concepts names (written in OWL by preference). It also defines three new attributes to annotate policy assertions directly. With this approach, each assertion could be linked with four types of semantic concepts. This complexity seems heavy to use compared to our simplified approach. Then, this annotation system considers all the assertions allows additional properties while that is not always the case.

SA-Policy does not limit semantic annotation to any particular language or ontology format. [PRU 04, PAR 05, KAG 03, USZ 04] defines usable ontologies for expressing policies. Those ontologies could easily replace our policy ontology which focusses on a simple example.

5. Conclusion and future work

This paper presents a simple semantic annotation mechanism for WS-Policy. This mechanism is voluntary close to SAWSDL's one, in order to unify semantic annotations in WSDL and Policies then facilitate the hang of this extension. Like SAWSDL, SA-Policy is independent of the ontology expression language and it requires and enforces no particular policy ontology representation.

In our future work, we intend to propose SA-Policy to standardization organism in order to make it official. At the same time, we plan to develop an open source Java library, called EasyPolicy, for managing WS-Policy and its extension for SA-Policy handling. A similar project was already done by the same team with WSDL and its extension SAWSDL. Those open source libraries, called EasyWSDL and EasySAWSDL, are based on an extendable architecture which easily can be adapted to manage policies expressions, assertions and semantic annotations [BOI 09].

6. Acknowledgements

This work was supported in part by the SOA4All project (http://www.soa4all.eu/), funded by the European 7th Framework Program.

7. Bibliography

[BEC 03] BECHHOFER S., VAN HARMELEN F., HENDLER J., HORROCKS I., MCGUINNESS D. L., PATEL-SCHNEIDER P. F., STEIN L. A., "OWL Web Ontology Language Reference", *W3C Recommendation, WWW Consortium*, 2003.

[BER 01] BERNERS-LEE T., HENDLER J., LASSILA O. *et al.*, "The Semantic Web", *Scientific American*, vol. 284, no. 5, 2001, p. 28–37.

[BOI 09] BOISSEL-DALLIER N., LORRÉ J.-P., BÉNABEN F., "Management tool for semantic annotations in WSDL", MEERSMAN R., HERRERO P., DILLON T., Eds., *On the Move to Meaningful Internet Systems: OTM 2009 Workshops*, vol. 5872 of *Lecture Notes in Computer Science*, Springer, 2009, p. 898–906.

[BRI 04] BRICKLEY D., GUHA R. V., "RDF Vocabulary Description Language 1.0: RDF Schema", *W3C Recommendation, WWW Consortium*, 2004.

[FAL 04] FALLSIDE D. C., WALMSLEY P., "XML Schema Part 0: Primer Second Edition", *W3C Recommendation, WWW Consortium*, 2004.

[FAR 07] FARRELL J., LAUSEN H., "Semantic Annotations for WSDL and XML Schema", *W3C Recommendation, WWW Consortium*, 2007.

[KAG 03] KAGAL L., FININ T., JOSHI A., "A policy based approach to security for the semantic web", *The SemanticWeb-ISWC 2003*, 2003, p. 402–418.

[KAG 04] KAGAL L., PAOLUCCI M., SRINIVASAN N., DENKER G., FININ T., SYCARA K., "Authorization and Privacy for Semantic Web Services", *IEEE Intelligent Systems*, 2004, p. 50–56.

[LAW 06] LAWRENCE K., KALER C., NADALIN A., MONZILLO R., HALLAM-BAKER P., "Web Services Security: WS-Security 1.1", *OASIS Standard*, 2006.

[LAW 09] LAWRENCE K., KALER C., NADALIN A., GOODNER M., GUDGIN M., BARBIR A., GRANQVIST H., "WS-SecurityPolicy 1.3", *OASIS Standard*, 2009.

[MAN 04] MANOLA F., MILLER E., "RDF Primer", *W3C Recommendation, WWW Consortium*, 2004.

[MAR 05] MARTIN D., PAOLUCCI M., MCILRAITH S., BURSTEIN M., MCDERMOTT D.,
MCGUINNESS D., PARSIA B., PAYNE T., SABOU M., SOLANKI M. *et al.*, "Bringing
semantics to web services: The OWL-S approach", *SWSWPC'04*, vol. 3387 of *Lecture
Notes in Computer Science*, 2005, p. 26–42.

[PAR 05] PARSIA B., KOLOVSKI V., HENDLER J., "Expressing WS Policies in OWL", *Policy
Management for the Web Workshop*, 2005.

[PRU 04] PRUD'HOMMEAUX E., "RDF for Web service policy assertions", *Workshop on
Constraints and Capabilities for Web Services Position Paper*, 2004.

[ROM 05] ROMAN D., KELLER U., LAUSEN H., DE BRUIJN J., LARA R., STOLLBERG M.,
POLLERES A., FEIER C., BUSSLER C., FENSEL D., "Web service modeling ontology",
Applied Ontology, vol. 1, no. 1, 2005, p. 77–106.

[STE 08] STEINMETZ N., TOMA I., "WSML Language Reference v1.0 - Final Draft", *ESSI
WSMO Working Group*, 2008.

[USZ 04] USZOK A., BRADSHAW J. M., JOHNSON M., JEFFERS R., TATE A., DALTON
J., AITKEN S., "KAoS Policy Management for Semantic Web Services", *IEEE Intelligent
Systems*, 2004, p. 32–41.

[VED 07a] VEDAMUTHU A. S., ORCHARD D., HIRSCH F., HONDO M., YENDLURI
P., BOUBEZ T., YALCINALP U., "Web Services Policy 1.5 - Attachment", *W3C
Recommendation, WWW Consortium*, 2007.

[VED 07b] VEDAMUTHU A. S., ORCHARD D., HIRSCH F., HONDO M., YENDLURI
P., BOUBEZ T., YALCINALP U., "Web Services Policy 1.5 - Framework", *W3C
Recommendation, WWW Consortium*, 2007.

[VER 05] VERMA K., AKKIRAJU R., GOODWIN R., "Semantic Matching of Web Service
Policies", *SDWP Workshop*, 2005.

[VIT 08] VITVAR T., KOPECKY J., VISKOVA J., FENSEL D., "WSMO-Lite Annotations
for Web Services", *ESWC'08*, vol. 5021 of *Lecture Notes in Computer Science*, 2008,
Page 674.

Shape Feature-Based Ontological Engineering Product Models

Najam Anjum*—Jenny Harding**—Bob Young***
—Keith Case****

Wolfson School of Mechanical and Manufacturing Engineering,
Loughborough University,
Loughborough, LE11 3TU, UK

* n.a.anjum@lboro.ac.uk
** j.a.harding@lboro.ac.uk
*** r.i.young@lboro.ac.uk
****k.case@lboro.ac.uk

ABSTRACT: *Ontologies are being used for product modeling in the manufacturing sector. This modeling of engineering components in the form of ontologies is more efficient and manageable if a component is divided into distinct shape features. Experience from industry shows that interoperable product models provide a good foundation for knowledge sharing between design and manufacture. Use of Common Logic to build feature-based ontological product models shows that once the individual features are defined completely, the aggregated component can be built with little effort. This component model can then be used to associate manufacturability knowledge with it to be shared with the designer and other interested parties. Use of a standardized feature library can further enhance the interoperability of these feature-based ontological models if the independent ontology development parties commit themselves to this standard library.*

KEYWORDS: *Ontological product models, manufacturability verification, Common Logic*

1. Introduction

The information technology revolution has brought with it the digitization of everything. This trend has affected each and every sector of the business world and the industry of manufacturing is no exception. Manufacturing of engineering components is modeled to make the designing, manufacturing, maintenance, use and disposal of a product more efficient and cost effective. Due to the growing trend of outsourcing and collaborative manufacturing, data, information and knowledge sharing is becoming essential for today's business. This sharing is often performed between geographically distant and technically different parties. The independent development of data and knowledge bases induces heterogeneity and gives rise to the problem of interoperability. Use of ontologies to alleviate this problem has been successful to some extent but still, due to the differences in the ways these ontologies are developed and the vocabulary they use, semantic and lexical heterogeneities occur. These heterogeneities are the biggest impediment in the way of building a seamless information and knowledge sharing system. This paper demonstrates a method of developing ontology-based models of engineering components for the purpose of manufacturing knowledge sharing. It is proposed that the interoperability can be enhanced by the use of a standardized shape feature library. The domain ontologies belonging to diverse sectors then commit themselves to this feature library for seamless manufacturing knowledge sharing.

This paper first presents a brief literature review to identify the gaps in the field of ontological product modeling and then elaborates on the proposed methodology.

2. Ontologies as models

Modeling is an essential part of the intellectual activity of human beings (Silvert, 2001). It is an approximation of reality (Studer *et al.*, 1998). The challenge of artificial intelligence in information science is therefore the challenge of formalization of this approximation. The fundamental questions to be asked and answered in this regard are about the existence of things. In the field of metaphysics, the systematic explanation of "being" as an answer to this question is called an ontology (Gomez-Perez *et al.*, 2004). In this sense, ontology is a particular system of categories accounting for a certain vision of the world (Maedche, 2002) and a model of discourse participants (Nirenburg and Raskin, 2004). In the field of information science it is a hierarchical arrangement of concepts and their relations, together with the constraints on those objects and relations (Alexiev *et al.*, 2005; Antoniou and Harmelen, 2008). Most importantly, ontologies provide a common terminology that helps to capture key distinctions among concepts in different domains (NIST, 2000). In the domain of manufacturing engineering, a common vocabulary is therefore needed to capture engineering components in a formalized state. Previous work in ontological product modeling lacks full utilization of the benefits of ontologies for product modeling, such as open world semantics (Bock *et al.*, 2009) and it is therefore imperative to explore more applications of ontologies in the modeling of products.

Ontologies for product modeling have been tested before in one form or another. Horvath *et al.* (1998), for example, formalize design concepts by using an ontology paradigm. These design concepts include, along with shapes, design situations and functioning of design objects. In another work, Staub-French *et al.* (2002) formalize a vocabulary to define different types of design conditions and a feature ontology for construction and building products. In another relevant work, Vegetti and colleagues (2005) define a PRoductONTOlogy (PRONTO) to define product concepts, their relationships and required axioms in the complex product modeling domain. In a further extension of this work, Gimenez *et al.* (2008) introduce new concepts related to the specifications of mechanisms for aggregating and disaggregating different kinds of product-related data needed for Extended Supply Chain (ESC) logistics, as well as representing such data along product abstraction hierarchy (Gimenez *et al.*, 2008). Another effort in the product ontology domain is the work of Tursi *et al.* (2007). They propose product ontologies using the IEC 62264 and STEP 10303 standards. Syntactic and semantic interoperability is then said to be achieved by finding correspondences between the terms in two ontologies. Bock and colleagues (2009) at NIST have defined OPML, an Ontological Product Modeling Language. This language claims to overcome the existing shortcomings of ontological product modeling techniques. It treats product models as ontological classifications and is capable of capturing partial and high-level product descriptions (Bock *et al.*, 2009). Another effort at NIST has developed a Product Semantic Representation Language (PSRL). PSRL serves as an interlingua to enable semantic interoperability (Patil, 2005b). It mediates between two heterogeneous ontologies (Patil, 2005a, 2005b) to find correspondences between similar terms. Mappings are then established to connect terms in two ontologies. The important part of this work is the feature-based modeling example Patil and colleagues have presented which is similar to the approach presented in this paper. In a more relevant work, Catalano *et al.* (2009) propose an ontology-based formalization of the product design process. The relevance of this work here is again due to the fact that they also use the shape of products to structure product design workflow. This use of shapes, however, is not as detailed and comprehensive as presented in this paper.

Ontologies as product models are also being used for manufacturability knowledge sharing and concurrent engineering. For example, the computerized concurrent engineering system of Yoo and Suh (1999) uses: 1 – an integrated product information model (IPIM) using the STEP standard; 2 – a hierarchical database to store these models; and 3 – an integrity constraint validation mechanism based on EXPRESS, which is a formal information modeling language from STEP. The way they have used these three components fully resembles an ontological product modeling approach. Product feature-level interoperability issues are addressed in the work by Ma *et al.* (2009). They have developed a collaborative product development system in which a domain classification ontology is used to describe information dependencies across CAD applications. In another work, Matsokis and Kiritsis (2010) convert a Semantic Object Model (SOM) into an ontology for better sharing and exchange of product lifecycle knowledge. SOM is a product item-oriented model capable of storing data of the product's lifecycle. Very recently Dutra and colleagues (2010) have proposed an ontology-based architecture for collaborative design. Their architecture supports conflict attenuation during the early stages of a collaborative design process.

The research work reviewed above is in no way exhaustive and many other efforts can be seen in this area. The main aim of this review was to establish that ontologies have been and are being used for product modeling. The results of these efforts, however, need some more refinement. The work presented in this paper, therefore, differs from most of these efforts primarily in its level of detail in which shape features are defined and the product is modeled through their aggregation. Furthermore, the demonstrated use of ontological product models in manufacturing knowledge sharing is also what makes this work stand out from the rest. The next sections elaborate further on the importance of shape features and their use to model engineering components.

3. Feature-based ontological modeling of engineering components

Not only can knowledge be preserved through ontologies, but ontologies also help in producing pre-packaged sets of information and knowledge available to be used as building blocks (Neches *et al.*, 1991). These building blocks of information and knowledge may become the underpinnings of feature-based modeling of engineering components in the form of ontologies. Product features are found to be very useful in encapsulating engineering intent into computer systems (Ma *et al.*, 2009). This is because once these product models are defined, the related knowledge can be attached to them for use. For example, in the field of manufacturing, a model of an engineering component can have manufacturability knowledge attached to it to be used by the designer for taking design decisions. The methodologies and software tools to link this manufacturability knowledge with product models for intelligent design is currently one of the main collaborative design research problems (Li *et al.*, 2001). Feature-based design and manufacturing offers an effective way of resolving this problem. Its benefits have been well recognized and CAD systems largely adopt it both in the mechanical and freeform domains (Catalano, 2009). This is endorsed by the existence of some commercial applications like FeatureCAM developed by Delcam plc. FeatureCAM is a suite of CAD/CAM software based on feature-based manufacturing technology (Delcamplc, 2010). This software identifies shape features in a component and then generates the machining data. This is, however, a manufacturing support software and not an interoperable application capable of allowing a seamless sharing of knowledge which is the main aim of the proposed methodology in this paper.

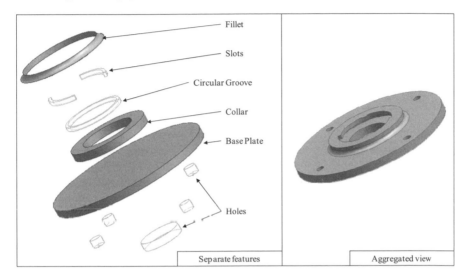

Figure 1. *Formation of a component through feature aggregation*

Feature-based technology involves the construction of an engineering component by joining together distinct shape features as shown in Figure 1. If these features are taken from a commonly understood feature library then the product model constructed can facilitate seamless sharing of knowledge attached to that model. The definition of these shape features in an ontological formalism is however not an easy task. The next section gives the detailed description of a methodology or language for defining features and resulting components in an ontological form.

4. A methodology for ontological definition of features and components

The feature-based ontological product modeling technique presented in this paper mainly consists of three components:

1 – the feature definition along with its characterisitcs, orientation, and placement in 3D space;

2 – the feature integration mechanism to form a component;

3 – the knowledge association mechanism to attach relavant shareable knowledge to the modelled component.

The task here is therefore to construct an ontology which includes the concepts, relationships, axioms and constraints required to define features, their associations and relevant knowledge. The first step towards the completion of this task is the selection of an ontology development formalism. The formalism selected here is the Knowledge Frame Language (KFL). KFL is a syntactic layer which sits on top of a logic syntax called ECLIF (Extended Common Logic Interchange Format)(HighfleetInc, 2010). ECLIF, as its name indicates, is an extension of the basic dialect called CLIF (Common Logic Interchange Format) which is one of the syntaxes defined in ISO standard 24707. This standard defines a family of logic-based languages under the name of Common Logic (ISO/IEC 24707:2007(E)). The following is a brief description of the KFL syntax.

4.1. *A KFL ontology*

A KFL ontology uses three types of directives to develop an ontology. These three directives are its class definitions, its relation definitions and its function definitions.

The classes in kfl are called properties and are defined as follows:

```
:Prop hole
:Inst Type
:sup    features
```

In the above statement, a shape feature named *hole* is defined which is a *type* of a class named *features*.

The second component of a kfl ontology is a relation which is defined as:

```
:Rel    hasDia
:Inst BinaryRel
:Sig    basePlate   diameter
```

Here a directive is passed to declare a binary relation *hasDia* which exists between a class named *basePlate* and *diameter*.

Finally, functions in a kfl ontology define additional entities by using one or more parameters. They are defined as follows:

```
:Fun    diameter_mm
:Inst UnaryFunction
:Sig    RealNumber -> diameter
```

These lines say that there exists a unary function called *diameter_mm* which is associated with the class named *diameter* and it takes *RealNumber* values.

Another essential component of a typical ontology is the axiom definition or rules. In a kfl ontology these entities exist as a combination of the three directives defined above. For example, the following lines state a rule which makes sure that whenever an instance of the class *basePlate* is defined, its diameter and height are defined as well. This rule makes use of the user defined class *basePlate*, and relations *hasDia* and *hasHeight*.

```
(=> (basePlate ?x)
(exists (?d ?h)
(and (hasDia ?x ?d)
(hasHeight ?x ?h))))
:IC   hard   "For   a   complete   description   of   a
'basePlate' both diameter and height are needed."
```

The last line here shows that this rule is a hard integrity constraint, hence "IC hard" which means that the height and diamter MUST be defined along with the definition of an instance of a *basePlate*. If these two parameters are not defined, the ontology editor gives an error message and terminates the process of instance declaration. The instance declaration in the kfl syntax is as follows:

```
(basePlateplate1)
(hasDiaplate1 (diameter_mm400))
```

Here an instance of the class *basePlate* is defined and is named as *plate1*. This instance is then assigned a value of 400 mm by using the relation *hasDia* and function *diameter_mm*.

A detailed description of how ontologies are written in a kfl syntax can be found in Changoora and Young (2010). Having described the ontology formalism, the three main components of the ontological product modeling technique are defined next.

4.2. Feature definition

Figure 1 illustrates a component divided into a number of features. For a complete definition of the component every single feature needs to be defined completely first. To do that the consideration of two essential elements in a product model is proposed. Firstly the dimensional characteristics and secondly the positional characteristics. The dimensional characterisitcs include the geometrical attributes like length, height, diameter etc. while the positional characteristics define the placement and angular direction of a feature in the 3D space. For the second element to be defined completely, it is proposed that a reference point and a reference line needs to be defined for every feature. Take for example the cylindrical feature shown in Figure 2. Its dimensional characteristics are defined completely by defining its height B, and its diameter A. For the positional characteristics a reference point RP with coordinates (x,y,z) and a reference line RL passing through the reference point with angles (α, β, γ) with x, y and z axes respectively are defined.

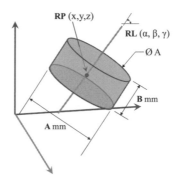

Figure 2. *Feature characteristics and orientation*

An example of the definition of a hole can be taken here as follows:

Description	Code
Defining a hole feature h1	`(hole h1)`
Assigning diameter to h1	`(hasDia h1 (diameter_mm 10))`
Assigning height to h1	`(hasHeight h1 (height_mm 20))`
Defining a reference point RP1	`(referencePoint RP1)`
Assigning coordinates to RP1	`(hasCoord RP1 (coord_mm 0 60 0))`
Defining a reference line RL1	`(referenceLine RL1)`
Assigning angles to RL1	`(hasAngle RL1 (angle_degrees 90 90 0))`
Associating RP1 to h1	`(hasRefPoint h1 RP1)`
Associating RL1 to h1	`(hasRefLine h1 RL1)`

In the above example a hole feature is completely defined by defining its dimensional and positional characteristics. For this to be valid, however, the concepts, relations and functions need to be defined first. Furthermore, some rules should also exist in the ontology which make sure that whenever a hole feature is instantiated, its dimensional and positional characteristics are defined completely. For the hole example above, thefollowing rule can be written:

```
(=> (hole ?x)
(exists (?d ?h ?rp ?rl)
(and (hasDia ?x ?d)
(hasHeight ?x ?h)
(hasRP ?x ?rp)
(hasRL ?x ?rl))))
:IC  hard  "For  a  complete  description  of  a  'hole'
diameter,  height,  reference  point  and  reference  line  are
needed."
```

As explained before, the "IC hard" directive makes it impossible to define a hole without defining its compulsory dimensional and positional characteristics. For the hole defined above the complete ontology can be seen in Appendix A. An important point to note here is that the position of the reference point and reference line within a feature needs to be standardized. This is necessary because the definition of a certain feature in an ontology of a different domain has to be based on identical assumptions. Otherwise it is impossible to establish the correct understanding of the knowledge shared because of the subjective perception of a feature by independent ontology builders. This issue is discussed in more depth in the sections to come. In the next section, the aggregation of features to form a component is defined.

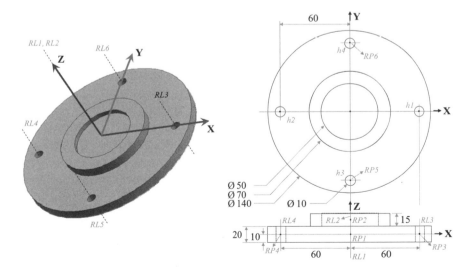

Figure 3. *An example component*

4.3. *Feature integration to form a component*

The positional characteristics of a feature model help in integrating them to form a single component. An engineering component in this regard is therefore a collection of individually defined features arranged in a way which gives the component its required shape and geometry. Consider the example part illustrated in Figure 3. Both the dimensional and positional characterisitics of all the features present in the component are clearly identified. The reference points and reference lines in these features are a certain distance and angle from each other. This means if one of the reference points is considered as a datum, all the other reference points can be positioned accordingly. Furthermore, as explained in the last section, the reference points and reference lines within a feature have to be fixed for use by independent parties to ensure the correct uderstanding of shared knowledge. In the example presented here, the reference points are fixed in the geometrical center of every feature while the reference lines pass through these reference points as shown in Figure 3. In this example, if RP1, which is the reference point of the base plate, is considered as datum reference point, then the coordinates of RP1 will be (0,0,0). Similarly if the reference line of the base plate is designated as the z-axis, all the other reference lines can be oriented accordingly. In this manner, the positions and orientations of other reference points will be as follows:

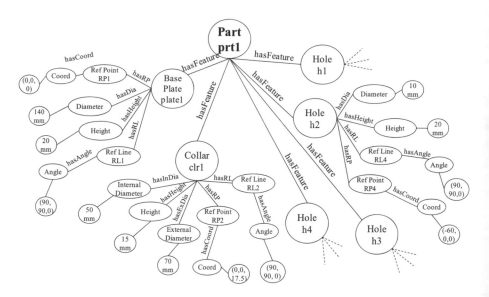

Figure 4. *Graphical representation of an ontological product model*

RP2 (0, 0, 17.5)	RL2 (90, 90, 0)
RP3 (60, 0, 0)	RL3 (90, 90, 0)
RP4 (-60, 0, 0)	RL4 (90, 90, 0)
RP5 (0, -60, 0)	RL5 (90, 90, 0)
RP6 (0, 60, 0)	RL6 (90, 90, 0)

The individual features and their positioning can be formalized in the same way as shown in section 4.2. The following lines, however, will need to be added for this aggregation of features to be a shareable ontological model of a component.

Description	Code
Defining the base plate feature	(basePlate plate1)
Defining the collar feature	(collar clr1)
Defining a hole feature	(hole h1)
Defining a hole feature	(hole h2)
Defining a hole feature	(hole h3)
Defining a hole feature	(hole h4)
Declaring the basePlate named plate1 as the datum feature	(isDatumFeature plate1)
Defining a component named prt1	(part prt1)
Attaching plate1 with prt1	(hasFeature prt1 plate1)
Attaching collar1 with prt1	(hasFeature prt1 collar1)
Attaching hole1 with prt1	(hasFeature prt1 hole1)
Attaching hole2 with prt1	(hasFeature prt1 hole2)
Attaching hole3 with prt1	(hasFeature prt1 hole3)
Attaching hole4 with prt1	(hasFeature prt1 hole4)

The code shown above is a reduced version of the original facts that need to be asserted to define the component completely. A complete description of all the features can be seen in Appendix B. Figure 4 shows the graphical form of the ontological model of the component in Figure 3.

4.4. *Knowledge association*

In the format used here to define the ontological product models of engineering components, knowledge can be associated in the form of rules. As a simple manufacturability example, consider a situation where a hole above a particular size cannot be drilled using the in-house facilities in a factory. If this knowledge is not made available to the designer at an early design stage, valuable time and money may get wasted in late design changes. This wastage can be prevented by building ontological knowledge bases in the design and manufacturing domain and creating a mechanism where manufacturability constraints existing in the manufacturing knowledge base scrutinize any design creations and modifications during the designing process. Feature-based ontological product models are very useful in these situations. The hole size constraint can be written in the kfl format as shown below:

```
(=>
    (and
            (straight_hole ?h)
            (= ?x (mm ?kx))
            (has_dia ?h ?x)
    )
            (lteNum ?kx 40)
)
:IC hard "Hole diameter should be less than 20mm"
```

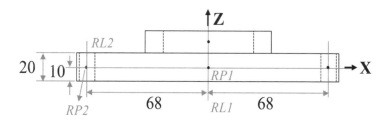

Figure 5. *Manufacturability knowledge example*

This is a very simple example but more complex examples where feature interdependency is involved can also be written in the same way. For example, a hole too close to the edge of the disc, as shown in Figure 5, may make a safe drilling process impossible. In this case a rule needs to be written that first explains the position of two features with respect to each other and then states the condition of non-manufacturability. This can be written as follows:

Description	Code
Starting the IF condition	```(=>```
Conditional AND	```(and```

Defining a basePlate feature along with its dimensional and positional characteristics	```(basePlate ?p)```
	```(hasDiameter ?p (diameter_mm ?dp))```
	```(hasHeight ?p (height_mm ?hp))```
	```(refPoint ?rp1)```
	```(hasCoord ?rp1 (coord_mm ?xrp1 ?yrp1 ?zrp1))```
	```(refLine ?rl1)```
	```(hasAngle ?rl1 (angle_degrees ?xrl1 ?yrl1 ?zrl1))```
	```(hasRefPoint ?p ?rp1)```
	```(hasRefLine ?p ?rl1)```

Defining the hole feature along with its dimensional and positional characterisitcs	```(hole ?h)```
	```(hasDiameter ?h (diameter_mm ?dh))```
	```(hasHeight ?h (height_mm ?hh))```
	```(refPoint ?rp2)```
	```(hasCoord ?rp2 (coord_mm ?xrp2 ?yrp2 ?zrp2))```
	```(refLine ?rl2)```
	```(hasAngle ?rl2 (angle_degrees ?xrl2 ?yrl2 ?zrl2))```
	```(hasRefPoint ?h ?rp2)```
	```(hasRefLine ?h ?rl2)```

Stating the conditions of hole and basePlate placements. Only the x coordinate of the hole reference point is different. The rest are equal	```(= ?xrl1 ?xrl2) (= ?yrl1 ?yrl2)```
	```(= ?zrl1 ?zrl2) (= ?yrp1 ?yrp2)```
	```(= ?zrp1 ?zrp2)```

Associating the two defined features with the same part	```(part ?prt) (hasFeature ?prt ?d)``` ```(hasFeature ?prt ?f)```

Calculating the thickness of the edge after drilling of hole	`(numDivide ?dh 2 ?result1)`
	`(numPlus ?result1 ?xrp2)`
	`(numDivide ?dp 2 result2)`
	`(numMinus ?result2 ?result1 ?result3)`

Closing the IF condition and opening the THEN condition	`)`
Stating the THEN condition which says that the edge left after drilling has to be equal or thicker than 5mm	`(gteNum ?result3 5))` `:IC hard "The hole drilled at the edge of the base plate should leave at least a width of 5mm for the edge to be strong enough."`

5. Discussion and conclusions

The brief review presented in this paper of the work being done on ontological product models seems to suggest that the inteoperability of these models depends mainly upon two factors. Firstly, the way the elementary shape features are formally defined and secondly, the way these shapes are used to model engineering components. This paper is all about the latter, i.e. it proposes a methodology of using shape features to define ontological models of engineering components. It is shown that if an engineering component is divided into distinct shape features, its modeling becomes very simple and suitable for it to be represented in the form of an ontology. The association of manufacturability knowledge, in this setting, is also very simple and straightforward. Since the component model takes the form of an ontology, all the benefits of an ontology for interoperability can be exploited. As far as the second factor, i.e. the definition of shape features, is concerned, a standard like ISO STEP 10303-224 (ISO/DIS 10303-224.3, 2003) can be used for feature definition and standardization. STEP provides a platform for feature-based designing and manufacturing, a formalized shareable ontological feature library, but still needs development. The technique presented in this paper is a step towards the development of such a standard library to be used by independent users to build their interoperable knowledge bases. This technique is fully adaptable if the STEP standard is used to define features. The integration of these features canthen be performed as demonstrated in this paper. Once a standard formalized library of shape features is available, enterprise interoperability can be achieved through compliance with that standard during the development of knowledge bases. Compliance, here, refers to both the compliance in the use of available shape features and compliance with the prescribed methodology of their use to model components and associating knowledge with them. Through this compliance, syntactic and semantic heterogeniety is prevented and thus interoperability achieved.

6. Acknowledgements

This research is funded by the Loughborough Innovative Manufacturing and Construction Research Centre (IMCRC).

7. References

Alexiev, V., Breu, M., de Bruijin, J., Fensel, D., Lara, R. and Lausen, H., 2005. *Information Integration with Ontologies: Experiences from an Industrial Showcase*, Wiley, England.

Antoniou, G. and van Harmelen, f., 2008. *A Semantic Web Primer.* 2nd edn., Mass.: MIT Press, Cambridge.

Bock, C., Zha, X., Suh, H. and Lee, I.., 2010. "Ontological product modelling for collaborative design". *Adv.Eng.Inform.*, 24(4), pp. 510-524.

Bock, P., 2001, *Getting It Right: R&D Methods For Science and Engineering*, Academic Press, San Diego

Catalano, C., Camossi, E., Ferrandes, R., Cheutet,V. and Sevilmis, N., 2009. "A product design ontology for enhancing shape processing in design workflows". *Journal of Intelligent Manufacturing*, 20(5), pp. 553-567.

Changoora, N. and Young, R.I.M., 2010. "The configuration of design and manufacture knowledge models from a heavyweight ontological foundation". *International Journal of Production Research*, 25(1).

DelcamPlc, FeatureCAM, [Homepage of Delcamplc], [Online]. Available: http://www.featurecam.com/ [24/12, 2010].

Dutra, M., Ghodous, P., Kuhn, O. and Nguyen Minh Tri, 2010."A Generic and Synchronous Ontology-based Architecture for Collaborative Design". *Concurrent Engineering*, 18(1), pp. 65-74.

Giménez, D.M., Vegetti, M., Leone, H.P. and Henning, G.P., 2008."PRoductONTOlogy: Defining product-related concepts for logistics planning activities". *Computers in Industry*, 59(2-3), pp. 231-241.

Gomez-Perez, A., Fernandez-Lopez, M. and Corcho, O., 2004. *Ontological Engineering: with example from the areas of Knowledge Management, e-Commerce and the Semantic Web.*, Springer-Verlag, London.

Highfleet Inc., 2010. *KFL Reference.* Highfleet Inc.

Horváth, I., Vergeest, J.S.M. and Kuczogi, G., 1998. "Development and application of design concept ontologies for contextual conceptualization". *Proceedings of ASME DETC,* 1998, pp. 1-16.

ISO/IEC 24707, 2007. *Information technology — Common Logic (CL): A Framework for a Family of Logic-Based Languages.* 1st edn. ISO/IEC 24707:2007(E).

ISO/DIS 10303-224.3, 2003. *Product Data Representation and Exchange: Application Protocol: Mechanical Product Definition.* ISO/DIS 10303-224:2003(E)

Li, W.D., Ong, S.K. and Nee, A.Y.C., 2002. "Recognizing manufacturing features from a design-by-feature model".*Computer-Aided Design*, 34(11), pp. 849-868.

Ma, Y., Tang, S., Au, C.K. and Chen, J.-., 2009. "Collaborative feature-based design via operations with a fine-grain product database". *Comput.Ind.*, 60(6), pp. 381-391.

Maedche, A., Motik, B., Silva, N. and Volz, R., 2002. "MAFRA - A MAppingFRAmework for Distributed Ontologies". *EKAW '02: Proceedings of the 13th International Conference on Knowledge Engineering and Knowledge Management. Ontologies and the Semantic Web,* 2002, Springer-Verlag, pp. 235-250.

Matsokis, A. and Kiritsis, D., 2010. "An ontology-based approach for Product Lifecycle Management". *Computers in Industry,* 61(8), pp. 787-797.

Neches, R., Fikes, R., Finin, T., Gruber, T., Patil, R., Senator, T. and Swartout, W.R., 1991."Enabling technology for knowledge sharing". *AI Mag.,* 12(3), pp. 36-56.

Nirenburg, S. and Raskin, V., 2004. *Ontological Semantics*, Massachusetts, Cambridge, The MIT Press, London.

NIST, 2000, The Process Specification Language (PSL): Overview and version 1.0 specifications, [Homepage of NIST], [Online]. Available: http://www.mel.nist.gov/psl/pubs/PSL1.0/ [8/24, 2009]

Patil, L., Dutta, D. and Sriram, R., 2005a. "Ontology-based exchange of product data semantics". *Automation Science and Engineering, IEEE Transactions on*, 2(3), pp. 213-225.

Patil, L., Dutta, D., Nistir, R.D.S., 2005b, *Ontology formalization of product semantics for Product Lifecycle Management.*

Studer, R., Benjamins, V.R. and Fensel, D., 1998. "Knowledge engineering: Principles and methods". *Data & Knowledge Engineering*, 25(1-2), pp. 161-197.

Silvert, W., 2001. "Modelling as a Discipline". *International Journal of General Systems,* 30(3), pp. 261.

Staub-French, S., Fischer, M., Kunz, J., Paulson, B. and Ishii, K., 2003. "A Feature Ontology to Support Construction Cost Estimating". *Artificial Intelligence for Engineering Design, Analysis and Manufacturing*, Vol. 17, No. 2.

Yoo, S.B. and Suh, H.W., 1999. "Integrity Validation of Product Data in a Distributed Concurrent Engineering Environment". *Concurrent Engineering,* **7**(3), pp. 201-213.

Vegetti, M., Henning, G. P., Leone, H. P., 2005, "Product ontology: definition of an ontology for the complex product modelling domain". *4th Mercosur Congress on Process Systems Engineering.*

Appendix A

Formalized ontology defining the shape feature concept of hole along with its necessary dimensional and positional characteristics and the constraints needed for their correct definition.

Description	Ontology Code

Defining the class named hole which is a type of shape feature. The superclass of this class named shape Feature needs to be defined earlier in the ontology	`:Prop hole`
	`:Inst Type`
	`:sup shapeFeature`

Defining a class named diameter which is a type of dimensionalCharacterisitcs. The superclass of this class named dimensionalCharacteristics needs to be defined earlier in the ontology	`:Prop diameter`
	`:Inst Type`
	`:sup dimensionalCharacterisitcs`

Defining a class named height which is a type of dimensionalCharacterisitcs	`:Prop height`
	`:Inst Type`
	`:sup dimensionalCharacterisitcs`

Defining a class named referencePoint which is a type of positional Characteristics. The class positionalCharacteristics needs to be defined earlier in the ontology	`:Prop referencePoint`
	`:Inst Type`
	`:sup positionalCharacteristics`

Defining a class named referenceLine which is a type of positional Characterisitcs	`:Prop referenceLine`
	`:Inst Type`
	`:sup positionalCharacterisitcs`

Defining a class named coordinates which is a type of positional Characterisitcs	`:Prop coordinates`
	`:Inst Type`
	`:sup positionalCharacterisitcs`

Defining a class named angle which is a type of positional Characterisitcs	`:Prop angle`
	`:Inst Type`
	`:sup positionalCharacterisitcs`

Defining a binary relation named hasDia between the classes hole and diameter	`:Rel hasDia`
	`:Inst BinaryRel`
	`:Sig hole diameter`

Defining a binary relation named hasHeight between the classes hole and height	`:Rel hasHeight`
	`:Inst BinaryRel`
	`:Sig hole height`

Defining a binary relation named hasRP between the classes hole and referencePoint	`:Rel hasRP`
	`:Inst BinaryRel`
	`:Sig hole referencePoint`

Defining a binary relation named hasRL between the classes hole and referenceLine	`:Rel hasRL`
	`:Inst BinaryRel`
	`:Sig hole referenceLine`

Defining a binary relation named hasCoord between the classes referencePoint and coordinates	`:Rel hasCoord`
	`:Inst BinaryRel`
	`:Sig referencePoint coordinates`

Defining a binary relation named hasHeight between the classes referenceLine and angle	`:Rel hasAngle`
	`:Inst BinaryRel`
	`:Sig referenceLine angle`

Defining the measuring unit through a function definition named diameter_mm. This function allows the diameter class to take real number values	`:Fun diameter_mm`
	`:Inst UnaryFun`
	`:Sig RealNumber -> diameter`

Defining the measuring unit through a function definition named height_mm. This function allows the height class to take real number values	`:Fun height_mm`
	`:Inst UnaryFun`
	`:Sig RealNumber -> height`

Defining the measuring unit through a function definition named coord_mm. This function allows the coordinates class to take real number values. Since it is a ternary function, three real number values can be taken for the signature class	`:Fun coord_mm`
	`:Inst TernaryFun`
	`:Sig RealNumber RealNumber`
	`RealNumber -> coordinates`

Defining the measuring unit through a function definition named angle_degrees. This function allows the angle class to take real number values. Since it is a ternary function, three real number values can be taken for the signature class	`:Fun angle_degrees`
	`:Inst TernaryFun`
	`:Sig RealNumber RealNumber`
	`RealNumber -> angle`

This rule makes sure that the height, diameter, reference point and reference line all characteristics are defined for every instance of class hole	`(=> (hole ?x)`
	`(exists (?d ?h ?rp ?rl)`
	`(and (hasDia ?x ?d)`
	`(hasHeight ?x ?h)`
	`(hasRP ?x ?rp)`
	`(hasRL ?x ?rl))))`
	`:IC hard "For a complete description of a 'hole' diameter, height, reference point and reference line are needed."`

This rule makes sure that whenever a reference point is defined, it is assigned the values of its x, y and z coordinates	`(=>(referencePoint ?rp)`
	`(exists(?c)`
	`(and (hasCoord ?rp ?c))))`
	`:IC hard "For a complete definition of a reference point, the values of its x, y and z coordinates need to be given."`

This rule makes sure that whenever a reference line is defined, it is assigned the values of its x, y and z angles	`(=>(referenceLine ?rl)`
	`(exists(?a)`
	`(and (hasAngle ?rl ?a))))`
	`:IC hard "For a complete definition of a reference line, the values of its x, y and z angles need to be given."`

Appendix B

This appendix shows the complete coding that needs to be written for a complete instance definition of the component shown in Figure 3 and graphically represented in Figure 4. For a description of the keywords used please see sections 4.1 and 4.2 of the paper.

```
(basePlate plate1)
(hasDia plate1 (diameter_mm 140))
(hasHeight plate1 (height_mm 20))
(referencePoint RP1)
(hasCoord RP1 (coord_mm 0 0 0))
(referenceLine RL1)
(hasAngle RL1 (angle_degrees 90 90 0))
(hasRP plate1 RP1)
(hasRL plate1 RL1)
(isDatumFeature plate1)
(collar clr1)
(hasInDia clr1 (inDia_mm 50))
(hasExDia clr1 (exDia_mm 70))
(hasHeight clr1 (height_mm 15))
(referencePoint RP2)
(hasCoord RP2 (coord_mm 0 0 17.5))
(referenceLine RL2)
(hasAngle RL2 (angle_degrees 90 90 0))
(hasRP clr1 RP2)
(hasRL clr1 RL2)
(hole h1)
(hasDia h1 (diameter_mm 10))
(hasHeight h1 (height_mm 20))
(referencePoint RP3)
(hasCoord RP3 (coord_mm 60 0 0))
(referenceLine RL3)
(hasAngle RL3 (angle_degrees
90 90 0))
(hasRP h1 RP3)(hasRL h1 RL3)
(hole h2)
(hasDia h2 (diameter_mm 10))
(hasHeight h2 (height_mm 20))
```

Continues in the next column......

```
(referencePoint RP4)
(hasCoord RP4 (coord_mm -60 0 0))
(referenceLine RL4)
(hasAngle RL4 (angle_degrees 90
90 0))
(hasRP h2 RP4)
(hasRL h2 RL4)
(hole h3)
(hasDia h3 (diameter_mm 10))
(hasHeight h3 (height_mm 20))
(referencePoint RP5)
(hasCoord RP5 (coord_mm 0 -60 0))
(referenceLine RL5)
(hasAngle RL5 (angle_degrees 90
90 0))
(hasRP h3 RP5)
(hasRL h3 RL5)
(hole h4)
(hasDia h4 (diameter_mm 10))
(hasHeight h4 (height_mm 20))
(referencePoint RP6)
(hasCoord RP6 (coord_mm 0 60 0))
(referenceLine RL6)
(hasAngle RL6 (angle_degrees 90
90 0))
(hasRP h4 RP6)
(hasRL h4 RL6)
(part prt1)
(hasFeature prt1 plate1)
(hasFeature prt1 clr1)
(hasFeature prt1 h1)
(hasFeature prt2 h2)
(hasFeature prt3 h3)
(hasFeature prt4 h4)
```

Wrapping Legacy Systems to Support SOA Migration Using Enterprise Service Bus

Timo Kokko – Jenni Vainio – Tarja Systä

Tampere University of Technology
Department of Software Systems
Finland
{timo.kokko,jenni.vainio,tarja.systa}@tut.fi

ABSTRACT: *Today there are a large number of so-called legacy systems which are coded over several years or even decades and are valuable business critical software systems. Maintaining those systems can be a daunting task since many of the systems lack documentation, the programmers no longer work in the organizations and the technologies can be very old. Still there is a constant need to develop new features to the existing legacy systems and to make them more interoperable with other systems. Service-oriented architecture is an architectural style that fosters the re-use of the existing legacy assets and enables co-existence of the old and new architectures. In this study we will use a bottom-up approach to wrap an existing legacy supply chain management system by using an enterprise service bus. We discuss the lessons learnt from this project, the impact of using a middleware solution and the feasibility of the chosen approach.*

KEYWORDS: *Service-Oriented Architecture, Legacy System, Migration, Enterprise Service Bus.*

1. Introduction

Migration from the legacy architecture to SOA has been widely studied and can be carried out iteratively and using many different technologies [1]-[7]. The existing application interfaces can be wrapped to be re-used along with the new service-oriented application services. Currently, Web services are the most prominent technology to implement the wrapping. Web service technology relies on standards agreed during many years of standardization effort and thus provides a reliable base to establish future architecture [8].

Message-oriented middleware (MOM) products have a long history in enterprise application integration and the feasibility of using Web services to promote the interoperability of applications has not gone unnoticed by the MOM vendors. Almost all MOM vendors have incorporated Web service technology into the integration platform [9]. In the era of SOA, the middleware vendors have updated their arcane EAI platforms to SOA platforms, which are referred to as enterprise service buses. The enterprise service bus concept and what it should contain is under debate, but it has also been regarded as a feasible approach to SOA implementation in the literature [10].

Along with the different technologies, there are also many different approaches to SOA migration. One can start from top-down modeling the business processes of the organization and identifying the business service candidates from the modeled business processes [11]. This approach, however, requires a considerable forward planning effort and thus according to recent studies is seldom used [12]. The bottom-up approach starts from identifying the service candidates from the existing applications. This, however, often results in services that are not as reusable as in the top-down approach. The meet-in-the-middle approach combines the two approaches by modeling the required service candidates business case by business case, thus resulting in more re-usable services than in the bottom-up approach, but in a shorter time than in the top-down approach [13].

In this paper we will present how an ordering process of an existing legacy system for supply chain management was migrated to support service-oriented architecture by wrapping the existing legacy interfaces as Web services, using an enterprise service bus and a bottom-up approach. After describing the wrapping process, we will evaluate the result of the migration effort and present best practices and lessons learned during the wrapping. Our results indicate that the bottom-up approach is a very fast and reliable way of reusing the existing business logic, when using an enterprise service bus to implement the wrapping, the further abstraction can be quite easily added later on, the performance impact of the service bus in the bottom-up approach is relatively small. The wrapping tools are still quite immature and a good documentation of the wrapping process can help to share the known issues and to shorten the lead time to develop the wrappings.

The remainder of the paper is organized as follows. In section 2, we review the literature related to SOA migration approaches and wrapping. In section 3, we present the legacy system and explain its structure and challenges. In section 4, we explain the actual wrapping process and the tools utilized in the wrapping. In section 5, we discuss the findings and finally, and in section 6 we present the conclusions.

2. SOA migration approaches

Several approaches have been proposed and experience reports presented on migrating legacy systems to Web services, e.g. [14]–[16]. These approaches use static reverse engineering techniques for identifying potential services, relying typically on data flow analyses, such as so-called data stripping, to identify all parts in the source code that affect a specific data structure or data content. Then, wrapping techniques are used to provide client applications with an accessible interface for the identified service. By wrapping, only minimal, if any, modifications to the original software need to be done. This was also one of the underlying aims in a case reported in this paper; minimizing the changes is both a safe and fast approach to migrate a legacy system to Web services or SOA in general. On the other hand, they do not really utilize all SOA benefits, since the subject system's structure remains the same, no matter how "SOA-like" it really is in practice.

Also run-time behavior analysis techniques can be used to aid the migration of legacy systems to Web services [17, 18]. These approaches are based on monitoring the user interactions while running the subject system, thus studying the subject legacy system as a black box and not requiring source code analysis. A summary of the interaction is typically given as a finite state automaton. The service wrapper is then composed by interpreting the state automaton. These approaches do not require any changes to the subject system.

A survey on approaches reported on migrating legacy system to SOA has been presented by Almonaies *et al.* [19]. On the wrapping-based techniques they also emphasize that those approaches are cost-effective and fast. As downsides, they point out, as also observed in our case example, that these approaches do not change the fundamental characteristics of the legacy applications and that they do not solve problems already present, such as problems in maintenance and upgrading.

When using wrapping to expose the functionality of the legacy system, there are many considerations to keep in mind. For example, the concept of a session, security, and the way the process in the user interface is maintained have to be dealt with somehow. Also, if wrapping is done bottom-up in a 1:1 ratio to the existing modules, the consumer applications can become too chatty and are bound to the legacy system's logic on how to call the underlying services. This is probably not a good solution for maintenance reasons and it may have serious performance impacts if fulfilling one operation causes several calls to the backend [20].

The use of Web services to wrap the legacy logic is standards-based and thus, reusable, but it is not the fastest technology that can be used. Using JMS or other more low level protocols could be more efficient, but could cause problems in terms of interoperability, because JMS libraries are often extended by tool vendors and require the use of proprietary libraries. Web services are also supported by most tool vendors and thus, provide a reliable platform for new SOA-based applications [21].

Modern middleware platforms combine the standard-based Web service approach and performance by exposing the lower level protocol handling as Web services to the consumer applications. Thus, the arcane and performing brokering architecture of the middleware platforms can be leveraged as distributed nodes across several data centers to improve reliability and load balancing. The complexity of the distributed nodes is abstracted and called the bus topology. The bus topology enables that the integration developers do not have to concern themselves with the underlying brokering infrastructure and can develop the integrations using SOA standards like WSDL, XML, XSLT, XPATH and XQUERY [9]. The use of the bus topology on top of the existing brokering infrastructure and the leveraging of the legacy interfaces as services have led to the coining of the term enterprise service bus [22].

The enterprise service bus is an SOA platform that works as a loosely coupled mediation layer between service consumers and providers [23]. They provide connectivity, sequencing, transformation, location transparency, quality of service, and security [24]. Connectivity is needed when working with heterogeneous backend systems that support only low level protocols like JMS. Sometimes the backend system does not even have an application interface that could be used for interoperability and a database connection is the only option. Sequencing is used when the ordering of the messages is required for the backend system and the backend cannot handle the ordering itself. Transformations are required when the consumer and provider do not understand the same message structure. The use of a canonical data model can often reduce the number of transformations between systems, but still the message has to be transformed if both of the systems do not use the same model. The location independence is an important feature that prevents the changes in the infrastructure from causing ripple effects to the whole application landscape. The location transparency is often addressed using intermediary services and routing which are provided by the enterprise service bus. Quality of Service is a critical factor in integrating mission critical systems. The Quality of Service provides business continuity through transactions, error handling and re-sending of the messages. Finally, security is a critical factor for any business critical system that contains sensitive information.

The use of an enterprise service bus enables the migration to start from the technical wrapping of the legacy functionality and enables the later abstraction of the services through mediation. Thus the enterprise service bus can be used to enable the meet-in-the-middle approach. The enterprise service bus can be used to create an application service layer, entity service layer and orchestration layer [25].

The application service layer is used to connect to the legacy application logic, the entity service layer is used to compose the application services into business entities and thus, hide the complexity, and finally the orchestration layer is used to create business tasks or process services.

3. The legacy system

The legacy system to be migrated, a supply chain management system, has ERP, SCM and WMS modules as well as book keeping which are all tailored to the different user organizations of the system. The system's development was started in the late 1980s and it was acquired from its original vendor in the late 1990s. The system is programmed in Advanced Business Language (ABL) and runs on the Open Edge application platform, provided by Progress Software. The legacy system has about 15,500 program files and consists of about 5.8 million lines of source code. Some of the code is common to all of the user organizations and some is completely tailored. The common source code also contains user organization specific variations and version history information which bloats the source code and makes it difficult to understand.

The legacy source code contains many language specific constructs like shared variables that are used for maintaining the session handling of the system that make the system difficult to learn and maintain. The shared variables make it difficult to comprehend what the program does. The data is transferred in shared database buffers, making it difficult to run a program separately from the whole application unless the buffers are initialized and the data is fetched before calling the program. Figure 1 describes the architecture of the system, which resembles closely the "big ball of mud" anti-pattern [26].

The code, even though it is hard to read and understand, let alone modify and maintain, has a great deal of value. It encapsulates a lot of valuable business logic; but the code, like many other legacy systems, lacks documentation. Because of the lack of documentation and the vast amount of code, the complete re-engineering of the system would be an enormous task, not to mention expensive and risky.

Fortunately, in the past, the legacy system's user interface has been renovated to support a Web user interface so the architecture has been migrated partially from monolithic architecture to client server architecture. This makes the wrapping easier, because the user interface logic is separated from the business and database access logic. The application logic between user interface and business logic is called business modules.

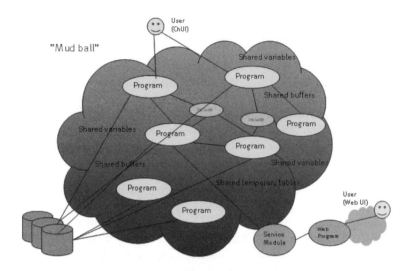

Figure 1. *Architecture of the legacy system*

The user interface logic consists of over 650,000 lines of source code. The user interface programs are hard to maintain since there is HTML, user interface code, JavaScript and also style sheets mixed together. This is the reason why the maintenance and development of the user interfaces has become time consuming and expensive. A more structured and powerful user interface technology is required to reduce the lead time of developing new user interfaces. It is also easier to find skilled developers for new user interface technologies.

In the past, the legacy system has been integrated into many systems, like SAP, and there are a large number of point-to-point connections implemented inside the legacy system's code base. There is also a home-grown business adapter, which contains proprietary transformation and communication logic that is hard to maintain. Since more and more connections are needed, the scalability of these home-grown integration solutions is starting to become limited. There has been a need for more advanced and flexible techniques.

4. Migration of the legacy system

The migration of the legacy system's ordering process was carried out in a project to an existing customer to enable shopping cart-like functionality and a new look and feel for the user interface. The legacy system's existing user interface was designed for B2B users and required training to be used efficiently. The user interface contained too much information for the end users and had to be simplified.

The wrapping process was stated with a comprehensive study of the requirements for the new interface. The requirements were turned into use cases presented in Figure 2. In the new user interface the user can search and list products, add the products into the shopping cart, and investigate product information more closely using a product card view. The user can list orders and view individual orders in more detail. The user can modify the number of products in the shopping cart, remove items from the cart, and empty the whole cart. When the shopping cart is finished, the user can send the shopping cart to be accepted by a user with acceptor role. The acceptor can confirm or decline the shopping cart. Once the shopping cart has been accepted the order is processed further in the legacy system.

Next, the entities were identified from the use cases and presented as a domain model, shown in Figure 2. As illustrated in the domain model, there can be several delivery addresses per customer from which the user can select the appropriate one for the order. An order may contain one or more order lines, each of which contains a product. The product always belongs to a product group which can be used as a search criterion. The domain model helped to identify the business entity services needed for the functionality.

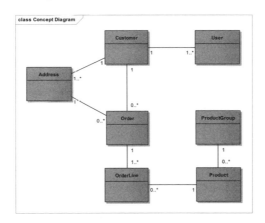

Figure 2. *Domain model of the shopping cart functionality*

The third step in the wrapping process was to identify the existing service modules in the legacy system that needed to be wrapped. Figure 3 illustrates all the functionality related to the handling of the shopping cart and service modules related to the functions. Creating Cart uses one legacy component sob609, which is the order creation component in the legacy system. AddProduct in turn uses two legacy components stb500 and sob620. Stb500 is used for the product information that is stored by sob620 to the order. ModifyCart is a complex task that requires the co-operation of six legacy components. Sob610 updates the order header information, sob620 the order lines, meb300 the comments of the order, stb582 product information and stb580 the product's warehouse information such as stock balance. Module help/webmenu.p is a special program used for populating selection menus.

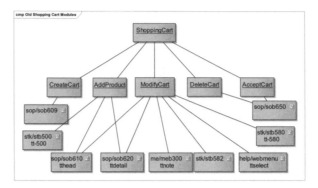

Figure 3. *Legacy service modules related to shopping cart*

Figure 4 shows the product modules and service modules related to the product functionality. Product information is also divided between several different modules. This is because there is so much information on different product properties. Also, there is a need to search larger databases quickly to find a product very fast. The search page has drop down menus, so there has to be a call to the help/webmenu. The quick search module is stk/stb582, which uses word indexes to find products. The basic information of a product can be brought up with stk/stb500, and stk/stb580 handles the stock information of products.

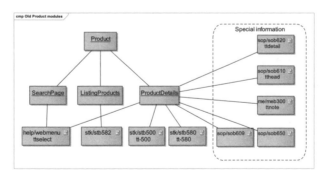

Figure 4. *Legacy service modules related to product*

After identifying the service modules to be wrapped, the data flows and interfaces between the components had to be analyzed. For instance, the order header information is handled by sop/sob610 and the lines by sop/sob620. This means that there have to be two calls when fetching the information of an order. For instance, the same modules fetching and saving the information they handle are used when listing and browsing order information. These two modules represent the normal interface of service modules; that is, they transmit data in input and output parameters and in a dynamic data structure called a temporary table. The whole interface is presented below:

- (input) method (fetch, next, previous, save, delete …),

- (input) session id (each session has a unique id number),

- (input-output) search method (which way to search data, 1, 2, …),

- (input) search parameters (semicolon separated list of search phrases),

- (input) number of results wanted (how many records),

- (input) handling instructions (special instructions),

- (input-output) record id (if we already know the record id),

- (input-output) temporary table (which has the data),

- (output) buttons available (for the UI, the directions we can offer to the user),

- (output) error message,

- (output) error field (which field caused the previous error message), and

- (output) error number.

There are also modules with a slightly different interface. They do not transfer temporary tables but only take the record id number to which the operation is to be targeted. This is the case for example with the module sop/sob650, which deletes and also accepts orders. It takes the order header address and performs the operations if it finds the corresponding record in the database.

After careful analysis, the actual wrapping could begin. Sonic ESB is an enterprise service bus product provided by Progress Software. Sonic ESB was used for the wrapping of the legacy service modules; because it supports native invocation of the ABL components run on Open Edge application platform. Sonic ESB, like many other service bus products, is Java-based and extends the JMS standard to provide a proprietary messaging solution. Sonic ESB is based on broker based communication to support event driven architecture, but also supports component-based centralized process orchestration.

We were very fortunate, because Sonic ESB could call the underlying service modules using native JMS invocation. This was possible, because both the application platform that hosted the legacy system and the service bus were from the same vendor. The wrapped programs required only annotation into the source code to indicate that the interface was to be used in the native invocation. The tooling automatically generated an intermediary program that called the legacy interface from the service bus.

After the annotations were added to the source code and the intermediary programs generated with the tooling, the parameters had to be mapped from the proprietary JMS message on the bus to the legacy systems format. This was done using a wizard provided by the tooling as illustrated in Figure 5. The message payload was XML, so the parameters to the legacy application interface could be extracted using XPATH. The editors were a bit buggy and sometimes the mappings were lost, which was very annoying especially if there were many parameters. On the other hand the tooling saved a lot of effort, because the parameters could be mapped graphically.

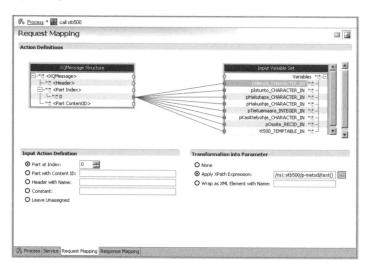

Figure 5. *Mapping request parameters with the tooling*

The same process of mapping parameters was repeated for the response messages from the legacy logic. This time the parameters were included as nodes to the XML document used as message payload on the bus.

After the service module was wrapped it could be incorporated as a step into a composite service that was used to orchestrate the service calls on the bus. The enterprise service bus tooling used graphical presentation of the service composition being configured, shown in Figure 6. The first step in the composite service is the native JMS call to the wrapped service module. The second step is a XSL transformation that transforms the output from the legacy invocation to a valid response message format for the user interface. The XSL transformation service is a native service provided by the platform. XSL is a powerful standard to implement transformations when the payload is in XML. The use of standards like XSL and XPATH is recommended, since they reduce the vendor lock-in that could be caused because of the proprietary messaging extensions used by the platform.

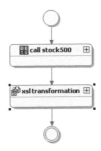

Figure 6. *Itinerary presenting a native service invocation*

The next step after defining the service composition is to define the interface for the service. In Figure 7 the interface parameters are defined for request and response. In this case, because the message is in XML, the request and response parameters are XSD types.

Process

Interface

Define request and response interface parameters, and their XML Schema type. Specify the expected ESB message bind

Request

Parameter	Type	Source in ...	Source N...	Example Document
p-metodi	all [http://www.w3.org/2...	Part	name	
p-istunto	all [http://www.w3.org/2...	Part	Id0	
p-hakutapa	all [http://www.w3.org/2...	Part	Id1	
p-hakuohje	all [http://www.w3.org/2...	Part	Id2	
p-tietuema...	all [http://www.w3.org/2...	Part	Id3	
p-kasittely...	all [http://www.w3.org/2...	Part	Id4	
p-osoite	all [http://www.w3.org/2...	Part	Id5	
tt-500	all [http://www.w3.org/2...	Part	idb	

Response

Parameter	Type	Source in ...	Source N...	Example Document
p-hakutapa	all [http://www.w3.org/2...	Part	Id2	
p-osoite	all [http://www.w3.org/2...	Part	name	
tt-500	all [http://www.w3.org/2...	Part	Id5	
p-sel-napit	all [http://www.w3.org/2...	Part	Id1	
p-virhemessu	all [http://www.w3.org/2...	Part	Id3	
p-virhekentta	all [http://www.w3.org/2...	Part	Id0	
p-virhenu...	all [http://www.w3.org/2...	Part	Id4	

Figure 7. *Web service configuration parameters*

When the interface for the composite service is defined, the composite service itself has to be wrapped as a Web service to be invoked from the new user interface layer. To expose the composite service as a Web service the tooling provided a wizard that could be used. In the wizard, the user has to type in namespaces, bindings and a name for the exposed Web service. When the wizard finishes, the wrapper service looks like the one in Figure 8. The WS protocol handling is implemented as a composite service itself, which calls the wrapped composite service as a sub-process. In the first step, the SOAP envelope is removed from the incoming message. In the second step, the wrapped composite service is being called as a sub-process, and finally the SOAP envelope is added to the outgoing response message. The wizard generates the WSDL file, but it must be edited for corrections and the schema needs to be added to the WSDL file.

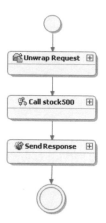

Figure 8. *Service composition wrapped as a Web service*

Finally, the composite service needs to be tested. We have used a product called SoapUI to test the Web services. It is simple to use and easy to learn. With SoapUI, one only gives the address of the WSDL file, and it opens a test case. One can then edit the SOAP message contents to call the service and the returning message is shown after a successful call. While tracking is on, on the ESB, one can see how the service works, and if it fails, which step it fails at. Also, if there are problems one can check the message contents on each step. Figure 9 shows a tracking sample of one case.

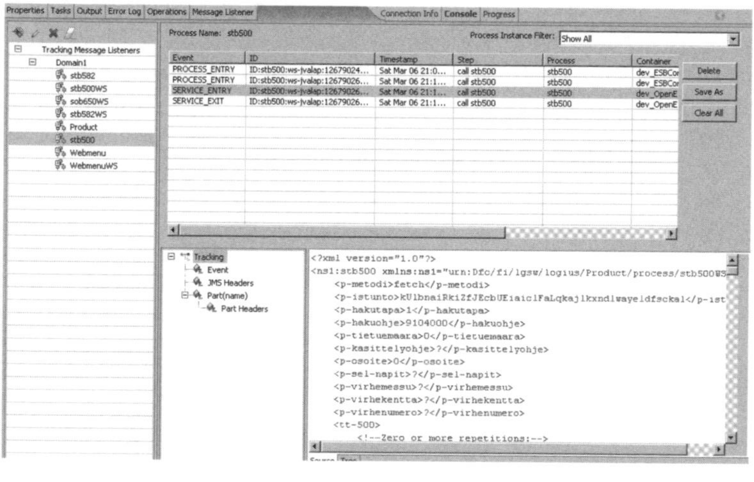

Figure 9. *Example of message tracking*

During the wrapping many annoying bugs were discovered in the tooling. For instance, all preprocessor commands had to be removed from the source code and logical data types were not recognized if the abbreviation "log" was used instead of "logical", even though this was permitted in the programming language syntax. Another annoying aspect discovered was that temporary tables with hyphens in their names were not mapped correctly; the outcome had no hyphen. This has to be repaired in the XSL transformations. While wrapping the modules, comprehensive instructions were written to help other developers to repeat the process and to avoid the underlying pitfalls. The enterprise service bus products can still be regarded as immature in terms of bugs and some time should be reserved for required workarounds.

5. Discussion and findings

As a result of the wrapping we have a new ordering process implemented with a new more powerful user interface technology, and yet it uses the old legacy system's business logic underneath. The existing legacy modules did not have to be altered except for annotations that had to be added to the legacy programming interfaces and a few syntax modifications which where shortcomings of the tooling. The wrapping has been carried out by wrapping the existing modules in the legacy system into reusable and replaceable web services.

The disadvantage of the chosen bottom-up approach was that the data transmitted between the user interface and the legacy modules was tied to the legacy system's data model. To avoid the contract-to-logic coupling, an intermediary canonical data model should have been used. However, defining and maintaining a standardized canonical data model requires a rigorous governance process and an adequate resourcing, which were not possible in the scope of the project. There can also be performance considerations when using especially industry specific canonical models.

Another issue to elaborate on is the granularity of the Web services that were exposed. Building the services in the bottom-up fashion as in this project, the consumer has to know some of the workflow logic on how to call the different services – and then also the workflow logic has to be implemented on the client's side. A better solution would have been to use a more granular composite service. This however was not possible in the given timeframe of the project.

Using the legacy system's session management for state deferral was also not the most efficient solution. Calls may take time since there are many steps between different systems. There have to be many calls from the UI into the legacy system. When, for example, a user wants to put the first product into the shopping cart, the UI first calls a service to create the cart as an order in the legacy system. Then it calls the product service to get all the information of the product and then adds the order line into the cart. After that, it calls the service to get the order header and maybe the order line too, if their information is needed in the UI. This means that this simple operation such as adding a product into a shopping cart can result in at least four Web service calls. This could be compensated for in the future by keeping the shopping cart state in a process engine and invoking the legacy backend only to create a new order when all the necessary information for the whole order has been gathered. This way there would be only one call to the backend to create the order.

Regardless of the shortfalls of the bottom-up approach and the granularity of the services, the impact of using the enterprise service bus to the performance of the overall solution was considered satisfactory. The latency of the whole solution was analyzed using a runtime governance tool. The runtime governance tool visualized the requests to the backend system as call graphs. From a call graph it was possible to see the latency of each step in the composite service. The latency of the enterprise service bus was around 100 milliseconds to 350 milliseconds depending on the load and complexity of the composite service, and the backend latency was from 1.7 seconds to several seconds. At least in this case the performance impact of the enterprise service bus was considered insignificant to the latency of the backend system. The analysis was carried out in a staging environment and in the production environment the round-trip latency was reduced to under a second.

Now that the existing functionality of the legacy backend system has been wrapped it is much easier to develop new functionality which does not require changes to the backend. For the modern user interface technology it is much easier to find developers than for the existing legacy system. The development is much more scalable and time schedules are easier to keep. Still, knowledge of the legacy system is required for maintenance reasons, but the new functionality can be developed on the side to new application services that use service-oriented principles from the beginning.

Although there were many bugs in the tools used for the wrapping that required a lot of time and effort to solve, wrapping the service modules was a lot faster and easier than re-engineering the existing modules. Most of the bugs have now been fixed and there exists instructions on how to perform the wrapping so in the future the it should be much easier. The re-engineering approach would take years to implement and it is much more cost efficient to do it iteratively.

From now on we can further develop the Web services that we expose to make them more general, and easier to use from the interface level. We can also start using the canonical data model, so that messages are transmitted in a general data model on the ESB, and this way we reduce the number of transformations needed in the long run.

We will next focus on developing the mediation layer further between the user interface and the legacy backend. It will be interesting to see how big performance impact the additional transformations from the legacy data model to the canonical data model will have. Another interesting topic is implementing the shopping cart functionality using process engine to store the status of the shopping cart. It is interesting to see how big performance hit the process engine causes and whether it is faster than the backend.

6. Conclusions

In this paper we discussed a modernization of an ordering process of an old legacy system. It has been developed for over three decades and its user interface was out-dated. The result of this process is that we now have a working technique to wrap up existing service modules in the legacy system. This way we can easily modernize the out-dated user interfaces by using any user interface technique that can use web services to get data. We have observed that besides the actual implementation, the wrappings, producing guidelines and documentation is very important, especially in a case of an iterative migration project.

The wrapped functionality can now be developed further in parallel with the new functionality implemented fulfilling the principles of SOA. Also, if the existing features are re-engineered, the service interface can remain the same, only replacing the business logic beneath. The use of middleware to decouple the user interface and the business logic has eased the refactoring and the use of multiple backend systems in subsequent projects.

One of the most important conclusions was that the performance of the ESB platform was considered sufficient for the future projects. The latency correlated to the complexity of the transformations and routing and there was still room for plenty of tuning and optimization. The performance impact will also motivate to keep the ESB layer as simple as possible which correlates to the best practices of designing ESB services. The business logic should not be incorporated on the bus and it should be used solely for mediation purposes.

7. References

1. H. Sneed. "Migrating to web services a research framework". In *Proc. of CSMR Workshop SOAM*, 2007.

2. H. Sneed, "Integrating legacy software into a service oriented architecture". In *Proc. of CSMR*, IEEE Computer Society, 2006, pp. 3-14.

3. T. Erl , *SOA: Principles of Service Design*, Prentice Hall, Indiana, 2007.

4. A. Winter, J. Ziemann. "Model-based Migration to Service-oriented Architectures - A Project Outline". In *Proc. of International Workshop on Service-Oriented Architecture Maintenance (SOAM)*, 2007

5. G. Canfora, A.R. Fasolino, G. Frattolillo, and P. Tramontana, "Migrating interactive legacy systems to web services". In *Proc. of CSMR*. IEEE Computer Society, 2006, pp. 24–36

6. H. Sneed. "Wrapping legacy software for reuse in a SOA", In *Multikonferenz Wirtschaftsinformatik*, 2006, pp. 345-360.

7. Y. Natis. *Applied SOA: Transforming Fundamental Principles Into Best Practices*, Gartner, 2007, ID Number: G00147098.

8. T. Erl *et al.*, *Service Contract Design And Versioning*, Prentice Hall, Indiana, 2008.

9. S. Tai *et al.*, *Using Message-Oriented Middleware for Reliable Web Services Messaging*. *Web Services, E-Business, and the Semantic Web*, Lecture Notes in Computer Science, 2004, pp. 89-104.

10. G. Hohpe, B. Woolf, *Enterprise Integration Patterns: Designing, Building, and Developing Messaging Solutions*, Pearson Education Inc., 2003.

11. G. Coticchia. "Seven steps to a successful SOA implementation". *Business Integration Journal*, 10(5), 2006, pp. 10-13.

12. T. Kokko, J. Antikainen, T. Systä, "Adopting SOA – Experiences from nine Finnish organizations", In *Proc. of CSMR*, 2009.

13. A. Arsanjani. Service-oriented modeling and architecture: How to identify, specify and realize services for your SOA, 2004. Online at http://www.ibm.com/developerworks.

14. J. Ziemann, K. Leyking, T. Kahl, and D. Werth. "Enterprise model-driven migration from legacy to SOA". In *Proc. of MKWI*, February 2006.

15. H. M. Sneed and S. H. Sneed, "Creating web services from legacy host programs". *5th International Workshop on Web Site Evolution (WSE)*, pp. 59–65, 2003.

16. G. Canfora, A. R. Fasolino, G. Frattolillo, and P. Tramontana, "Migrating interactive legacy systems to web services," in *Proceedings of CSMR 2006*. Washington, DC, USA: IEEE Computer Society, 2006, pp. 24–36.

17. E. Stroulia, M. El-Ramly, and P. G. Sorenson, "From legacy to web through interaction modeling," in *Proceedings of ICSM 2002*, October 2002, Canada. IEEE Computer Society, 2002, pp. 21–29.

18. D. Bovenzi, G. Canfora, and A. R. Fasolino, "Enabling legacy system accessibility by web heterogeneous clients" in *CSMR 2003*, March 2003, Italy. IEEE Computer Society, 2003, pp. 73–81.

19. A. Almonaies, J. Cordy, and T. Dean, "Legacy System Evolution towards Service-Oriented Architecture", *Interrnational Workshop on SOA Migration and Evolution (SOAME)*, March 2010, pp. 53-62.

20. G. Lewis, E. Morris, L. O'Brien, D. Smith, and L. Wrage. Smart: The service-oriented migration and reuse technique. Technical report, CMU/SEI-2005-TN-029, 2005.

21. Sonic Software Corp., Amber Point Inc., Bearing Point Inc., and Systinet Corp., "A New Service-Oriented Architecture (SOA) Maturity Model", Online at http://www.omg.org/soa/Uploaded%20Docs/SOA/SOA_Maturity.pdf, 2005.

22. R. Schulte, *The Enterprise Service Bus: Communication Backbone for SOA*, Gartner, 2007, ID Number: G00143223.

23. T. Erl , *SOA: Design Patterns*, Prentice Hall, Indiana, 2009.

24. Amberpoint Inc. *et al.*, *An Implementor's Guide to Service Oriented Architecture - Getting It Right*, Westminster Promotions, 2008.

25. T. Erl, *Service-Oriented Architecture: Concepts, Technology, and Design*, Prentice Hall, Indiana, 2005.

26. [bbmud] B. Foote and J. Yoder, "Big Ball of Mud". *Fourth Conference on Patterns Languages of Programs (PLoP '97/EuroPLoP '97)*, Monticello, Illinois, September 1997.

Index of Authors